IMPLEMENTATION
AND THE
POLICY PROCESS

Recent Titles in
Contributions in Political Science

Implementation and the Policy Process

OPENING UP THE BLACK BOX

Edited by

Dennis J. Palumbo
and
Donald J. Calista

PREPARED UNDER THE AUSPICES OF THE
POLICY STUDIES ORGANIZATION
Stuart S. Nagel, *Series Adviser*

CONTRIBUTIONS IN POLITICAL SCIENCE,
NUMBER 252

GREENWOOD PRESS
New York • Westport, Connecticut • London

Library of Congress Cataloging-in-Publication Data

Implementation and the policy process : opening up the black box /
    edited by Dennis J. Palumbo and Donald J. Calista ; prepared under
    the auspices of the Policy Studies Organization.
        p.   cm.—(Contributions in political science, ISSN 0147-1066
    ; no. 252)
        Includes bibliographical references.
        ISBN 0-313-27283-2 (lib. bdg. : alk. paper)
        1. Policy sciences.   2. Bureaucracy.   I. Palumbo, Dennis James.
    II. Calista, Donald J.   III. Policy Studies Organization.
    IV. Series.
    H97.I46   1990
    320'.6—dc20   89-23640

British Library Cataloguing in Publication Data is available.

Library of Congress Catalog Card Number: 89-23640
ISBN: 0-313-27283-2
ISSN: 0147-1066

First published in 1990

Greenwood Press, Inc.
88 Post Road West, Westport, Connecticut   06881

Printed in the United States of America

∞

The paper used in this book complies with the
Permanent Paper Standard issued by the National
Information Standards Organization (Z39.48–1984).

10 9 8 7 6 5 4 3 2 1

Contents

Part II: Implementation Politics and the Organizational Context

Part III: Epistemology, Methodology, and Implementation

Illustrations

Acknowledgments

The editors would like to thank Marian Buckley, Keith Campbell, Mary Cullen, and Tammy Stein of the College of Public Programs' Auxiliary Resource Center at Arizona State University for their help in word processing some of the chapters of this book, the bibliography, and the tables and figures. In addition, we would like to acknowledge the help of Rosemarie Tempestilli of Marist College who helped with the mounds of correspondence and typing; without her assistance, the book would not have been possible.

Introduction:
The Relation of Implementation
Research to Policy Outcomes

Dennis J. Palumbo and Donald J. Calista _____

Over the last fifteen years public policy analysis has witnessed the emergence of a new subfield. It focuses on the role of implementation as a distinct phenomenon in the creation of policy outputs. Two discoveries have distinguished the field: one is that prior to the discovery of implementation, the significance of implementation for public policy had been overlooked (Hargrove, 1975). The second is that surprised observers have finally recognized implementation's independent effect on policy outcomes (Bardach, 1979). This independent effect acknowledges that the government is more than a ''cash register'' that adds up the various pressures put on it; the bureaucracy itself is an important contributor to public policy as well. Acknowledging its prominence, however, produced consternation among early researchers who tried to make sense of why implementing programs of the Great Society, particularly, usually failed (Pressman & Wildavsky, 1973). More recently implementation researchers have called for a major reevaluation in understanding the process of policy formation itself (Palumbo & Calista, 1987). This book begins where this latter point leaves off.

The book serves two purposes. First, it presents an overview of why implementation research has contributed to a major reconsideration of the field of public policy analysis. Second, it offers conceptual frameworks that employ implementation research to develop a fuller understanding of the entire policy process.

Earlier observers assumed that whatever implementation was, it had to be both conceptually and empirically separated from policy formation. Policymakers dictated what they wanted and implementors fulfilled them—or did not. Policies were viewed as givens that were to be implemented whatever flaws the policies themselves might have. Implementors were supposed to produce outcomes for which they were to be held accountable. Over time, implementation researchers found that policy outcomes were not only shaped by the implementation process itself, but, in some instances, were actually determined by it.

While the evidence for these findings were often faulted because the research largely represented case studies, cumulatively the story became overwhelming: Public policy outcomes could not be understood fully without recognizing the influence of implementation. Often, observers found that implementation was important because policy formulators (i.e., legislators) overlooked the role of implementation. They misunderstood or ignored the peculiar requirements for political coalition-building in implementation (Bardach, 1975); they imposed inappropriate organizational structures on implementors (Elmore, 1978); or they didn't understand the impact that street-level workers have on the delivery of services (Lipsky, 1980). This book speaks to joining the divide between the assumptions of the earlier and later implementation researchers. As a subfield, implementation research cannot go on without developing a perspective that contributes to public policy analysis as a whole. This book's purpose aims at clarifying that relationship. It goes a step further than the most recent research that establishes and sometimes overemphasizes the impact of implementation on policy. The book's main purpose is to caution against the error of assuming that implementation is the main factor in policymaking and that once implementation is taken care of, policies will be effective. We attempt to place implementation in the broader policymaking process and show its relationship to the other parts of the policy cycle (i.e., design, problem definition, formulation, evaluation).

This book originated in a two-stage project by the editors. The first stage was a symposium that summarized the major contributions the field has made to date and addressed problems for future research. This was published as a symposium in the *Policy Studies Review* (Palumbo & Calista, 1987) entitled *What Have We Learned from Implementation Research? Where Do We Go from Here?* The articles in that symposium capture a lot of the excitement generated by implementation research over the last fifteen years. Most of the articles argue that implementation is a complex process involving more than managing government programs. Their principal concern was to explain the conditions under which implementation can become successful. Unlike many earlier observers who singled out the way bureaucrats or bureaucracy contributed to failure, the symposium articles introduced more generic conditions that constrain or confound implementation outcomes. Some of these conditions include multiple perceptions of policy intentions by the various stakeholders (Love & Sederberg, 1987), inadequacy of resources (Elmore, 1987b), ineffective organizational structures (Ferman & Levin, 1987), and inability to create sustaining political linkages (Yanow, 1987).

Some of the articles in the symposium develop critiques that emphasize the benefits of making implementation a more central variable for public policy analysis. These critiques reveal, however, that not all observers agree on what role implementation might play in a broadened definition of the field. Not unexpectedly, there are essentially two viewpoints that correspond to the two prevailing assumptions in implementation research. One viewpoint stresses the top-down version of implementation. It suggests that an emphasis on the role of implementation in policymaking undermines the foundations of democratic politics. Despite the problems faced by implementation that may require adaptation or changes in programs, elected representatives are the only ones who can legitimately make policy—otherwise the "will of the people" will be stymied (Linder & Peters, 1987a). A related critique views implementation from the vantage point of the amount of discretion available to public administrators (Burke, 1987). It views implementation along a continuum of control over policy outcomes by public administrators; this approach sees control over bureaucracy occurring more as a default of certain policy situations than by design of democratic politics.

Overwhelmingly, the articles in the symposium identify with a bottom-up approach to implementation. In particular, this view is that the actions (and conditions) of street-level bureaucrats and client behaviors must be incorporated into policymaking. The delivery of services shapes policy outcomes more than the design of policy. In this view, implementation failure is more complex than just the result of bureaucratic incompetence. The behavior of bureaucrats must be understood as byproducts of the complex political, organizational, social, and economic context in which they work. Bureaucrats' varying positions of power in determining outcomes (or in defining objectives) can often be traced to the nature of the policy environment itself. Indeed, these critiques show how attempts to control implementation by employing top-down control over bureaucrats often has dysfunctional results (Calista, 1987). Some of the contributors call for acknowledging the importance of these real-world conditions in rethinking policy design (Love & Sederberg, 1987). Others assert that the problem is more far-reaching; it is epistemological. That is, as long as public policy analysis remains wedded primarily to positivist traditions, then implementation success and failure will never be fully understood (Fox, 1987).

The second stage of this project has been to focus more on the positive contributions of implementation research. The result is this book. One purpose is to develop explanatory models that cut across the research dichotomies of the prevailing top-down and bottom-up approaches. A second goal is to establish an agenda for future research. Procedurally, the editors organized a workshop under the Policy Analysis Section of the American Political Science Association's meetings in Washington, D.C., in 1987. The object of the meeting was to summarize the PSR Symposium and to offer proposals for advancing implementation research. Following that discussion, the editors developed a list of nine questions that were circulated to individuals attending that meeting and to other researchers in the implementation field.

QUESTIONS OF POLICY DESIGN

The nine questions are grouped into subsections within which related chapters fall. While each of the chapters generalizes about the field, each focuses on different levels of analysis. Accordingly, the chapters are organized by questions that move from the more empirical to more methodological and theoretical concerns.

The initial questions deal with how the nature of policy intentions relates to policy outcomes and the role of implementation in that translation. These questions concern policy design issues:

• To what extent is policy failure or success a result of design rather than implementation?
• Is the top-down bias that pervades our thinking about implementation unrealistic and conservative in its orientation?
• Has implementation research contributed to a conservative bias in our attitude about government?
• Is there a solution to the top-down versus bottom-up, and the adaptation versus fidelity dichotomies?

The chapters in this section are of two kinds. Two deal with policy designing issues and the other two with empirical aspects of implementation research.

The first chapter, written by the editors, reviews the field. It discusses the question of how we can determine when a policy has succeeded or failed. It is empirically derived in that it calls for recognizing the fact that adapting and redesigning implementation inevitably result from the symbolic nature of policy formation. The latter is not disparaged; instead, Palumbo and Calista show how they can be employed to develop a fuller range of strategies aimed at reaching successful outcomes.

Søren Winter (Chapter 2) summarizes the implementation literature with an eye towards building a model that shows how the constraints of implementation processes create linkages with policy formation. He suggests there are various phases to implementation. Superficially, it appears similar to earlier models. It differs from them in its dynamic quality. Successful implementation is multilinear: It depends on the interrelationship among actors in the various stages of implementation. Indeed, Winter assumes that policy intentions will be clarified as they pass through each stage. Thus, implementation is a series of interactions and interpretations between the outputs of policy formation and the effects of organizational and interorganizational impacts, between the latter and street-level bureaucratic behaviors, and between the latter and target-group behaviors. At best, then, implementation is a series of junction points that produces outcomes which cannot be predicted from policy intentions.

The third chapter by Barbara Ferman might have set the course of implementation research along different lines had it been published earlier. The fact that it is written now suggests that there is a need to put implementation research into a broader theory of democratic politics and regimes. She discusses the fact that the American system of government requires conflicts during implementation. In her view, the top-down and bottom-up positions are both ''correct'' and reflect the unsettled characteristics of the American constitutional structure. She invokes Madisonian concepts of Republican politics to show that the gap between policymaking and implementation is not a failure but a testimony to the success of the constitutional design of the Founding Fathers.

Chapter 4 by Stephen Linder and Guy Peters is a far-reaching statement that traces the intellectual roots of the top-down and bottom-up views of implementation and contrasts this with an approach that they call the "design perspective." They suggest that there has been a tendency in implementation research, particularly in the bottom-up perspective, to conflate empirical and normative statements. It is wrong, they say, to take empirical findings about the importance of street-level workers in implementation, and build this into a normative theory about how implementation should proceed.

The last chapter in the policy design section, by Robert Nakamura, deals with the symbolic dimension in implementation. While much implementation research focuses on policies that are intended to change behavior in target populations (i.e., getting firms to hire hard-core unemployed workers), Nakamura focuses on a policy that is purely symbolic—a policy specifically directed at changing people's attitudes or perceptions. This fits in nicely with the idea that policy is not an empirical reality but a political construction of how those in power would like others to view the policies they support.

IMPLEMENTATION POLITICS AND THE ORGANIZATIONAL CONTEXT

Most subjects of the chapters in this section would not have been considered worthwhile as little as ten years ago. They represent implementation's special contribution to the policy field. The chapters discuss how policy implementation adapts to changing organizational, intergovernmental, and ideological circumstances. The authors' generalizations focus on the contribution implementation research makes to understanding the entire policy process. The questions addressed are:

• How are organizational structures related to successful and failed implementation?
• Under what conditions should implementors be given discretion?
• Is there a particular point that determines whether implementation will succeed or fail?

The first chapter in this section by Glenn Rainey, Jr., discusses the importance of understanding organizational structures for implementation. He focuses on human service agencies, but his findings clearly apply elsewhere. He describes the conditions under which one organizational form develops and the role that actors at the bottom in this process play. Rainey also points to issues that implementation researchers might consider in developing taxonomies and concepts of implementation.

Evelyn Brodkin's Chapter 7 explicitly introduces politics into the implementation context. She proposes a concept called social politics, which essentially says that implementation has its own politics that are different from legislative politics. Hence, the multiplicity of interests and constraints that create policy intentions will continue to shape them during implementation. Most important, the institutional and organizational structures have an impact on how politics are played out.

Chapter 8 by Bryna Sanger and Martin Levin challenges conventional thinking about the biases and predispositions that pervade most thinking and action regarding management of implementation. They suggest that male-dominated assumptions about appropriate managerial behaviors eliminate an alternative view, one that can be associated culturally with women.

John Burke in Chapter 9 discusses a different set of realities but reaches similar conclusions; he offers a typology of situations when discretion should be exercized by implementors. He focuses on the discretion available to public administrators and uses the concepts of responsibility and accountability to create that typology. Burke does not make normative judgments about this situation as a failure of democratic politics. In fact, he urges caution in attempting to apply inappropriate controls in implementation. Discretion moves from the existence of a formal-legal set of controls that constrain bureaucratic behavior severely to how personal, political, and moral values dominate implementation. Burke joins Winter (Chapter 2) on one central point. By arguing, respectively that implementation can be organized either into a typology of discretionary controls or a series of interactive phases, they agree that policy implementation is not contingent on policy intentions—it yields its own dynamic in producing successful outcomes.

Chapter 10 by Carl Carlucci deals with implementation in one of Burke's four cases: Where accountability is strong and external sources are responsible for governing the exercise of discretion. The case is whether state legislatures responded (in 1980) to the requirement for congressional redistricting by adopting computer-driven technology to aid the process. Carlucci hypothesizes that in addressing new technology, a stage between its adoption and implementation exists. This stage he calls acquisition. He finds that not all adopters are acquirers in that they become nonusers of the technology. In Winter's model, then, a policy output does not exist until adopters become acquirers, and then implementation begins. In relation to Burke's typology, Carlucci suggests that there is a neutral ground that precedes understanding the amount of discretion available to public administrators. While it appears that reapportionment is a formal-legal type of implementation, to lump all the fifty states together as implementors of computer-assisted reapportionment overlooks the important difference between acquirers of the technology and the "mere" adopters.

IMPLEMENTATION, EPISTEMOLOGY, AND METHODOLOGY

The last section includes chapters that capture and extend the observations of the other contributions. They also develop generalizations and suggest various lines of future research. The questions addressed are:

- Has the epistemological orientation of implementation research, which has been primarily positivist, led us astray in our conclusions about implementation "failure"?
- How has implementation research improved our knowledge of public administration?
- Is it possible to discover general "laws" of implementation, or is implementation always contextual and specific?

Chapter 11 by Mary Ann Scheirer and James Griffith concerns the implementation of a federal program at the local level. It deals with the fluoridation program for school children. They find that the normal statistical analysis based on linear regression models does not capture the full range of implementation outcomes, including both successes and failures. Scheirer and Griffith were unable to find support using regression analysis for some of the factors that Rainey believes may be crucial to implementation, possibly because in health fields were the degree of accountability to external sources is high, professionals dominate. Professional discretion makes determining outcomes difficult to standardize to fit regression curves. Because there may be many paths to successful implementation, linear, additive models underlying regression are a poor fit and cannot detect the important variables.

The multiauthored Chapter 12 by Malcolm Goggin and others contributes to the conceptual shift toward developing increased levels of generalization. These authors assert that implementation research is in its "third generation" and propose a method that focuses on the interrelationships of variables for understanding implementation at the state level. What is important about their proposal is not only the specifics of the methodological recommendations they make, but also the ability to integrate them into the models suggested earlier by Winter and Burke. The suggested methods can assist in discovering how well implementation phases and discretion typologies are doing as antecedents to evaluating outcomes and suggesting refinements.

The next two chapters offer additional evidence for broadening the understanding of implementation. Chapter 13 by Charles Fox begins with a critique of implementation. He not only criticizes the implementation field, but offers specific suggestions to improve research—and to enhance outcomes. Principally he finds fault with positivist philosophy and rationalist methodology, some of which can also be found in more empirical framework suggested by Goggin et al. Fox finds no use for a scientific philosophy that eschews the subjective—in effect limits the value of qualitative methods. He ends by forcefully arguing that empirical findings would be strengthened by adopting a phenomenological approach to implementation.

The final chapter both summarizes the implementation contributions and proposes an interpretive model that forwards future research. Dvora Yanow suggests that researchers must become more fully appreciative of a phenomenon they have avoided acknowledging. Implementation amounts to recognizing its capacity to be a series of (continuous) interpretive logics. Implementation is multifaceted by design—much as Ferman asserts in Chapter 3—and cannot be explicated by looking at it through one lens. It must be observed through four lenses: political, structural, systems, and human relations. Employing more than one lens reveals how much further implementation research has gone in illuminating the entire policy process.

These overviews of the chapters cannot substitute for reading them. Their value to implementation research and to the policy field generally can only be appreciated by a thorough reading. The future research agenda for implementation will be both individually and collectively influenced by what the chapters say.

_____ PART I

Implementation and Policy Design

Opening up the Black Box:
Implementation and the Policy Process

Dennis J. Palumbo and Donald J. Calista

In the fall of 1988, the U.S. Congress passed the Family Security Act (FSA) that was described as a break with past social welfare policies. Supporters claimed that it would "break the cycle of dependency." The act required that people receiving welfare assistance (who numbered 3.7 million adults on Aid to Families with Dependent Children in 1988) enter a program called Job Opportunities and Basic Skills (JOBS). They were not actually required to work under the proposed legislation because such a stipulation would mean not only having jobs available for recipients, but also providing day-care facilities for their children, since 80 percent of the recipients were women. Instead, recipients were required to undergo remedial education, job training, and counseling. To make the bill palatable to conservatives in Congress, supporters had to call it a "workfare" program.

What will determine whether or not this legislation will be successfully implemented? Conventional wisdom says that successful implementation occurs if: (1) the act correctly identifies the reasons why people wind up on welfare; (2) the act contains unambiguous directives that organize implementors to maximize the likelihood that the eligible welfare recipients will behave as desired; (3) the administrators implementing the legislation possess the necessary managerial and political skills, and commitment to its goals; (4) the program is actively supported by organized constituency groups and key legislators throughout the implementation process; and (5) the relative priority of statutory objectives is not undermined over time by conflicting public policies or by changes in relevant socioeconomic conditions that limit the statute's purposes or political support (Sabatier & Mazmanian, 1979).

Only two of these five conditions of "ideal type" implementation are related to the performance of administrators—conditions 2 and 3. The others refer to policy design (condition 1) and political and socioeconomic conditions in the environment in which implementation takes place (conditions 4 and 5). Yet, bureaucrats (implementors) often take the blame when there is a gap between promise and performance in a policy, and there almost always is such a gap. There are a number of reasons why such gaps occur. The main ones are:

1. Much legislation passed at the national, state, and local levels is symbolic; it is usually a promise that something can be done about an intractable social problem that has lingered on the public agenda for years (i.e., welfare dependency).
2. Legislation is often not based on a sound program theory that correctly identifies what design conditions will get the target groups to behave in the desired fashion because we do not have such theories.
3. Socioeconomic and political conditions change so that the solution promised in the legislation may not be appropriate a few years later (i.e., the economy loses unskilled manufacturing jobs that welfare recipients could fill).
4. Administrators discover during implementation that a different type of program or organizational structure would work better than the one envisioned in the legislation.
5. Insufficient resources are committed to the program.
6. Implementors don't have the know-how to make the policy work.

Because there is an inevitable gap between the promises in legislation and the programs actually delivered, early implementation studies concluded that most government programs failed. Such studies, however, focused on implementation at the point of delivering a policy; hence, the fault lay with bureaucrats. Or, as the second edition of the landmark 1973 study, Pressman and Wildavsky (1986), noted in its subtitle: "How Great Expectations in Washington are Dashed in Oakland; or Why It's Amazing That Federal Programs Work At All. . . ." Unfortunately, many conservatives took this to mean that government couldn't do anything right (Bardach, 1979). Often, administrators were blamed for program failure as bureaucrat bashing continued to remain popular during the conservative 1980s. Such voices only echo the accusation that implementation is the "Achilles' heel" of government (Williams, 1980); administrators are seen as playing the "easy life" or engaging in "diversion of resources" games (Bardach, 1979).

But by the late 1980s, more than fifteen years after the initial implementation studies, researchers discovered that these earlier views were wrong (Fox, 1987; Schwartz, 1983). They were wrong, first, because they assumed that policy implementation could be separated from formulation and design and the other parts of the policy cycle. They falsely accepted the traditional politics-administration dichotomy promulgated by Woodrow Wilson in the mid–1880s instead of adding a new perception of the role of implementation in public policymaking. As Robert Denhardt noted:

The study of policy implementation represents a regression in the study of public organizations: the distinction between policy making and policy implementation exactly parallels the old politics—administration dichotomy; and the uncritical acceptance of such a distinction by many students of the policy process neither recognizes the role of bureaucracy in framing public values nor addresses the issues of democratic accountability raised by this activity. (1984, p. 133)

It is now accepted doctrine that administrators play as great, if not a greater, part at all stages of the policymaking process as do executives and legislators. The doctrine of separation of powers ensures that not only will there be a tug-of-war between legislatures and executives in determining policy directions but that implementors will not always be the winners in these struggles, even though they have tactical and strategic advantages. Moreover, as courts have come to play more activist roles at the level of implementation, administration is sometimes called to join one branch against the other. If there is a gap between a policy's promises and its implementation, it may be due to a difference in political party ideology or group and personal attitudes and perceptions about what a policy should be. This is a normal part of the American constitutional design (see Chapter 3, this volume), not an illegitimate usurpation of power by "bureaucrats."

Another reason why the earlier implementation studies were wrong is that they assumed that problem definition and policy design are usually clear and unambiguous. But this seldom happens. Problem definition and policy design are political activities, and therefore, they are products of conflict that results in bargaining and compromise. In these charged situations, it is not possible to identify correctly the causes of the social problem that a policy purportedly seeks to cure. Moreover, what is identified as a cause of a social problem depends on the ideology of the person or groups doing the identifying. In the War on Poverty programs, for example, policymakers—the politicians who must run for office—identified the cause of poverty as being individuals' lack of training and education; some more conservative policymakers even suggested character flaws such as laziness or defective genes, although they were reluctant to say so without qualifications. Many poor people, on the other hand, saw their situations as resulting from racial discrimination and lack of jobs (Ingraham, 1987). Seldom is there a perfect fit between the problem as defined by legislation, the design of a policy aimed at alleviating it, and the implementation delivered by that policy.

A third reason why the early implementation studies were wrong is that the definition of implementation was too narrow in most studies. Implementation involves more than just the governmental agencies that are officially responsible for carrying out a program; they involve, in addition, private agencies and groups that often are contractors for carrying out policies; the target groups themselves (e.g., welfare recipients, criminals, students, old people, polluters, price fixers, sick people, drug users, smokers), and, of course, the socioeconomic, cultural, and political conditions in the environment in which policies are supposed to operate.

Implementation is not and cannot be seen as purely technical. Implementation must be viewed as an "exercise in continuous problem solving" (Ingraham, 1987, p. 149). This view holds that implementors actively shape public policy. And this is as it should be; the traditional view that implementors (i.e., administrators, private agencies, interest groups, state and local governments, target groups) should not be involved in making policy is false. Public administrators cannot be properly understood as the deliverers of decisions made earlier by separate groups or bodies of "real policymakers." Moreover, when policies are changed through political and organizational conditioning and given more specific content during implementation, this does not connote policy failure.

Policy failure comes from several sources; it is due as much to inadequate problem definition or policy design as it is to administrative misfeasance, malfeasance, or nonfeasance. Moreover, administrative failures may now be seen as stemming from the inattention paid by legislators to program constraints during policy design. Problems, or failures, in implementation, therefore, are as much a consequence of flaws in the policy formulation process and in the environment in which implementation takes place as they are due to specific problems of administration per se.

When implementation success or failure is attributed to administration alone, the knowledge provided by organizational analysis can shed light on how to improve implementation. This involves such topics as leadership, management styles, and strategic planning. But to the extent to which implementation success or failure is a part of the overall policymaking process, such knowledge is no longer adequate. More global understandings are required. In providing some of this knowledge, implementation research has somewhat opened the "black box" of the policymaking process. These advances are the subject of the rest of this chapter.

THE POLITICAL NATURE OF IMPLEMENTATION

Shioji was a completely political man; he understood better than almost anyone of his generation that Nissan was not only a manufacturing organism but a political organism as well, with all kinds of tiny interlocking personal relationships and dependencies. Power could be exercised through these dependencies; there were always favors to trade. (Halberstam, 1986, p. 399)

A great deal of the early research on implementation ignored or misunderstood the relationships among its political, organizational, and behavioral aspects. The research seemed to assume that implementation occurred in the absence of these relationships. There are some exceptions. Nakamura and Smallwood (1980), for example, focused on politics in the broadest sense, on "the conflicts over values which permeate many, if not all, aspects of public life, and the role of politics in resolving these conflicts" (1980, p. 2). They described the various policy environments in which implementation occurs, such as the policy formulation, implementation, and evaluation environments.

Implementation, however, is political in several other ways. Politics takes place within the subgovernments that influence implementation (Heclo, 1978; Kingdon, 1984). Implementors are a key part of these political networks and play a major role in interpreting policy directives. There are distinctions, however, between the kinds of politics that influence the organizational and behavioral dynamics of programs and of the politics that shapes those dynamics among legislative committees and executive staffs (see chapter 7, this volume).

Another way politics enters implementation is in the trading that occurs among the ''tiny interlocking personal relationships and dependencies'' within each bureaucracy (public or private) involved in implementing policies. Agreements must be sought among them. Sometimes opposition consists of loyalists and sycophants who are complete supporters of what they think the directors want, or of deviants who put their own spin on policy that changes it slightly in an attempt to gain power. The range of responses includes those who knowingly undermine or counteract the policy, to those who say they advocate more effective ways to achieve the policy's goals, to others who are passive and indifferent and for whom inaction secures their stake against those seeking changes. As long as resources remain scarce—including providing expertise—none of these political behaviors should be surprising.

Implementation must contend with this multiplicity of behaviors. Administrators will be ineffective if they act as if they are carrying out policy objectives as stated ''on the books.'' Pure technocrats think that organizations exist only for the purpose of achieving goals. But organizations are social enterprises that also serve human ends. Administrators, no less than legislators, seek power, esteem, and monetary rewards that invariably shape how (or which) goals are achieved. This is not, nor should it be, considered dysfunctional for policy or the public, for it is exactly what occurs in the private as well as the public sector.

Implementation and the American Constitutional System

The Reagan administration seems to have understood the political nature of implementation better than previous administrations. It sought to redirect many policies through implementation rather than by seeking new legislation, which it knew it could not get. The Environmental Protection Agency (EPA) is a case in point.

The 1970 legislation that created the EPA was vague. Although the EPA policy arena functioned in what can be viewed as a technical area that presumably circumscribed bureaucratic discretion, the articulation and interpretation of acceptable guidelines proved enormously complex. Implementors developed wide discretionary powers that could not be controlled by congressional oversight.

The Reagan administration used this discretion fully to achieve its environmental objectives. The EPA became a favorite target of Reagan's 1980 campaign rhetoric, and he vowed to curtail it if elected. After the election, the civil servants in the EPA who were not replaced by Reagan faced an uncomfortable situation. On the one hand, they were members of the executive branch of government whose chief officer was President Reagan, who opposed serious enforcement of environmental laws. On the other hand, they were responsible for carrying out the environmental laws that had been passed by Congress over the previous decade. Moreover, Congress in 1980 wanted the EPA to implement the Superfund cleanup provisions of the law vigorously and also to issue air quality regulations according to the timetable established in 1970. That legislation stated explicitly that Congress did not want costs to be taken into consideration during implementation. The Reagan administration disagreed (Marcus, 1980, p. 86).

The EPA became involved in this political battle. The atmosphere created by Reagan appointees who headed the EPA discouraged civil servants from serious enforcement of social environmental laws. They were encouraged to use their discretion to reduce the scope of effective enforcement (Rohr, 1988, p. 171).

Thus, the EPA served two political masters. It could not be a single, monolithic public servant in which all members agreed on or fulfilled the same goals and objectives. This fissure between the president and Congress paralleled the public's disagreements about what was most important. Marcus notes that "The goals of public health—lessening the impact of common cardiovascular illnesses, such as emphysema and heart disease—were in conflict with the average driver's concern to get to work, go shopping, visit friends, and use his automobile without restriction'' (1980, p. 136).

The various deadlines set by the EPA were not met, not only because of these conflicts, but also because of the EPA's reliance on other agencies to carry out its regulations. It depended on an uncooperative Justice Department to bring compliance lawsuits forward. It also had to contend with the decreasing resistance of its counterpart state agencies that were worried about losing basic industries, so they dragged their feet. In other words, the macroimplementation conditions over which EPA administrators had no control greatly hindered effective implementation. Nor were the microimplementation conditions favorable toward implementation. The Reagan appointees were not only uncommitted to the goals of the legislation; they were outright hostile toward the career EPA administrators who might have tried to implement the goals. The latter turned to their allies in Congress and to sympathetic lobby groups to prevent the agency's goals from being completely immobilized. As Rohr notes: "Eventually, high-ranking officials from the EPA's political leadership became so flagrant in disregarding their agency's mission to clean up toxic waste sites that career officials were able to "blow the whistle" to key congressional committees which undertook investigations that led to the resignation of four officials and a criminal conviction for a fifth'' (1988, p. 171). In other words, EPA bureaucrats had to depend on gaining political support from congressional representatives to increase their legitimacy in confronting Reagan appointees.

EPA implementation, although outrageous, is, nonetheless, fairly typical of most implementation. For example, the Reagan administration succeeded in changing agency goals by reshaping implementation in a number of other policy areas as well. These included changes in the policy of the Office of Surface Mining, which allowed stripmining to take place on a large scale; and in the National Highway Traffic Safety Administration, which rescinded the requirement for all motor vehicles made after 1982 to be equipped with passive restraints and air bags.

Whether these cases are viewed as successes or failures is a matter of political and ideological perspective. Implementation success cannot be objectively examined solely by measuring differences from policy intentions. Policy intentions are a matter of perceptions, and implementation is not a matter of technical fulfillment of some clearly stated policy objectives. Instead, implementation helps to unfold perceptions of policy intentions in the ongoing political and organizational contexts of public administration. By examining how these contexts apply to the realities of public administration, implementation research has shown how the "inputs" of policy design are transformed into "outputs" of policy redesign. Policy redesign not only makes goal modification unavoidable (Stone, 1980), it actually becomes desirable in certain situations (Berman, 1980). Moreover, the degree to which greater or lesser goal incongruence will occur can be predicted from different contexts of public administration. For one, implementation can be examined by observing that public administration contexts contain differing amounts of discretion by bureaucrats. This discretion in decision making can be seen as functions of the way the variables of accountability and responsiveness relate to political authority. There will be policy arenas in which discretion is highly formal and legal, thereby limiting not only bureaucratic discretion but goal modification as well (see Chapter 9). Discretion in the implementation of environmental policy is quite a different matter. It invites goal incongruence because executives and legislators—at all levels—disagree over how much responsiveness they want from public administration. Goal incongruence also occurs because it is difficult to obtain accountability in that policy arena; there is little agreement about what are the appropriate elements of technological and organizational design. In effect, accountability is muddled and discretion negotiated. It is, therefore, not easy to say whose political goals represent the priority for implementation. Implementation turns out to be a matter of perspective in that public administration must create the appearance of wholeness while the operating reality dictates balancing competing views of priorities.

Nevertheless, the problem of the responsible use of administrative discretion remains the central moral concern of the literature in public administration (Rohr, 1988, p. 170). Implementation research cannot really solve this moral concern; it simply concludes that policymaking occurs during implementation. The problem with stating "ideal type" implementation conditions described earlier is that they are essentially static. They spell out how implementation responsibility can be achieved according to the old politics—administration dichotomy. But these conditions seldom, if ever, can be met. Therefore, policy will continue to be redesigned during implementation. By increasing the understanding of how policy outcomes develop, implementation research has opened up what goes on in the "black box" of the policymaking process.

IMPLEMENTATION AND POLICYMAKING

Implementors are involved at every stage of the policymaking process: agenda setting, problem identification, formulation, implementation, and evaluation. They are often the most powerful groups in setting the policy agenda. They are consulted by legislators and interest-group representatives when policy is just being shaped. Bureaucracies frequently initiate policy; they also force policy choices on legislators, especially by creating or analyzing impending crises (i.e., crime waves or prison overcrowding). Their influence over setting agendas also extends to the budget requests that shape program directions.

One source of implementors' power is their expertise (Weber, 1949). They know the technical details of social programs and have the data to show how existing programs are progressing. They may be consulted by legislators, particularly at the local level, simply to approve or disapprove policies proposed by other administrative agencies (Miller, 1984; Romer & Rosenthal, 1978). But the principal source of their power is their influence over policy subgroups or networks that create policymaking intentions (Meltsner & Bellavita, 1983; Milward, 1980). Members of these subgroups include professionals, bureau chiefs, administrators of line agencies, university professors, consultants, suppliers, and legislative and executive staffs. They can determine what will get onto the policy agenda and how an issue or problem will be defined. They do this by making the policy issue highly technical and unintelligible to the uninitiated and thereby erecting barriers to participation by outsiders, or by defining the problem to suit their interests.

In some issue networks that form within policy areas, administrators are the most powerful members. For example, administrators in the U.S. Department of Agriculture (USDA) were a part of a small issue network that redesigned food stamp policy during the 1960s and 1970s. The network included advocacy groups and food experts as well as USDA administrators. But USDA officials actually determined the eligibility requirements for food stamps, the benefit structure, and the amount of coupons that became available to individuals and families. They could do this for more then a decade because the members of Congress were apathetic about these questions and because liberals and conservatives in Congress could not reach a consensus (Berry, 1984).

Public administrators often have issues on their agenda that ultimately define both legislative and executive agendas. Administrators are uniquely situated to propose solutions to ongoing troublesome issues. Usually, the costs and benefits of these proposals get hammered out between administrators and legislative and executive staffs. Prison overcrowding is a good example. This problem affects most states today and is, therefore, high on the agenda of most criminal justice agencies. Many professionals in these agencies help devise solutions in conjunction with local officials that are ultimately sanctioned by state legislatures. For example, in a number of states (Kansas, Oregon, Colorado) judges, lawyers, probation officers, county attorneys, and reform groups helped develop and design community corrections programs at the county level that the legislatures in these states eventually adopted (Palumbo, Maynard-Moody, & Wright, 1984). Policy formulation in these cases was done primarily by the implementors of these programs. In turn, much like the dependence of legislators and executives on top-level administrators, street-level bureaucrats possess know-how that higher-level administrators must carefully cultivate in order to provide optimal policy outcomes.

Opening the black box now reveals that formulation is clearly a small part of policymaking (Palumbo, 1988). Much policy is made during implementation itself. Although this occurs in various ways, the principal way is by street-level bureaucrats who create policy through the multitude of decisions they make in interacting with the public (Lipsky, 1980). They possess discretion that cannot be completely controlled because there are never enough resources to provide close, frequent, and direct supervision with the host of street-level bureaucrats, and also because they are physically separated from their superiors. There are no precise performance standards in existence that specify exactly how an engineer, teacher, cop, parole officer, prosecutor, judge, public health nurse, social worker, and the many other street-level bureaucrats should do their job. In sum, policy formulation occurs during implementation by bureaucrats developing routines and shortcuts for coping with their everyday jobs.

IMPLEMENTATION AND PROGRAM EVALUATION

Program evaluation also has progressed in the past decade from the simple input/output model of operationalizing variables to a more global view. It now looks at "throughputs" to try to understand what actually goes on in a program (Cook & Shadish, 1986). It has done this by focusing on process questions rather than strictly on outcome or impact questions. Evaluators have discovered that before they can conclude that implementation is considered a distortion or a failure, it is important to learn what program theory informs policy intentions. Program theory connects policy intentions to tacit assumptions about implementation. Policy formulation, then, requires understanding implementation in its multifaceted dimensions. As Bickman (1987, p. 9) observes: "The policymaker must know if the multiple ways a program was implemented at different sites provide similar feedback on validity of the program." Thus, only as the theory underlying the program becomes clarified can outcomes be realistically validated. Nor can the prevailing notion that policy implementation leads to unintended outcomes be treated as an administrative distortion or failure, for, if a program has been only partially implemented, it cannot be judged either a failure or success until analysis uncovers why it has not been fully implemented. Consequences might be unintended if causes other than inadequate implementation have been eliminated; these include determining the appropriateness of the underlying theory informing policy formation as well as developing an appropriate evaluation design. Poor evaluation design may erroneously conclude that a program has failed when it has not.

Program evaluation research has gone a long way toward contributing to opening up the black box of implementation. This opening focuses on two distinct elements. One is the extent of implementation. As suggested above, this involves questions about context: whether the elements adopted by a program actually reach or serve the right clients or target groups and provide adequately for a sufficient proportion of them (see Chapters 10 and 11). The primary concern regarding the extent of implementation is who and how many clients or target groups are experiencing the program's services. Again, it is necessary to specify the program theory in order to determine whether the right clients or target groups are being reached or are receiving the program's resources, benefits, or punishments (Bickman, 1987; Chen & Rossi, 1980). The question of benefiting from a program now includes a more realistic picture of how much the policy design required redesign to produce satisfaction.

The second opening of the black box focuses on the process of implementation, which deals with the organizational processes that deliver a program (Elmore, 1978; Scheirer, 1987). The latter can be further subdivided into the categories of macro- and micro-implementation. Macro-implementation refers to the variety of organizations involved in implementing a program. For example, implementing a community corrections program requires the efforts of the courts, district or county attorney, sheriff, probation department, state department of corrections, community groups, and offenders; macro-implementation can also include federal agencies. Micro-implementation refers to what goes on inside the local agency primarily responsible for program implementation.

When considering macro-implementation processes, the major theme that emerges from the literature is that program objectives are often interpreted differently by those at the various levels of an implementation chain; these levels include federal agencies, officials of state and local governments, and community and business groups (Pressman & Wildavsky, 1986; Salamon, 1981; Scheirer, 1988). The many voices that are raised by these groups during implementation (Love & Sederberg, 1987) make it apparent that there isn't something factual to be discovered about the process of implementation. Instead, policies are both interpreted and influenced by the character of those implementing organizations (Yanow, 1987; see also Chapter 5). Implementation outcomes, then, represent a confluence of actions among parties that may only superficially agree about mutual objectives. Implementation research has helped to understand this process of macrolevel program implementation. But it also creates problems for evaluation. In a system in which there are multiple actors and voices, each claiming to have the legitimate interpretation of a policy, there are no criteria or standards against which to measure its success or failure (Linder & Peters, 1987a). What a policy is, then, cannot be known until the aggregation of intention and implementation unfold.

At the micro-implementation level the unfolding process is called adaptive implementation. This concept has grown largely out of the conflicts between the top-down versus bottom-up views of implementation. The top-down approach assumes that program goals can be specified by policymakers (viewed as legislators) and that mechanisms can be set up to ensure their implementation (Mazmanian & Sabatier, 1981). Supporters of the bottom-up view contend that the street-level bureaucrats have a better hold on what clients need, and therefore, can play a major role in shaping program goals (Elmore, 1982; Johnson & O'Conner, 1979). While there have been attempts to integrate the two perspectives, there does not appear to be an easy solution; it is not possible to have both faithful adherence to policy directives of legislation and, at the same time, adaptation of the directives at the lower levels to fit what street-level bureaucrats see as the most appropriate clients or client needs. For example, the Elementary and Secondary Education Act of 1965, and its 1967 and 1974 amendments, were passed as an antipoverty bill aimed at helping the poor and disadvantaged. But the categories of aid were so inclusive that many school districts used the funds as general aid to education. Similarly, the Education for All Handicapped Act of 1975 was aimed at providing financial incentives for states to enroll and educate handicapped children, and particularly at providing education in the least restrictive environment appropriate to the handicapped child's needs. But in implementation, schools took shortcuts and did not always follow the mandate of the law (Weatherly, 1979). Similar to the jobs program in Oakland, California, described by Pressman and Wildavsky (1986), federal programs seldom are carried out exactly as specified by the legislation. This gap occurs because the legislation often has broad and vague mandates and because local jurisdictions will adapt the legislation to fit their needs, and there is little the federal government can do to force them to do otherwise. This is also a function of organizational relationships; most federally initiated programs are so loosely coupled (Weick, 1976) that organizational adaptation during implementation becomes inevitable.

As Salamon (1981, p. 160) notes, most federal programs are implemented through "third parties such as special districts, banks, hospitals, corporations, states and cities. Instead of a hierarchical relationship between the federal government and its agents, therefore, what frequently exists in practice is a far more complex bargaining relationship in which the federal agency often has the weaker hand." This factual reality reflects the normative basis for understanding microimplementation in the American federal system. At all stages—from design to redesign—pubic policy represents a mixture of levels of government as well as private and quasi-private agencies involved in implementing programs (Grodzins, 1963). Moreover, these findings do not mean that at the macro level adaptive implementation usually violates normative expectations about maintaining democratic controls over administrators and bureaucrats. Not only has implementation research shown that the politics-administration dichotomy is untenable empirically, it also demonstrates that the political character of democratic policymaking does not suffer. The outcome of adaptive implementation is more like a draw. On one hand, it may invite unresponsiveness to fulfilling policy intentions because they are experienced as inappropriately operationalized. On the other hand, adaptive implementation may create appropriately achievable operational goals despite the flaws of policy design (Calista, 1986a).

Because adaptive implementation (Berman, 1980) is normal and not an aberration, it is difficult to reach external validity in program evaluation (Palumbo & Olivario, 1989). Earlier evaluation studies were primarily concerned with internal validity and did not pay much attention to external validity, that is, to generalizing to future application of the program (Cronbach & Associates, 1980). However, according to some evaluators, policymakers are not so concerned with whether all variables have been controlled as they are with whether the program will work in future applications. But if adaptation is a necessary element of implementation, then achieving external validity may not be possible. As Palumbo and Olivario (forthcoming) note: "Moreover, even if a program works fairly well in one location, we usually want to improve it in the next location." Adaptive implementation, nonetheless, will continue to create problems for program evaluation as well as for the traditional constitutional issue of bureaucratic responsibility.

CONCLUSIONS

Implementation research has opened up the black box of policymaking in a number of ways. There is no doubt that implementation research has finally laid to rest the politics-administration dichotomy. Early implementation research fostered this view when it assumed that implementors were supposed to simply carry out previously made policy directives. More recent research demonstrates that implementation is a legitimate part of the policymaking process—a part that can be neither diminished empirically nor de-legitimated normatively.

Implementors are crucial to the policy networks that shape policy. Their participation in policymaking is no less political or technical than occurs in the process of policy formation. There is usually a conflict between legislators and implementors, especially in cases of divided government (i.e., Republican presidency and Democratic Congress), which occurs often. But the conflict is not confined to these situations. Conflict is inevitable because goal modification during implementation is unavoidable and, from the bottom-up perspective, desirable. Some conflict occurs because middle- and lower-level administrators have their own views about what the objectives of a policy are; in many instances, implementation becomes a process by which superiors must make converts out of followers. At risk is the zealousness by which common purposes can be pursued.

Implementors are involved in every stage of the policy cycle, from design to redesign. Implementors not only help define issues and solutions at the agenda-setting stage; they help to create policy during formulation. Most significantly, they shape policy because of the enormous and irreducible discretion they have, particularly at the street level.

Implementation research has spread to a number of disciplines from its original development by political scientists. Evaluation research has found that implementation has helped open up the limitations of input-output program evaluation. It is now considered essential in order to identify the intervening variables that contribute to specific program outcomes. Implementation research also enables evaluators to understand how programs are interpreted by the many voices involved in policy implementation. Finally, it tells us that we may not be able to achieve external validity in program evaluation.

More than fifteen years have passed since the first seminal studies of implementation were conducted. Although there has been considerable criticism of implementation research during this time (Palumbo & Calista, 1987), it has contributed a great deal to understanding the policymaking process. This research is still in the early stages. Certainly implementation is no longer the unknown quantity lying between formulation and evaluation, the "missing link" (Hargrove, 1975). Instead, implementation research has gone full circle—it now challenges policy analysis to develop frameworks that integrate formulation and implementation without violating their integrity as distinct concepts.

This chapter opened by posing a question about whether the Family Security Act (FSA) of 1988 can be successfully implemented. This question can now be answered. From the vantage point of top-down implementation as an "ideal type," the FSA is already disadvantaged. A most significant issue is the funding targeted in 1988 at $3.34 billion over a five-year period—about $668 million a year. If success is to be measured by acquiring bona fide employment for a large percentage of the 3.7 million people affected, then the funding is inadequate (i.e., the extent of implementation is insufficient). If only 3 million of these persons qualify for aid under the act and the funds are spent on them (assuming no replacements over these first five years), then there will be roughly $223 per individual plus whatever the states contribute. If we assume the states contribute an equal amount, how much then can be bought for about $446 per person? Not much. The only way to increase the amount of funds per individual would be to decrease greatly the extent of implementation which, of course, will also defeat the goals of the act. Some states may employ what amounts to a voucher system, providing funds directly to some recipients. Applied indiscriminately, these funds will do little except provide for some training in low-paying jobs in the service industry. Gaining such employment may provide psychological but not many economic benefits, for the jobs may not even move families above the poverty line. These circumstances, among others, led the act's sponsors to express reservations about not raising hopes too high in expecting any near-term success (*New York Times*, September 18, 1988). Are there any lessons from implementation research that can tell what needs to be done not to disappoint the sponsors too much?

To their credit, the sponsors favored giving states considerable latitude in generating purposes and structuring actions. This certainly satisfies the adaptive implementation requirement to encourage states to establish favorable administrative and managerial climates. Some states have already moved along the frontier contained in the legislation; the objective for these states would be to raise the national standard and through incentives such as demonstration projects to support them in further experimentation.

At the same time, however, such opportunity to adapt FSA to local circumstances can be used to defeat its purposes. There are several possibilities. One is that some states, being pressed for funds due to budget shortfalls, may use the federal funds to replace their existing efforts rather than extend them. To the extent to which they do this there will be a net *reduction* in the effort to help people on welfare—an outcome that is certainly contrary to the act's intentions. A second possible negative adaptation is "creaming." Some localities may elect to spend their funds on the most trainable and employable individuals. While this may help these particular individuals, it will greatly reduce the extent of the FSA, although some might argue that this outcome is really a part of the intentions of some policy formulators (Robertson, 1984).

On the positive side, some jurisdictions may use the funds to provide programs in addition to their existing efforts, thereby exceeding the extent of implementation over that of other localities. Some may even find innovative ways of training some clients and removing them from the welfare rolls. Ostensibly, these constructive ways of implementing the act will fulfill or even exceed the policy. Whether the positive and constructive adaptations are sufficiently great to offset the negative adaptations, however, is impossible to say. There is no doubt, however, that both forms of adaptation will occur.

From an epistemological perspective, the interesting question is how well these adaptations are perceived by the Congress, by the president, and by the states and localities. To be sure, disagreement will develop even among those localities where negative adaptations occur. These will not be seen that way by all the groups, organizations, and individuals involved. In other words, agreement will not exist either about the outcomes, nor about who is to blame for what some observers will call negative outcomes. Implementation is multifaceted; therefore, the judgments about whether or not implementation has succeeded will contain elements of political, organizational, and behavioral dimensions about which ideological and technical disagreements prevail. What observers see will be a function of those dimensions.

At the broadest level, the success of the act's implementation depends on how accurate the underlying program theory is. Similar to most welfare policies, FSA is based on the theory that individuals are the cause of their own welfare dependency. The problems that are supposed to be corrected by the act stem from inadequacies in education, job skills, motivation, and lack of day-care facilities for the welfare-dependent women. But this theory may well apply to only a small proportion of the approximately 3.7 million individuals. There is also a conflicting theory that the act seems to reject; that is, that a major cause of welfare dependency is the lack of adequate jobs in the changing American economy (Wilson, 1988). If this theory is correct, the FSA will fail during implementation. The failure will not be due to faulty implementation but to faulty problem definition and policy design. Nonetheless, there will not be universal agreement among all stakeholders that the failure, if it occurs, would be due to these aspects of the policymaking process. Indeed, if the ideology of antitax and antigovernment sentiment still abounds, it will be "those ineffectual bureaucrats" who will shoulder the blame.

Finally, since implementation as well as policy formulation involves the politics of symbolism, there will be instances where the appearance of success will occur. Such instances may be sufficient to justify the continuation of the policy and even vindicate its program theory in the minds of some stakeholders. Nevertheless, we can be sure that the FSA will not end welfare dependency. This is because there isn't a theory in existence that identifies the causes of welfare dependency or what incentives or tools will succeed in getting the intended target groups to behave the way the act wants. This is not meant as a counsel of despair; we do not say that it is impossible to discover the correct theories and methods by which both policy formulation and implementation can be guided. We do say that it is a political rather than a technical process, and, similar to all political processes, it is a matter of power and conflicting interests.

2

Integrating Implementation Research

Søren Winter

Even though implementation research has been dominated by case studies, some progress has been made in the development of theory during the last fifteen years (Palumbo, 1987; Lester et al., 1987). There are many interesting theoretical ideas, such as the importance of the number of decision points (Pressman & Wildavsky, 1973), conflicts in interorganizational settings (Bardach, 1977), street-level bureaucracy (Lipsky, 1980), validity of the causal theories of the policy and structuring the implementation process (Mazmanian & Sabatier, 1981; 1983).

Implementation has been analyzed from many different perspectives characterized by the special lens applied by each particular scholar. Yanow (1987) identifies four different lenses focusing on the behavior of the individual implementor: dynamics within and between groups, design of organization, and interdependencies among organizations respectively, and she herself adds a policy culture lens as a fifth important perspective.

There are several analytical frameworks (e.g., Van Meter & Van Horn, 1975; Mazmanian & Sabatier, 1981; 1983; Lester et al., 1987), and there are various major approaches that often are categorized into two: top-down (e.g., Mazmanian & Sabatier, 1981; 1983) and bottom-up (e.g., Hjern & Porter, 1981; Hull & Hjern, 1987; Elmore, 1982; 1985). However, this dichotomization is probably too rough to do justice to the many different perspectives that can be found. Each approach contains its own combination of theoretical conceptions and methodology.

An earlier version of this paper was presented at the Conference of the Nordic Association of Political Science, August 16–19, 1987, Copenhagen, in the workshop on "Guidance, Control and Evaluation."

Figure 2.1

The Implementation Process and Determinants of the Implementation Result

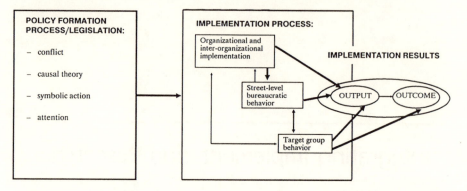

However, there is too little accumulation in implementation theory. There is a substantial theoretical pluralism including various perspectives, research strategies, and theoretical findings but very little overall accumulation in our knowledge of implementation processes (Alexander, 1985; Lester et al., 1987; Palumbo, 1987).

Some efforts to integrate the top-down and bottom-up approaches have been undertaken (Sabatier, 1986; Hull & Hjern, 1987), but the results are both research strategies that demand more data-collection and analysis than can normally be done within one study, and sets of variables that hardly are enough to explain implementation outcomes in a satisfactory way. For instance the synthesis model seems to ignore Lipsky's identification of street-level bureaucratic coping strategies as an important determinant of implementation outcomes. Alexander (1985) has also stimulated accumulation by proposing a rather abstract framework to identify important processes and linkages in the policy-program-implementation process.

This paper approaches accumulation in implementation theory by identifying the most promising theoretical elements that really have contributed to our understanding of implementation—as well as a few variables that have received too little attention—all of which ought to be included as a part of a more general theory of policy implementation. Yet it is far too early to form such a theory. Our systematic knowledge of implementation processes is still too limited. What we are trying here is only to present a preliminary model to explain implementation outcomes by identifying some of the key variables and by suggesting how these variables can be brought together into one model. According to this model, illustrated in Figure 2.1, the key factors that determine implementation outcome are to be found in four main sociopolitical processes or conditions: (1) the character of the policy formation process prior to the law or decision to be implemented, (2) the organizational and interorganizational implementation behavior, (3) street-level bureaucratic behavior, and (4) the response by target groups and other changes in society. These processes or conditions also represent different phases or levels in the policy formation and implementation processes.

The model is relatively simple with only four sets of key variables to explain implementation outcomes. It attempts to concentrate the analysis on a few important variables and to avoid the very long list of potentially relevant factors that are so common in implementation studies (Goggin, 1986). But admittedly, the model gets more complicated when we proceed to analyze each of the four variables separately, as well as linkages among these variables.

The aim of the model is to identify and integrate the most important implementation variables for the purpose of getting a comprehensive view and stimulating future theory development; it does not intend to offer a synthesizing research strategy or a methodological recipe. One's preferred methodology tends to affect one's theoretical conceptions, and the synthesis approaches made by both Sabatier (1986) and Hull and Hjern (1987) seem to be affected by their respective research strategies and methodologies.

Therefore, as an alternative it might be interesting to start by identifying and combining the most promising theoretical elements and to leave the methodological issues as a secondary consideration. However, various strategies must be adopted to analyze all the variables of our model, and in most cases there will probably be too few resources to handle all the variables thoroughly in one study. The model is intended to have a rather general applicability across different countries and policy areas. In particular, it is relevant for both the implementation of human service policies and regulatory policies, though the relevance of some of the variables may vary among those policies as we shall see later. However, the model focuses on the implementation of "material" policies that seek to change conditions in society, whereas it does not fit very well to the analysis of implementation of reorganization policy.

IMPLEMENTATION OUTCOME: DEFINING THE DEPENDENT VARIABLE

In implementation studies it is not always clear what the dependent variable is, and there is little agreement about the proper standard of evaluation for the purpose of deciding whether the implementation was a success or a failure (Linder & Peters, 1987a). Three main kinds of behavior can be identified when we look for an evaluation standard: process, output, and outcome/impact or changes in society (Linder & Peters, 1987a). This behavior can then be compared either to the official (and/or the unofficial) goals of the policy mandate, to the problematic behavior in the society to which one or more policies address themselves, or to the interests of the various actors who have a stake in the implementation process.

Most implementation scholars compare behavior with official policy goals. Not only do the "top-down" scholars belong in this group, but also some of the scholars that perceive implementation as a conflict-bargaining game (Bardach, 1977), and even some "bottom-up"-people (Weatherly & Lipsky, 1977; Lipsky,

1980; Winter, 1986a). As in process evaluation, the actual implementation actions can be compared to the envisaged ones. The character and quantity of the output or performance of the delivering apparatus can be compared to the policy objectives (Lipsky, 1980; Winter, 1986a), and in a similar way the impact on target group behavior can be related to the policy goals (Mazmanian & Sabatier, 1981; 1983). In our opinion output and even more outcome/impact are the most relevant variables, as neither process nor output compliance can assure goal achievement ("The surgery was successful but the patient died").

However, the identification of policy goals represents a major problem in policy evaluation and implementation analyses. Policy goals are often so vague or conflicting that they are useless as standards by which to evaluate implementation behavior and outcomes (Palumbo & Nachmias, 1983). Also, the real goals may be quite different from the official goals stated in legislation. To the observer, official goals are often of limited value because so many participants in the implementation are motivated by quite competing interests (Hjern & Hull, 1982; Elmore, 1982; Sabatier, 1986).

Another strategy to cope with the evaluation-standard problem is to use the goals or interests of the various actors in the implementation process (Hjern, Hanf, & Porter, 1978; Hjern & Porter, 1981; Premfors, 1981)—or even the interests of all actors involved in the formation of policy as well as implementation without making any distinction between the two processes (Sætren, 1983). The various interests included in such a "stakeholder" model probably explain better than formal policy goals what is going on in the implementation process. Moreover, this strategy pays attention to the fact that programs are often not executed in isolation but in interaction with other policy programs with similar or different objectives affecting the same actors and target groups (Hjern & Porter, 1981).

A third strategy is to avoid policy goals and focus on problem solving instead. Then the evaluation criterion is not goal achievement but the extent to which implementation structures contribute to the solving of problems in society. This has been the strategy of two of the bottom-up advocates, Hjern et al. and Elmore. Though it is tempting to use such a strategy to avoid the ambiguity of policy goals, there are also some important problems involving questions not only about facts but also about values. It is impossible to define a problem or solution without explicitly or implicitly referring to some political values. These values may be the analyst's own—with important implications for the relevance of the research—or they may be inspired by the problem definitions and/or goals of the policymakers (Hull & Hjern, 1987; Elmore, 1985). But in the latter case the distance from goal-directed implementation research is not very great.

Which of these strategies is most appropriate depends on the purpose of the analysis in question. The "stakeholder" strategy describes what really happens, but it fails to take into account that, from a democratic point of view, objectives stated in legislation are important and must be taken seriously. Implementation studies may further democratic control of government if they investigate whether the official policy goals, as stated to the parliament and the public, are indeed implemented (Winter, 1986a; Mazmanian & Sabatier, 1983; Sabatier, 1986). For this reason the present study employs the official goals set down in law and administrative rules as the evaluation standard for outputs and outcomes. The study does not, however, ignore the importance of conflicting interests in the policymaking and implementation processes. The character of both the policy-formation process and the interorganizational networks in the implementation process are included in the model in the explanation of implementation results. Even though we choose the official goals as our evaluation standard, however, the variables of our model are also likely to be relevant for explaining implementation outcomes according to other evaluation standards.

Implementation research has revealed an abundance of failures. Particularly the first generation of studies reported mostly negative results. Typical is Bardach's (1977) statement that "even the most robust policy—one that is well designed to survive the implementation process—will tend to go awry. The classic symptoms of underperformance, delay, and escalating costs are bound to appear."

The pessimistic conclusions to a significant extent can be attributed to the special perspective of most implementation scholars (Lester et al., 1987). They typically ask why the program objectives have not been completely achieved, in contrast to the "classic" evaluation analysts who are interested in measuring if and why a given program has had any effect at all. While many evaluation analysts have reported disappointing results, the question that implementation specialists typically ask is bound to lead to even more pessimistic conclusions.

However, recent evaluation and implementation literature paints a somewhat brighter picture. Studies covering a longer time frame have found that some programs that were failures at first gradually become more successful as the policy proponents make use of experience and experimentation to remedy deficiencies (Kirst & Jung, 1982; Mazmanian & Sabatier, 1983; Sabatier, 1986). Second-generation studies have also paid attention to the variability in implementation outcomes among countries (Elmore, Gustafsson, & Hargrove, 1986), local settings, and policy areas (Goggin, 1986; Sabatier, 1986; Lester et al., 1987; Hull & Hjern, 1987) and even across different subelements of the same program (Winter, 1986a).

HOW POLICY FORMATION AFFECTS IMPLEMENTATION

When implementation scholars explain why the objectives of a policy program have not been met, most studies have referred to failures during the implementation process. Such failures are attributed, for instance, to the conflicting interests of implementation actors or lack of implementation capacity. The fact seems to be, however, that irrespective of the commitment and resources of the agencies in charge of implementation, some policies are impossible to implement from the outset.

This recognition has stimulated an interest in policy design as a variable that affects the implementation outcome (Mazmanian & Sabatier, 1981; 1983; Linder & Peters, 1987a; 1987b; Elmore, 1985; Palumbo, 1987). The design focus is very interesting, but it very easily turns into a rationalistic exercise where implementation researchers tell policymakers that their policies are not rational because the causal theory of the policy is either invalid or missing, or because they have not structured the implementation process sufficiently to secure compliance by participating implementors (Mazmanian & Sabatier, 1981; 1983).

We know, however, that policies are very rarely made in a rational way, and therefore the actual character of the policy-formation process may be very important to explain why some policies are impossible or difficult to implement from the outset. If we really want to understand how and why policies are implemented, we cannot just start by looking at the design. We must also understand why the policies were constructed the way they were. Though Hargrove (1975) earlier called for more implementation research to provide the "missing link" in policy studies, most later implementation studies have isolated themselves from studying the links or interactions between policy formation and implementation (Yanow, 1987). Some of the rare exceptions are Mayntz (Blankenburg, 1985); Lundquist (1980); Elmore, Gustafsson, and Hargrove (1986); Calista (1986a), and Winter (1986a).

Apparently, ignoring the link between policy formation and implementation is a consequence of the division of labor between subdisciplines of political science and policy studies. Scholars specializing in policymaking and legislative processes have rarely shown any interest in what happens after the laws are passed, and scholars specializing in implementation and policy evaluation have typically restricted their interests to the implementation process.

In the absence of any established theory concerning the effect of policy formation on implementation, Winter (1986b) has derived a set of hypotheses about such linkages from three well-known models of policymaking: the rational decision-making model, the conflict-bargaining model, and the garbage-can model (Olsen, 1972; March & Olsen, 1985). These models are normally seen as conflicting. However, it may be possible to gain insight from all three models for the purpose of constructing one integrated set of politically realistic hypotheses about the impact of the policy-formation process on the implementation outcome.

First, successful implementation is likely to be negatively related to the degree of conflict in the policy-formation phase (Calista, 1986a). Policy-formation processes are often characterized by conflicts among actors, who each follow their own interests, and agreement about goals is rare. In such a situation the actors typically engage in a bargaining process (Lindblom, 1959), and their decision is a product of their individual interests, the intensity of these interests, the unequal distribution of resources among the participants, and their ability to form coalitions. Most decisions are compromises, and they concern means rather than goals. Accordingly, conflictual policy formation tends to discourage any clear definition of goals while at the same time new formal goals may be invented in order to legitimize compromises.

As the means are part of the bargaining and compromising game, the chosen implementation structure is not likely to maximize any goal achievement even if clear goals have been formulated. In fact, an ineffective means or implementation structure may be compensation for important actors if they accept policy goals and principles that they do not like. Indeed, policy opponents may engage in structuring the implementation process quite as often as policy proponents do (Mazmanian & Sabatier, 1981; 1983). Policy opponents may be quite skilled in getting the implementation process structured in such a way that the policy is not implemented effectively. For instance, choosing local governments as controlling authorities seems to have made industrial interest organizations much more willing to accept environmental regulation policies, because they trust local governments to be more "flexible" and to take the well-being of the local enterprises more into consideration than state authorities (Blankenburg, 1985).

Second, successful implementation is more likely if the policy proponents in the policy-formation process have based their decisions on a valid causal theory about the problematic behavior to be regulated by the policy and the relationship between the policy instruments and that behavior (Pressman & Wildavsky, 1973; Mazmanian & Sabatier, 1981; 1983). The application of a valid causal theory presumes first that such a theory exists, and second that it has been applied by the policy proponents in analyzing the consequences of the policy decision. It does not, however, presume that all proponents agree about the theory application, except that each knows what he is doing and has been thinking about consequences in relation to his own values.

Many policy problems in the modern welfare state are "wicked" problems that are ill defined and intractable (Hoppe et al., 1987). It may be difficult to grasp exactly what the problem is as well as its causes and consequences, and it may be even more difficult to find policy instruments that can affect the problem. However, policymakers often feel that it is their duty to respond to all kinds of problems in society, especially "wicked" ones. This may be one reason why some policies are adopted that rest on an insufficient causal theory or that even are of purely symbolic nature.

Demonstrating a willingness to act may be more important than actually solving problems. Therefore, it is an evident third hypothesis that an implementation success is unlikely if the policy was adopted for symbolic reasons.

Fourth, successful implementation is likely to be positively related to the level of attention by the policy proponents in the policy-formation process. Most actors in a policy-formation process are only part-time participants faced by competing claims for attention from other private and public roles. Participants are also often exchanged with new ones. Their level of attention is, furthermore, affected by the length of the decision-making period, the number of participants, and the number of competing issues on the agenda (Olsen, 1972; March & Olsen, 1984;

Kingdon, 1984). Therefore, attention to one particular policy is also affected by the way policies are grouped into reform packages (Winter, 1986b).

If the attention is diverted from a given policy, the policy decision process tends to become less instrumental. The connection among participants, values, problems, choice opportunities, and solution tends to become more accidental, resembling the garbage can model (March & Olsen, 1984; Kingdon, 1984). Causal theories and analyses of consequences are less likely to be applied, and symbolic action is more likely. Therefore, limited attention tends to produce decisions where no direct relationship and internal consistency among policy formation, policy goals, design, and implementation can be expected (Winter, 1986b). In a case study of the decentralization of the Danish Disablement Insurance Tribunal, Winter (1986b) found some support for these hypotheses. Particularly, the hypothesis about limited attention explained the failure of the reform to achieve its goals of speeding up decision making and decreasing administrative costs while preserving a uniform decision-making practice. The decentralization of the tribunal was not an isolated reform but only a small part of a massive legislative package concerning the entire social welfare system. Other issues in this larger package attracted most of the attention of the many participants in the policy-formation process. Though this process lasted for thirteen years, the decision to decentralize the tribunal was given only a few minutes of debate.

In the 1960s and 1970s, "decentralization" was a symbol that enjoyed wide and uncritical support as a democratic value in its own right and as an instrument to improve services and reduce administrative decision-making time and costs. The decentralization of the tribunal fitted beautifully into this pattern of beliefs. But symbols are difficult to implement! The decentralization reform was impossible to implement from the outset.

These hypotheses may be a start in examining the linkages between the policy formation and implementation processes, but we need much more research in order to get a better understanding both of conditions for implementation and of the whole policy process covering both problem identification, policy formation, implementation and feedback (Alexander, 1985) and the linkages between those phases.

ORGANIZATIONAL AND INTERORGANIZATIONAL IMPLEMENTATION BEHAVIOR

Policy outcomes are not only influenced by the prior policy-formation process but also by several conditions in the implementation phase, to which we now turn. One set of variables to explain implementation outputs and outcomes has to do with the way organizations alone or in interorganizational relationships respond to policy mandates. Almost always policy implementation requires the participation of one or, more frequently, several organizations, public and private. Organizations have various institutional interests to attend to. These may be in accord with the objectives or mandate of the policy in question, but often influential participants in the implementation process give priority to goals that conflict with the policy (Bardach, 1977). This situation frequently leads to problems of coordination, delays, implementation failures, and the spending of public funds for purposes other than those prescribed.

While the role of private interest groups requires no further comment for the present purposes, the role of public authorities does. Policy implementation often involves state and local governments headed by politicians who disagree with the objectives of programs adopted by the national government. Thus, most implementation studies in the United States and Europe report implementation problems arising from the lack of coordinated action among federal, state, and local governments (Pressman & Wildavsky, 1986; Bardach, 1977; Williams & Elmore, 1976; Elmore, 1978; Sabatier, 1986). Furthermore, federal and state bureaucracies have interests of their own to protect. Examples are the need for bureaucracies to seek their own survival and growth, reluctance to abandon traditions and routines (Elmore, 1978), attachment to previously established programs that may be in conflict with new ones (Winter, 1986a), and loyalty to traditional coalition partners (e.g., interest organizations).

Organizational and interorganizational implementation behavior can be studied according to different levels of analysis (Yanow, 1987; Lester et al., 1987), but for the sake of simplification we treat both organizational and interorganizational behavior as one set of variables without distinguishing between them. The common core of the argument is that the implementation output and outcomes are affected by organizational interests and incentives of the organization or organizations that participate in the implementation process.

Most implementation studies have used the institutional interests of and conflicts among organizations as the central variables to explain implementation output and outcome (Williams & Elmore, 1976; Palumbo, 1987; Lester et al., 1987). This is easy to understand, both because the variables are very relevant and because conflicts and bargaining among actors in policymaking are among the most popular research perspectives within different subdisciplines of political science. According to this view, policymaking—whether in the policy-formation or implementation phases—and policy outputs and outcomes are determined by the interests and resources of the participants. Implementation is seen as a continuation of the political game played out in the formation of policy, albeit in another arena and also to some extent involving different actors.

Here it should be noted, however, that in the implementation phase the relationship among the participants may be quite different from that in the policy-formation phase. Some actors may be much more powerful in the implementation phase than they were in the policy-formation phase as in our environmental protection example above. And as Bardach (1977) argues, implementation games are much more defensive than policy-formation policymaking games because the actors are "more concerned with what they in particular may lose than what all in general may win." Moreover, compromising coalitions that were necessary for the participating organizations to affect the policy tend to break up in the implementation phase (Nakamura, 1987). Implementation is most often regarded as a threat to established interests. Because of the defensive character of the implementation game, Bardach thinks that coalitions are much more rare than they are in the formation of policy. Characteristic features of the implementation phase are fragmented and isolated maneuvers and countermaneuvers.

As a general comparison of policy formation and implementation these observations are probably correct. However, the presence of coalitions in the implementation phase may vary across issue areas, nations, and even different stages of the implementation process. Patterns of actor interaction vary from sector to sector (Damgaard, 1981). For example, in Denmark, relationship among the central actors, the social partners, in workers' safety and health programs tend to be hostile while they form strong coalitions in vocational training programs.

Compared to the United States, implementation in the Scandinavian countries tends to be less complex and is less affected by involvement from both volunteer organizations in social service delivery and the courts while municipalities and interest organizations participate to a considerable degree. Many American implementation studies convey an impression of "pressure-group" politics in which the government is responsible for implementation but is deterred by external pressure applied by interest organizations (Mazmanian & Sabatier, 1981, 1983). In Scandinavia, on the other hand, interest organizations are most often directly and mandatorily involved in the implementation process. In Denmark interest organizations are represented on several hundred boards and committees, which are consulted or even assigned responsibility for implementation (Johansen & Kristensen, 1982). In some cases, the administration of a public program is entirely turned over to interest organizations. One example is the administration of unemployment benefits (which for the most part are financed by the state).

As mentioned above, most implementation studies focus on conflicts among participants in the implementation process. Even different implementation approaches share an emphasis in the importance of interorganizational relations. Therefore, such different approaches as the "top-down" perspective by Mazmanian and Sabatier and the "bottom-up" approach by Hjern and collaborators both focus on such interactions. What separates the two is their methodology, their evaluation standard, and the extent to which they think policy proponents can structure the implementation process to avoid conflicts and implementation failures. We have discussed the evaluation standard problem above, and we shall later return to the issue of structuring the implementation process.

The "top-down" approach largely restricts its attention to actors that are formally involved in the implementation of a specific program. Thus, the actors are defined in a formal, programmatic way. Also in keeping with the "top-down" perspective the analyses start at the top and do not always reach the delivery-level actors. The "bottom-up" approach, on the other hand, begins with the definition of a certain problem in society and proceeds with the identifications of actors that affect this problem. The actors are defined not in terms of their attachment to a specific program but in terms of their relevance to a specific problem. The special "snowballing" technique of the approach is well suited to identifying informal public and private organizations and actors that the formal "top-down" research strategies tend to ignore (Sabatier, 1986).

However, just as the "top-down" approach favors actors at or near the top of the implementation system, the "bottom-up" approach, resting on the assumptions that delivery-level activities are the most important in determining policy results, favors what happens at or close to the delivery level. Consequently, in their backward mapping the very time consuming "bottom-up" analyses do not always reach the top agencies (see, e.g., Hull & Hjern, 1987). While we agree that delivery-level behavior is very important for the outcome—a point that will be further emphasized in the following section—top-level behavior or nonbehavior will in our opinion affect the conditions for delivery-level activities in important ways. An ideal research strategy would, of course, be to combine the two approaches. Since, however, the "bottom-up" strategy is excessively expensive and time-consuming, this is rarely possible (Sabatier, 1986). One solution to this problem is to combine parts of the two approaches. Winter (1986a) has done so in a study of the implementation of a youth employment program in Denmark.

While implementation studies have been successful in describing how the complexity of action in interorganizational settings hampers implementation, these studies have not been of much positive help to policymakers interested in avoiding implementation conflicts (Elmore, 1982; Mazmanian & Sabatier, 1981; 1983). But some attempts to provide policymakers with information on how to structure the implementation process have, after all, been made.

Mazmanian and Sabatier (1981; 1983; Sabatier, 1986) emphasize the importance of the hierarchical integration within and among implementing institutions combined with the specification of the formal decision rules of the implementing agencies. This approach is tempting, especially when we are dealing with the federal system of the United States, which is characterized by myriads of conflicts with state and local governments. But although it might be tempting to conclude that such a situation calls for the establishment of "Weberian" ideal-type true hierarchical structures, it would hardly be a practical alternative.

First, the implementation structure can rarely be created from scratch. The involvement of many actors in the implementation process is often merely the result of a power game that legislators cannot ignore. Local governments are involved in the implementation process just because they are powerful enough to be included, or because other important political actors want to rely on local governments for policy implementation, (see the environment protection example above).

Second, legal hierarchical subordination does not guarantee successful implementation. Though formal subordination may represent a power resource for the top executive, the behavioral public administration research has demonstrated that subordinate agencies may have countervailing resources, such as action invisibility, expertise, and ability to form coalitions. The power of hierarchical control is limited (Elmore, 1982; Hjern & Porter, 1981; Hjern, 1982b). As the next section will suggest, this principle also applies to efforts to control the behavior of street-level bureaucrats by stipulating rules and regulation. On the other hand, and dependent on the incentives, legally independent local governments may sometimes be more helpful in implementing national policies than the agencies of the central government. For example, in connection with the youth employment program in Denmark, local governments have created relatively more job offers than have state institutions (Winter, 1986a; 1987).

Mazmanian and Sabatier's term "hierarchical integration" must, however, not be understood too literally. The hierarchical control seems to depend primarily on number of veto/clearance points involved in the attainment of program objectives and the sanctions and inducements that are provided to overcome resistance. The two authors also believe that goal attainment will be improved if implementation is assigned to agencies which support the objectives and give them a high priority, and if formal rules are made to allow citizens in favor of the program to participate in the implementation process.

In an evaluation of more than twenty applications of the Mazmanian/Sabatier framework, Sabatier finds considerable empirical evidence in support of the notion that it is important to select implementing institutions supportive of the new program or, alternatively, to create a whole new agency (Sabatier, 1986). This finding raises doubts about the soundness of the wisdom that has been common since the early 1970s both in the United States and Denmark, namely that social services need to be integrated into comprehensive social and human service centers for purposes of improving implementation (Winter, 1978; Calista, 1986a). Integrating various service programs and institutions may mean that some programs are given a lower priority. The implementation literature throws a new light on the old organization theory problem of specialization versus coordination.

Sabatier's evaluation, however, provides support for the idea that the number of veto points is important (see also Pressman & Wildavsky, 1973). In this light, Bardach's (1977) idea of creating a "fixer" might be mentioned as a structuring device. Such a fixer is an influential person, agency, or group of people not only closely monitoring the program performance, but also serving as helpful in straddling strategic veto points.

To sum up, implementation failures are more likely if the implementation structure includes organizations that have institutional interests and incentives that are conflicting with the policy goals. To some extent it is possible for policy proponents to structure the implementation process to avoid conflicts and implementation barriers. However, we have earlier seen that not only policy proponents but also opponents attempt to structure the implementation process to fit their own values. But though policy proponents often cannot manipulate the structuring freely, they may get some valuable insight from the implementation research that may enable them to control the implementation process better.

Until now we have used an organizational and interorganizational level of analysis for explaining implementation outcomes. We have seen how these outcomes are affected both by the character of the policy-formation process that preceded the legislation and by responses of single or interacting organizations involved in the implementation. Very often, however, it is impossible to explain the implementation outcome in a satisfactory way if we ignore individuals as actors (Yanow, 1987). In the next two sections we analyze how individual street-level bureaucrats and the target population respond to public policies. In order to be implemented, policies must not only be transformed by organizations but also by individual field workers and citizens in the target groups.

When organizational response is the level of analysis, individuals in those organizations are assumed to follow organizational interests in doing their work. But when changing our level of analysis to the individual level, we discover that individual field workers may follow other rationales than the organizational ones. Hjern and Porter (1981) have found that people in organizations who have specialized in administering a certain program or problem area often are more loyal to programmatic than organizational goals (Winter 1986a). On the other hand Lipsky has made the observation that field workers or street-level bureaucrats tend to lose sight of programmatic goals because of the pressure of the daily work situation (Lipsky, 1980).

THE BEHAVIOR OF STREET-LEVEL BUREAUCRATS

Since Michael Lipsky's study (1980) the policymaking process has been turned on its head by regarding street-level bureaucrats as the real policymakers. Laws and programs are nothing but statements and have no social existence until they are translated into action aimed at delivering services to or regulating the behavior of citizens. And most programs require street-level bureaucrats to perform the delivery or control functions. Street-level bureaucrats are public officials who in their work interact directly with members of the target groups and who often enjoy considerable discretionary powers.

One fairly universal problem is that street-level bureaucrats feel that their own resources are chronically and seriously insufficient to meet the demands placed on them (Weatherly & Lipsky, 1977). A typical response to the conflict they experience is to employ a number of conscious or subconscious coping strategies. Street-level bureaucrats will use tricks such as limiting information about services, making clients wait, making access difficult, and imposing a variety of other psychological costs on clients. A slightly different kind of coping strategy is to concentrate on a limited number of selected clients, types of programs, and solutions. According to Gresham's Law programmed activities tend to dominate more loosely programmed activities (March & Simon, 1958). Accordingly, street-level bureaucrats tend to give priority to easy, programmed routine cases at the expense of more complicated, nonprogrammed, and time-consuming cases (Winter, 1986a). By the same token, higher priority is given to cases where the client is demanding a decision than to cases involving preventive action, reaching out, or follow-up activities. Another coping mechanism is "creaming," a concept implying that "street-level bureaucrats often choose (or skim off the top) those clients who seem most likely to succeed in terms of bureaucratic success criteria" (Lipsky, 1980), but who may not be the most needy ones. Other coping mechanisms are rough categorization of clients, routinization, domination of clients, passing clients on to other authorities, and down-grading of client perception and program objectives.

Such coping strategies are so common among street-level bureaucrats that the implementation of policy programs is distorted in a systematic way. Lipsky and his colleagues have demonstrated that these strategies are employed by very different professions within very different policy programs (Lipsky, 1980; Weatherly & Lipsky, 1977; Weatherly, 1979; Prottas, 1979). Others have found quite similar behavior in the implementation of social welfare and youth employment programs in Europe (Winter, 1981; 1986a; Rasmussen, 1986; Christensen, 1987).

Lipsky and collaborators have made a very significant contribution to implementation research in showing that street-level bureaucrats are very important—perhaps the most important—actors in the policy process. This finding ought to be included in any theory or research framework concerning policy implementation. It is a serious weakness that particularly the top-down approach (Mazmanian & Sabatier, 1981; 1983; Sabatier, 1986) but to some extent also the bottom-up perspective of Hjern and collaborators (Hull & Hjern, 1987) have paid very little attention to Lipsky's finding concerning the coping mechanisms of street-level bureaucrats.

Yet the street-level bureaucracy theory is too narrow to be satisfactory alone. Additionally, the theory has not been very successful in explaining why the coping behaviors occur and why substantial variations exist. Correspondingly, Lipsky has not been able to offer any convincing constructive suggestions as to how to reduce coping behavior (Winter, 1985).

In their early analysis Weatherly and Lipsky (1977) seemed to regard the actual workload per street-level bureaucrat as the independent variable and suggested that coping behavior could be cut by increasing staff. Lipsky has later become skeptical about the usefulness of merely increasing the staff in efforts to control coping behavior. He maintains that the demand for services will grow along with delivery capacity (1980). A Danish study of a social welfare reform shows that even though the actual and the perceived workload per social worker varies considerably among the local welfare agencies, there is no correlation at all between the two variables. More important, the actual workload cannot explain variation in reaching-out activities, one of the activities assigned a high priority in the reform (Winter, 1984; Plovsing, 1985). It appears that perceived workload can better explain coping behavior than can actual workload, but the relationship between the two variables is very complex and difficult to sort out.

If coping behavior is closely related to perceptions and attitudes, our understanding of the dynamics of street-level bureaucratic behavior might be improved by introducing organizational culture as an explanatory variable (Winter, 1985;

Christensen, 1987; Yanow, 1987). Adherence to routines and resistance to policy change may be understood as coping strategies. But such behaviors can also be interpreted as part of an organizational culture (see also Elmore, 1978, and Allison, 1971), just as perceptions of excessive workloads may be shaped by the culture.

If the coping behavior is rooted in the organizational culture, a logical strategy would be to change the culture. However, students of organizational culture disagree about whether it is possible for managers to affect any lasting changes (see, e.g., Peters & Waterman, 1982; Christensen & Kreiner, 1984; Schein, 1985). We believe that Schein is right in maintaining that it is difficult but not impossible to change the culture of an organization. One obvious precondition for successful change is that managers gain insights into the culture of their organization. In any event, it seems evident that implementation studies that combine a focus on the behavior of "street-level bureaucrats" with serious attention to organizational culture could add significantly to our understanding of implementation processes and problems (see also Yanow, 1987).

TARGET-GROUP BEHAVIOR AND SOCIOECONOMIC CONDITIONS

Finally, implementation is very much affected by the way in which the target groups respond to the policy. This target-group behavior constitutes the primary focus of most policies. Most regulations and policy programs attempt to solve problems in society by changing the behavior of the citizens, but people's behavior is determined by many other factors, in addition to policy. In fact, policies may often affect the target group behavior only marginally (Elmore, 1982). By the same token, changing socioeconomic and other conditions in society may affect implementation; for example, the implementation of both social welfare and employment policies is very dependent on changes in the economy and on the labor market.

Yet, most implementation research has paid very little systematic attention to how target-group behavior and unexpected societal changes impact on implementation. Some implementation scholars have been interested in following the implementation process within the public sector only to the point of delivery without paying any attention to the effect or outcome. However, the impact of public services on target groups obviously is a relevant implementation problem—and in the implementation of regulatory policies, those processes can hardly be understood without paying attention to the response of the target groups.

However, even when implementation scholars attempt to explain implementation output rather than outcome, the behavior of target groups is an important variable. For example, in a youth employment training program the output—training—is conditioned by the willingness of the target group to participate. Therefore the target groups are also actors in the implementation process.

Though a few implementation scholars have begun to focus on target-group behavior, we have very little systematic knowledge of these processes. The

"bottom-up" scholars have, naturally, paid some attention to target-group behavior (Hull & Hjern, 1987; Elmore, 1982). They stress that the behavior of
clients is affected by many other factors in addition to those of a particular
program. However, while most "top-down" implementation studies focus very
little on target-group behavior, the top-down approach by Mazmanian and Sabatier does pay some attention to this phenomenon. First, the framework emphasizes that policies are likely to fail if they do not incorporate a valid causal
theory that explains how policy objectives are to be attained. The authors conclude that "inadequate causal theories lie behind many of the cases of implementation failure" (Mazmanian & Sabatier, 1983, p. 26; Sabatier, 1986;
Pressman & Wildavsky, 1973). Such a theory must also cover target-group
behavior. In this connection, Mazmanian and Sabatier believe that the probability
of implementation failure increases with the amount of behavioral modification
required to achieve statutory objectives and that this amount is a function of both
the number of people in the target group and the degree of change required of
them. Several empirical applications of the framework have, however, convinced
Sabatier (1986) that a certain departure from status quo ante is necessary to
arouse enough commitment to get anything done.

If we accept that the reactions of target groups are important to implementation,
then it becomes necessary to ask how implementation scholars can gain a greater
understanding of these reactions. A first requirement is, of course, that target-
group behavior be included in implementation studies (e.g., Elmore, 1986; Winter, 1986a; Hull & Hjern, 1987).

Second, implementation scholars might get some insight from the enormous
evaluation literature. Many evaluation studies contain a great deal of information
on how target groups have responded to policy programs. In spite of the fact
that evaluation scholars engage even more rarely than implementation scholars
in development of generalizations and theories applicable beyond the single case,
evaluation studies have focused on target-group behavior. These studies have
looked not only on how a target group as a whole responds to specific programs
but also on how behavior varies between individuals according to attributes such
as educational and social background. For example, it has been demonstrated
that people with little education and a poor social background are less likely to
benefit from social services than more educated and wealthier people even when
these social services are targeted primarily at the former category. Creaming is
done not only by street-level bureaucrats but also by the self-selection of the
target groups themselves.

Third, within the discipline of sociology of law, where interest in theory
building generally has been greater, several scholars have studied target-group
responses to regulations and services. These studies show how crucial the communication of regulations and right to services is. In the course of the last decades,
the number of new or revised statutes has multiplied every year, and a considerable portion of these statutes are not known to their target groups. Many people
are ignorant of their rights as well as their duties.

When, however, a statute is known to the target group, it is important that the members are motivated to comply with that statute. The behavior that is subjected to regulation is not independent of group norms internalized by the individual members through socialization. As a general rule, the successful implementation of a statute is more likely when its prescriptions are in accord with already existing behaviors and norms (Aubert, 1982; Dalberg-Larsen, 1973; cf. also Mazmanian & Sabatier above).

However, the relationship between statutes and target-group reactions varies according to policy area. An important distinction in this connection is whether the policy aims at regulation or the provision of services. Generally speaking, target groups expect greater benefits from services and the granting of allowances than from regulation. Accordingly, service-oriented policies are likely to enjoy a greater degree of goal attainment than regulatory policies (Aubert, 1982; Dalberg-Larsen, 1973). However, communicating the right to services is, as mentioned above, often a problem, and unfortunately the least privileged groups are the least likely to be reached by appropriate information. Another problem is stigmatization, which demotivates some people from receiving services and benefits to which they are entitled.

Compliance with regulation often involves considerable costs for the target group. However, the ability of these costs to impede compliance depends not only on their size but on the perceived likelihood that the public authorities will apply negative or positive sanctions. The effect of sanctions and punishment has been a popular research topic within sociology of law and criminology, and several studies have questioned the validity of the common belief that punishment prevents crime (Aubert, 1982). The use of incentives may be a more effective tool to bring about a change in behavior than prohibition and hypothetical sanctions. However, some regulation, such as industrial and agricultural subsidies and protection, does not imply costs but benefits for the target group. Here the prospects for successful implementation are much better, even if a considerable change in behavior habits is required.

Target-group behavior may also vary with different types of target groups. As already mentioned, behavior and norms vary with education and social background. Not infrequently regulatory policies are aimed at target groups that include private companies, and obviously these have far greater resources to secure benefits and avoid costs than do ordinary people. It seems reasonable to expect that firms are much more powerful in their interaction with street-level bureaucrats than are poor clients in welfare bureaucracies.

CONCLUSION

Implementation research still is a young specialty in political science. Although much has been accomplished in the years that have passed since Pressman and Wildavsky (1973) published their pioneering work, the presence of different competing schools or approaches to problems of implementation continues to be a conspicuous feature of this specialty.

The present study represents an effort to summarize and integrate some of the most important implementation findings into one working model. From among the myriad of variables affecting implementation this model incorporates four specific processes or conditions that seem to be of special importance in determining implementation results: The prior policy-formation process, organizational and interorganizational implementation behavior, street-level bureaucrats' coping behavior, and target-group response and changes in society. These processes can be found in different phases of the policy process by which policies are formulated, adopted, implemented, and both delivered to and perceived by the citizens.

While all four variables are important in explaining most implementation outputs and outcomes, their relative importance may vary across policy areas. For example, the role of the street-level bureaucracy is probably most important in human and social services, whereas the target-group response is probably more critical in the implementation of regulatory policies. However, more studies focusing on variations in implementation across policy areas and political systems are needed (see also Goggin, 1986, and Lester et al., 1987).

So far we have integrated the various implementation theory elements only in the sense that we have identified and collected four sets of variables that are so crucial to implementation failure or success that they ought to be included in any future theory on policy implementation. In order to get to a really integrated model, it is also necessary to specify if and how these four variable sets are interrelated. At the present stage we can only offer some preliminary suggestions (see Figure 2.1).

The character of the policy-formation process may affect all three other variables. The implementation structure is often shaped by compromises in the policy-formation phase, but frequently policymakers pay so little attention to organizational questions that inadequate implementation structures become the inevitable result (Calista, 1986). The formulation of vague, symbolic, and conflicting goals may contribute to the street-level bureaucrats' feelings of powerlessness and the development of coping strategies, and the absence in policy formation of adequate causal theories about how to solve problems in society may be responsible for unexpected target-group responses.

The behavior of street-level bureaucrats is often affected by their organizational setting and by interorganizational relations. The external and internal division of labor and interorganizational conflicts have a substantial impact on the range of discretionary and coping behavior that these bureaucrats can employ (Winter, 1986a). Interorganizational conflict tends to be reflected in street-level bureaucratic behavior, but on the other hand, one can also find situations where field workers from different organizations cooperate and share a higher sense of common loyalty to program objectives than to their own "mother institutions" (Hjern & Porter, 1981; Winter, 1986a).

The working conditions of street-level bureaucrats are also in a complex way affected by how resources have been mobilized in their organizations and in interorganizational networks at higher levels. However, the simultaneous focusing of our model on interorganizational behavior and street-level bureaucratic behavior also reveals that interorganizational conflicts do not always have any impact on street-level bureaucratic behavior. Such conflicts may just be a game that, although taken very seriously by the actors involved, has no implications whatsoever for the way a policy is delivered to the citizens (Winter, 1986a). Thus, implementation studies that employ a narrow interorganizational perspective but ignore street-level bureaucratic and target-group behavior tend to overestimate the impact of these networks on the implementation result (see also Goggin, 1986).

The interorganizational networks found in the implementation phase (and in the policy-formation phase as well) may also affect target group behavior. Though the participation of interest groups in the implementation game may distort implementation, such participation may nevertheless serve the useful purpose of getting a particular interest group sufficiently involved and committed to recommend its members to conform with the policy. And finally, interorganizational implementation networks tend to affect future policymaking processes. Once organizations or agencies have gained access to the implementation network, they are in a very strong position to lay claim to participation in future policy revisions. And then they will normally try to affect both policy and implementation structure.

Street-level bureaucrats may affect target-group behavior with their coping strategies, by which services are rationed and held back. Coping behavior also impacts on the interorganizational networks, for instance when street-level bureaucrats attempt to reduce their work loads by refusing to cooperate fully with other agencies and by getting rid of clients by passing them on to other authorities (Lipsky, 1980; Winter, 1986a).

Street-level bureaucrats rarely affect the policymaking and revision processes, and then usually only in indirect ways except when they are constituted through professional and technical associations or unions as interest groups, or as individuals (acting on behalf of others) going "public" by communicating (leaking, perhaps) information to the media. The presence of coping behavior may, however, inspire policymakers to introduce measures designed to reduce the discretionary powers of street-level bureaucrats. Significantly and unfortunately, the personal experiences of fieldworkers in dealing with their clients and their working conditions are rarely taken into consideration when policies are developed and revised (Elmore, 1982).

This is one reason why valid information about target-group behavior is usually absent from policymaking processes. Studies on the use of evaluation analyses in policymaking also reveal that evaluation results about policy impact are for the most part ignored when they first appear, although they may have a cumulative long-term impact on policymaking (Weiss & Bucuvalas, 1980; Cronbach et al.,

1981). Target-group attitudes may be reflected in interorganizational networks through the positions taken by the interest organizations involved, depending, of course, on the extent to which the target groups have organized themselves and on the responsiveness and influence of their organizations. And finally, target group behavior may affect the behavior of street-level bureaucrats. Cases where the behavior of clients violates the virgin ideals of relatively young field workers may give rise to generally cynical perceptions of clients.

A first step in employing the model may now be taken. It is to suggest interrelationships among the four independent implementation variables. The most important appear to be the impact of the policy-formation process on all three other variables, the impact of organizational and interorganizational implementation behavior on both street-level bureaucratic and target group behavior, and the impact of street-level bureaucracy on target group response.

Implementation research is still such a young field of research, and the complexity of implementation processes is so great, that it is rather natural that implementation scholars have focused on many different variables and approaches to get a deeper understanding of implementation processes. More of that kind of research is still needed. But we also need to gain an overview and more integrated understanding of what implementation is about, what the most essential variables are, and how implementation is linked to the process of policy-formation. This paper is a modest attempt to stimulate such efforts.

3

When Failure Is Success: Implementation and Madisonian Government

Barbara Ferman

This chapter reexamines the policymaking-implementation gap by focusing on the political and organizational contexts of the process. The analysis indicates that the implementation process closely mirrors the Madisonian framework of Republican politics. Consequently, the gap between policymaking and implementation is not a sign of failure. Rather, it is a testimony to the success of the American political system as initially conceived by the Founding Fathers.

Politically, policymakers and implementers operate in very different environments. This factor affects the behavior of the two groups, which in turn influences the direction of the policymaking-implementation process. The major impact is to lead the processes in two different directions, thereby creating a gap.

The organizational analysis includes an examination of various organizational models. Specifically, it looks at how each model depicts the implementation process and the recommendations for improving the process. This consideration reveals the weakness in the recommendations as well as in some of the models themselves. By selecting models that represent top-down and bottom-up views of implementation, the organizational analysis indicates the limits to the "forward-mapping" as well as "backward-mapping" approaches to the policymaking-implementation problem.

Combining the results of the political and organizational analyses indicates a certain universality to implementation problems. The most significant finding is that the factors that contribute to the gap between policymaking and implementation are manifestations of the Madisonian system of American politics and government. The implication of this finding for implementation theory is that we should view implementation in a very different light—implementation is another check in the American system of government. Like the entire system of checks and balances, it can be a source of delay and diversion of objectives, but it also protects against the concentration and abuse of power. Moreover, the delay factor can be beneficial to the extent that it guards against the commitment of egregious errors by allowing more time for analysis and testing.

THE POLITICAL CONTEXT OF IMPLEMENTATION

Madison's Victory: Policymakers versus Implementers

Fearful of the oppressive potential of centralized power, the Founding Fathers devised a political system to prevent factions from overrunning minorities that makes such collective activity nearly impossible. The separation of powers, the federalist structure of government, and the different constituencies of elected officials served to institutionalize a system of checks and balances designed to guard against the worst abuses of power. While this system has been fairly successful in stymieing serious threats to democratic rule, it has also been the source of institutional incapacity. Some critics have argued that power has become so fragmented that it is virtually impossible to get anything done in the American political system (Lowi, 1969).

This criticism probably finds its best support in the policy sector where fragmentation increasingly has come to dominate the policymaking and implementation arenas. As in the political system at large, a major source of fragmentation in the policy sector is the phenomenon of different constituencies. Policymakers and implementers must satisfy two very different groups. Thus, their incentive structures, priorities, and behavior diverge.

The constituents of the policymaker are the media and the general public, both of which are highly responsive to symbolic gestures. Indeed, the media are often partners in crime in the development of those gestures. Government bureaucrats, by contrast, have constituencies that consist of their staff and the specific client groups they serve, both of which are interested in material resources (wages, working conditions, services).

The demand aspect of constituencies creates very different incentive structures among policymaking officials and implementing bureaucrats. The distinction is probably the sharpest when the former is an elected official. Typically, an elected official is concerned with the political salability of a policy and the impact it will have on his constituency. Moreover, the electoral imperative conditions a short-run orientation and creates pressure for action. This often results in symbolic politics, which allocates rewards on the basis of which side you are on. David Mayhew illustrated how "position-taking" has become a major preoccupation of congressional representatives (1974).

This type of behavior is prevalent even when the policymaker is not an elected official. In his study of public executives Lynn argued that "a policymaker may regard as appropriate a strategy that emphasizes changes in public or legislative *perceptions* of a program over changes in program *designs* or *budgets*." He goes on to say that, "Actual change in governmental actions is not necessary for a policymaker to claim success. The creation of favorable impressions may be enough" (Lynn 1987, p. 38, emphasis added). Indeed, when dealing in the arena of symbolic gestures, it probably is enough.

In its extreme, this type of incentive structure can lead to a "proclaim and abandon" approach. This pattern characterized Lyndon Johnson's behavior in the new towns and Model Cities programs as well as the behavior of Thomas P. O'Neill and Francis Sargent in the Defense Employee Reemployment Program (DERP) in Massachusetts (Glynn, 1977). These officials announced their projects, received public attention and credit for them, and then moved on to the next item of business (Levin & Ferman, 1985).

By contrast, government practitioners, who must implement these programs, are very concerned with program designs and budgets—the nuts and bolts of policy. In fact, material resources are to implementers what symbolic resources are to policymakers. Both groups may be equally unconcerned with actual policy content. What they are concerned with is what it means for them in terms of their respective environments. The elected official's environment rewards image. The practitioner's environment, as Bardach aptly demonstrated through his "games" metaphor, emphasizes concrete items like budgets, jurisdiction, and manpower (1977).

The different constituencies of policymakers and implementers create different sets of demands and thus condition different incentive structures. These factors combine to produce two different types of politics as well.

The Politics of Policy Adoption

American politics is coalition politics. This has important ramifications for policymaking in general and for policy adoption in particular. The need to forge broad coalitions out of many diverse factions means that the policy must have broad appeal. This can be accomplished through the use of vague language, the endorsement of broad goals, or a wide dispersion of resources. Vague language permits different supporters to "attach their own different meanings to the action" (Lynn, 1987, p. 35). For instance, the Housing Act of 1949, which became the foundation for urban renewal, was seen by liberals as a response to the "social crisis" in the slums while conservative supporters viewed it as an economic tool to eradicate commercial and residential blight (Judd, 1988). Broad goals can serve this same purpose and at the same time avoid the divisiveness characteristic of narrower, more specific goals. Title I of the Elementary and Secondary Education Act (ESEA) was redefined as "general aid" for education for this very purpose (Murphy, 1971). Finally, spreading resources over a broad range of groups "buys" support. The Model Cities program went from two cities in the original Reuther proposal to 150 cities in order to get the necessary congressional support. This strategy, of expanding the scope of benefits, is typically characteristic of programs targeted for the poor. Middle-class people are included in the scope of benefaction in order to secure greater political support for the policy.

The Politics of Implementation

The results of the politics of policy adoption create many problems for implementers, who face a very different political situation. Broad goals and ambiguous language present both opportunities and dilemmas. On the positive side, they avoid the straitjacket effect that very narrow goals and specific language might produce. The discretion can provide the skillful implementer with opportunities to shape the policy in a way that maximizes resources. During the 1970s, many mayors used Comprehensive Education and Training Act (CETA) funds to supplement their budgets, thereby softening the effects of the recession.

On the down side, the variety of possible interpretations opens the door for criticisms of performance from clients, taxpayers, or even public officials. Moreover, broad goals, especially those in social service policies, are often difficult, if not impossible, to achieve. By contrast, specific objectives and language can sometimes make it easier for the implementer to perform the task. Orfield discovered, for instance, that educational administrators in the South were more receptive to implementing desegregation policies after the issuance of guidelines (Orfield, 1972). In the case of unpopular policies, clear guidance from above offers the bureaucrat protection; one can always blame Washington.

The opportunities and dilemmas provided by clarity in legislation can be seen in the mayoral experience with categorical and bloc grant programs. Categorical programs provided local officials with little discretion. On the positive side mayors did not have to take the responsibility, hence the "heat," from their constituents for unpopular funding decisions. Bloc grant programs, which gave mayors significant discretion, forced them to address their constituents and assume responsibility for funding decisions. However, the discretion inherent in bloc grants made them a much stronger political resource for mayors than categorical grants.

The dispersion of resources, which results from the politics of policy adoption, also creates problems for implementers. The flipside of dispersion is dilution; funds are doled out over a larger target area, but each recipient's share is reduced. This becomes problematic in several ways. First, it is more difficult to do a job with less resources. Commenting on the recent compromise in the Urban Development Action Grant (UDAG) program, which will spread resources over a greater number of cities, the executive director of the National Council for Urban Economic Development stated, "I'm afraid the program may be in the process of self-destructing because now it is doing everything possible to satisfy all possible constituencies" (*National Journal*, February 27, 1988, p. 599).

Second, and perhaps more significant, it effects the politics of the implementation process. The constituency, environment, and incentive structure of implementers all tend to run in the direction of material resources. The politics of implementation is primarily a politics of material resources. Thus, the requirements for successful activity in the policy formulation arena are at odds with the requirements for successful activity in the implementation arena.

The Victory Continues: Policymakers versus Policymakers

Even when we narrow our focus to the policymaking community itself, we find a diversity of actors whose incentives and behavior are shaped by different constituencies. The professionals who flourish in Heclo's issue networks are performing for an audience of their peers; hence, professional norms and criteria heavily influence their activities. Elected officials and their appointees are judged by the electorate and thus guided by political and electoral concerns. Career bureaucrats are preoccupied with issues of organizational survival and health, which condition yet another type of behavior.

The different incentive structures and behavioral patterns lead in different directions and thus further fragment the policymaking process. Professionals, for instance, are rewarded for uncovering greater complexity while elected officials face a need to simplify issues. Professionals also seek to challenge accepted practices, which flies in the face of the politician's need for gathering consensus and appearing confident. Moreover, the challenge of traditional concepts often involves continuing experimentation and debate, which conflict with the politician's need for closure (Heclo, 1978).

The policymaking community also exhibits substantive fragmentation. The proliferation of governmental policy has stimulated the development and active participation of many new groups. Thus, what were once broad, monolithic policy areas have now been broken up into many narrower interests. In health care for example, "Public policy has not only uncovered by also helped to create diverging interests among hospital associations, insurance companies, medical schools, hospital equipment manufacturers, local health planning groups, preventive medicine advocates, non-teaching research centers, and many others" (Heclo, 1978, p. 96). What was joined by commonality has been torn asunder by policy-stimulated conflict.

THE ORGANIZATIONAL CONTEXT OF IMPLEMENTATION

The field of implementation analysis has produced many recommendations for narrowing the gap between policymaking and implementation. These recommendations, in a broad sense, divide along their respective assumptions about the source of implementation failure. If the problem is the "street-level bureaucrat," then efforts must be aimed at the work environment of these actors (Lipsky, 1978). If the problem is a leakage in authority, then the solution lies in improving management controls (Allison, 1971). If implementation problems are in essence coordination problems, then the solution lies in improving institutional arrangements (Pressman, 1975).

These conclusions can be categorized along a directional dimension—implementation is seen either as a top-down process or a bottom-up one. Thus, identifying the source of implementation failure is directly related to the organizational model employed by the analyst. This connection served as a primary impetus for Elmore to develop his insightful typology (1978). His fundamental premise was that organizational structure and characteristics effect implementation outcomes. In a more recent analysis of policy instruments, Elmore expanded this typology to incorporate backward- and forward-mapping strategies (1985). The significance of Elmore's typology can be seen in its application. In a recent examination of organizational reform efforts, which used Elmore's framework, Calista demonstrated the important relationship between organizational design and the ability to implement structural reforms (Calista, 1986a).

Accepting this relationship, the organizational context of implementation can now be discussed. The various organizational models are considered in terms of their assumptions about organizational behavior, the implementation process, implementation failure and their recommendations—direct as well as implied—for improving the implementation process. While the models included here are ideal types, they are, nevertheless, valid representations of the two broad perspectives—top-down and bottom-up approaches.

The point about ideal types is significant in another context, however, which bears directly on the thesis presented here. Models are for educational or illustrative purposes. Organizations, on the other hand, exist within a given political system. As products of the people and institutions that operate in that system, organizations will mirror the basic characteristics of that system. This does not suggest that we will not find variation among organizations. Indeed, there are organizations that resemble each of the models presented here. The point is, rather, that the most prevalent types will be those that most closely approximate the larger political system. For purposes of implementation theory, it is important that we have a realistic assessment of how organizations work in practice. Following Elmore's approach, the models which are the closest in character to our political system are those in which the policy-implementation gap is the least likely to be narrowed.

Rational Model

The rational, or systems management model, depicts organizations as "efficiency maximizers." The achievement of goals is facilitated by the organization's behavior (goal-oriented) and its hierarchical structure. Within this structure, decision-making, authority, and responsibility follow a stringent top-down path. Therefore, control is an essential feature of effective organizations.

According to this model, implementation failures result from a breakdown in controls or "poor management." This may manifest itself in ill-defined policy, unclear delegation of responsibility, or a failure of accountability mechanisms. Hence, the answer to bad implementation is good management.

The rational model paves a rather smooth road for implementation. If we are dealing with a management issue, which is correctable, then policy formulation need not be shaped by implementation strategies. In fact, such a process would reverse the logical order of things—top down. Conversely, plugging the holes in the management structure should facilitate an implementation process that is practically automatic.

The simplicity and neatness of the model are at the root of its seductive power as well as the branch of its shortcomings. Unfortunately, reality is not so simple, individuals are not so one dimensional, and organizations are not so neat. As Lynn argued, the rational model "has no behavioral basis and no empirical support" (1987, pp. 24–25). This harsh indictment is perfectly understandable when we consider some of the "hidden" assumptions of the rational model. Value maximization, for instance, assumes that all priorities are known, that they can be ranked, and that there is agreement on the selection and the ranking. Anyone who has experienced indecisive moments knows that priorities cannot always be ranked by the individual decision maker let alone a group of decision makers who may have varying agendas. But the rational model precludes consideration of different agendas. If we can truly prioritize objectives, then there can be only one agenda. But who decides? According to the rational model this agenda exists objectively, and the decision maker's task is to discover it.

The rational model assumes the possibility for unrealistic amounts of coordination; unrealistic particularly in our fragmented political system. The Model Cities program, for example, was intended to coordinate all existing urban programs. However, it ran into congressional opposition, interest-group resistance, interagency conflicts, and internal contradictions. In short, the objective was doomed from the start.

Equally faulty is the model's assumption that problems remain the same and that there is one ultimate solution. The density of policy sectors and the frequency of unintended consequences nullify such a static picture of policy.

Bureaucratic Process Model

The bureaucratic process model is also characterized by a top-down process. Its key features, however, are discretion and routine. Workers exercise discretion in their decisions and develop operating routines for dealing with their tasks and responsibilities. The existence of discretion and routines tends to fragment organizational power.

The absence of the hierarchical structure found in the rational model makes implementation a somewhat bumpier process. Nevertheless, the responsibility and capacity for improving implementation are still at the top and can still be depicted as management issues. Top-level executives must identify where discretion exists and which routines are impediments to implementation. The job, then, is to devise alternative routines which are more likely to promote the true ends of the intended policy.

This model appears to be a prime candidate for shaping policy formulation around implementation strategies. Indeed, a major recommendation of proponents of this model is that policymakers must understand the work environment of service deliverers. While it is acknowledged that coping mechanisms will never be entirely eliminated, it is believed that they can be reoriented in ways more conducive to achieving policy goals.

There are several problems with this assumption. First, policymakers will not take the time to understand bureaucratic coping mechanisms. Their incentives have already led them away from any concern with implementation issues. But even if they could be persuaded to investigate this area, there is the problem with the coping mechanisms themselves; they vary with the nature of the work. The coping mechanisms of police will differ from those of teachers, which will differ from those of social workers, and so forth. Further, there is variation within each profession. Teachers in white, upper middle-class schools will have different coping mechanisms from teachers in poor, minority, inner-city schools.

National policy cannot be so specific as to contain provisions for the various coping mechanisms found regionally, ethnically, racially, culturally, and economically. One of the early debates in implementation studies, in fact, concerned this very issue: how much discretion should local governments be given in executing national policy? Those arguing for wide discretion pointed to the issue of local variation and the concomitant need to shape policy to local conditions. Thus, it appears that our travels have taken us back to the beginning.

Organizational Development Model

In contrast to these two models, the organizational development model paints a "bottom-up" process; initiative and implementation begin at the bottom of the organization. The key structural element is not hierarchy or discretion and routines but rather the small work group. For this group to be effective, it must contain "mutual agreement on goals, open communication among individuals, mutual trust and support among group members, full utilization of members' skills, and effective management of conflict" (Elmore, 1978, p. 7).

Implementation failure in this model results from a lack of consensus among implementers on the policy goals and/or from the separation of policymaking from implementation. Recommendations for improving implementation center around lower-level personnel issues (fostering individual commitment, autonomy and sense of involvement) and around developing lower-level organizational capacity.

The central role played by lower-level personnel makes effective planning contingent upon coordination between the policymaker and these personnel. This is precisely the recommendation from those who cite the planning-implementation gap as the true culprit. And, rather than providing control, the policymaker would be cultivating a policy partnership with these bureaucrats. Once again, the problem of political incentives arises; policymakers will not take the time to coordinate with the implementers.

Given the recurrent problem of political incentives, the best that we can hope for is that the federal government will provide the necessary resources to "enhance the internal capacity of organizations at another level to respond to the necessity for change, *independent of the requirements of specific policies*" (Elmore, 1978, p. 217, emphasis added). The emphasis is crucial. Organizational capacity will have been increased, but capacity does not guarantee results. Thus, we will still face the gap between policy intent and implementation reality.

The reason this gap will exist is directly related to the problem with the model's assumptions. The emphasis on cooperation and consensus comes at the expense of conflict. Even a cursory look through the literature on bureaucracy reveals how misguided such an assumption is. According to Bennis, "The fundamental deficiency in models of change associated with organization development [is that they] systematically avoid the problem of power, or the politics of change" (Elmore, 1978, p. 217).

Conflict and Bargaining

This model addresses the major shortcoming of the prior model. Rather than consensus, conflict and bargaining are at the heart of organizational structures. Organizations are depicted as "arenas of conflict in which individuals and sub-units with specific interests compete for relative advantage in the exercise of power and the allocation of resources" (Elmore, 1978, p. 217). Within such a setting, policy serves as a catalyst for the bargaining process. The various actors are not committed to the policy, but rather to bargaining as a mechanism for acquiring advantage and resources, a situation reminiscent of the congressional pork barrel.

This scenario renders implementation less a means for realizing policy goals than a mechanism for securing individual objectives. Implementation is a "series of strategic moves by a number of individual units of government, each seeking to shape the behavior of others to its own ends" (Elmore, 1978, p. 219).

While this may explain a lot about how organizations operate and how the subunits within them behave, it is not very helpful from a policy or implementation perspective. Policy is merely the result of conflict, and successful implementation is a relative notion. The latter is particularly problematic for approaches seeking to narrow the gap between policy and implementation. If we cannot apply some objective standard for measuring implementation effectiveness, there is little we can do objectively to improve the process. Moreover, if implementation is a process dedicated solely to the competition for resources, power, and advantage, then any mention of policy is akin to a foreign intrusion; policy is indeed irrelevant.

Despite the apparent irrelevance of policy, the bargaining and conflict model most closely approximates the American political system. In fact, the picture painted by this model can be viewed as the implementation equivalent of the policy adoption process. While Congress, as an institution, may exhibit a stronger commitment to policy goals than one finds in the conflict and bargaining model, the overriding organizational need to forge broad coalitions often makes the bargaining aspect the most important part there as well. And this is reinforced by the electoral needs of individual congressional representatives, which place a heavy emphasis on satisfying constituent demands. Describing the legislative process, Yates suggested that "the different players in the policy game compete to see who can get which of their policies and programs advanced and their bureaucratic needs fulfilled. It [the legislative process] is filled with rules and procedures designed to order the competition for resources and the scant time and energies available for new policy formulation" (1985, p. 219).

The most significant aspect of Yates's description is the resemblance it bears to Elmore's description of the conflict and bargaining model of organizations. In both stages—policymaking and implementation—an inversion takes place in which process becomes more important than policy outcomes. This inversion tends to characterize the entire American political system. Indeed, a major criticism of our political system has centered around this confused interchangeability among process and results. As in the conflict and bargaining model, the American political system's area of greatest consensus is found in the commitment to the democratic process. Viewed through the lens of Madisonian politics, this process is one of competition, bargaining, and conflict.

THE POLICY-IMPLEMENTATION GAP REVISITED

Examining the policy-implementation gap from the dual perspectives of political and organizational contexts reveals several significant findings. First, there appears to be a certain universality to those factors that contribute to the gap. Second, the factors that are the most recurrent, like the phenomenon of divergent constituencies, are direct products of the Madisonian system of American government. This last finding is consistent with some of the major theories of implementation, particularly those that paint the policy-implementation process as continuous (Elmore, 1987) rather than dichotomous (Mazmanian & Sabatier, 1983). A common feature of all of these, however, is the proliferation of checks and balances that continually alter policy.

Notes from Theory: Conceptual Models of Implementation

According to the incrementalist model, policymaking is a continuous process subject to constant modification and tightly intertwined with implementation (Lindblom, 1980). New policies are the result of marginal changes in existing policies. These changes occur because of the "mutual partisan adjustments" that take place among the various participants in the policy process—interest groups, program executives, and legislators. Each of these groups, as this chapter has stressed, has its own constituency. The need to satisfy these constituents is the fuel that fires the mutual partisan adjustment process.

Implementation as "pressure politics" views the process as a continuation of the politics of policy adoption. The players are the same. In fact, implementation provides the "losers" of the first stage with a second chance to alter the policy to their liking. These attempts by the opponents stimulate a reaction from the legislation's supporters, who seek to protect the bill in its adopted form. Thus, the implementation process is a "system of pressures and counter-pressures" (Bardach, 1977, p. 38). This depiction is not very different from the Madisonian system of checks and balances.

The interactive or adaptive model of implementation emphasizes the adjustments to goals and strategies made by participants all throughout the process. Using the "game" metaphor, Bardach suggests that these adjustments are the result of the various participants pursuing their stake in the process (1977).

The focus on implementation as evolution provides more support for the continuous rather than dichotomous view of the policy-implementation process. According to this view the predominant aspect of the process is policy redesign. "At each point we must cope with new circumstances that allow us to actualize different potentials in whatever policy ideas we are implementing. When we act to implement a policy, we change it" (Majone & Wildavsky, 1984, p. 197).

Summing Up: An Alternative View of Implementation

These conceptual models reinforce the political and organizational evidence on the policymaking-implementation process. Taken together, the data suggest that the gap between policy intent and implementation outcomes may not be so bad after all. To a large extent, the gap is the result of policymakers and bureaucrats doing what they have to do to get things done in our political system. Bending the rules can lead to desirable outcomes. Bureaucrats, especially street-level bureaucrats, must exercise discretion in order to humanize the system. Their behavior is analogous to machine politicians who provided brokering services for their constituents to soften a formal and at times incomprehensible system of municipal government. The casework activities of congressional representatives also fit this mold.

The real limit on narrowing the gap is not the bureaucracy or the administrators or elected officials or the electoral imperative, but rather the sum total. These individual factors are merely products of a consciously designed system. This has important ramifications for policy prescriptions. If the true culprit is our political system, changes in one part (e.g., limiting bureaucratic discretion) will not alter the system and will probably create more difficulties in one little area. In effect, the policy process lives with the negative consequences of our good intentions.

The evidence presented here suggests that the policy/implementation conflict is another example of the Madisonian victory. Conflict and policy alterations resulting from vague language may actually represent another level of input in the policymaking process, perhaps the most significant one. The conflict that surrounds policy at the implementation stage is usually among those people who will be directly affected by the policy—bureaucrats, citizens in general, and the target population in particular. Since they are directly affected, there will be less symbolic politics and more thrashing out of issues. Thus, perhaps we should view implementation as the final distillation in a political process whose major feature is competition. This conception also has heuristic value as implementation becomes the real world test of laboratory ideas (Levin & Ferman, 1985, pp. 14–16).

This perspective can be challenged on the grounds that it is overly political and injurious to the public interest. However, even if we remove all discretion from the implementers and all conflict (assuming it is possible) from the multiple levels, policy will still be the result of politics—legislative politics. Since our legislators are not cast in the Burkean mold, congressional policymaking will not embody the public interest either. Implementation politics, however, will better approximate the interests of the "affected" publics. This may be the closest we can come to a "public interest." Viewed in this light, implementation politics is an integral part of the American political system as envisioned by the Founding Fathers.

4

Research Perspectives on the Design of Public Policy: Implementation, Formulation, and Design

Stephen H. Linder and B. Guy Peters _____

All public policies have an underlying design. That design may be implicit and not consciously understood as such, but it will be present. As policy studies have become more concerned about the designs that shape policy, the term "policy design" has come to be used in at least two ways. In one meaning it is a process term, concerned with how and at what point in the policy process designing is carried out. The other meaning of the term is as a product—a blueprint or template that shapes policy, especially the instruments of government intervention. This chapter discusses the implications of these two approaches for understanding public policy. We will place special emphasis on designing in the implementation phase of the policy process. We will contrast the likely results of designing occurring there with designing occurring at the formulation stage, and then contrast both process approaches with a design perspective more concerned with the substance of policy.

IMPLEMENTATION RESEARCH AND POLICY DESIGN

Our knowledge of policy implementation has expanded considerably over the last decade, but that expansion has not been cumulative. Debate continues over empirical and methodological emphases, as well as over the appropriate normative basis by which to judge public sector governance (Burke, 1987). Some find virtue in central management of policy and employ a "top-down" perspective that values implementors' compliance more than their discretion, while others admire local dynamics and project their view upward from the "bottom" of service delivery systems. While the former view posits that implementation should produce results closely linked to the desires of policy "formators" (Lane, 1983), the latter focuses on the preferences and operating patterns of field staffs and clients. While the distinction between formulation and implementation may be difficult to discern in real-world policymaking, the separation retains analytical usefulness, due in no small part to its role in clarifying the design implications of the "top-down" and "bottom-up" views and their various hybrids.

Implementation research, despite intramural differences, has stood the Wilsonian dichotomy between politics and administration on its head. Not only does politics pervade administration, as widely acknowledged since the 1950s, but from the implementation perspective politics appears to make its home there. The rhetorical pendulum, however, may have swung too far in an anti-Wilsonian direction. The popularity of implementation research has diverted attention from other features of the policy process to the point where implementation has become, for many, the logical center of gravity for policymaking as a whole. For some, the necessary conditions for policy success reside with implementation (Bardach, 1980; Mazmanian & Sabatier, 1983; Hoppe, van de Graaf, & van Dijk, 1987), while others (Majone & Wildavsky, 1978; McMahon, Barrett & Hill, 1983) find implementation success a sufficient condition for overall success. Still others search in implementation, as ethnologists might, for the true meaning and definition of the policies themselves (Hjern & Hull, 1982). In all this, the aspect of policymaking to which authoritative policy decisions are usually ascribed has become displaced and consequently devalued.

The point of view of many implementation studies not only de-emphasizes the role of actors and events situated elsewhere in the policy process, but also tends to conflate empirical findings with normative claims about the design and governance of public policy. The presumption appears to be that once implementation is understood and properly orchestrated, policy is unlikely to fail. By implication, policy failure becomes synonymous with a failure to accommodate implementation issues properly. The analytical force of this presumption orients thinking about the policy process around implementation, and ignores the possibility that policies fail because of fundamental errors that have nothing to do with implementability, or perhaps that ambiguity in some problems defies consensus on a workable solution (see for example, Fox, 1987).

Two negative consequences arise from concentrating on implementation issues as a way of addressing questions about the appropriate design of policy. First, our conceptions of policy may become restricted to only what can be easily implemented; that is, implementability may be elevated in analysis from a constraint on effectiveness to a dominant criterion for judging policy proposals. Here, empirical points about necessary conditions for problem-free or cooperative implementation assume the status of a normative assertion. In effect, what we should do becomes circumscribed and, in the extreme, defined by what we can do well or, more often, by what we have always been able to do in the past. The trouble with this injunction is not only its conservative, mortmain flavor but its capacity to "crowd out" other, more appropriate, normative concerns that do not offer the same tempting promises of easy success.

Once converted into normative claims, conditions considered necessary for successful implementation begin to assume the status of sufficient conditions for the ultimate success of the policies themselves. Satisfying the requirements imposed on policy by its implementation prospects begins to displace more substantive purposes of policymaking and what appears good for implementation appears a priori good for policy. This is similar to arguments that reflexive, self-maintenance goals in organizations may dominate the purposive goals for which those organizations were established (Mohr, 1967; Niskanen, 1971). Here implementation and formulation do indeed merge, but that merger may have the same unhealthy consequences as the dominance of purposive by reflexive goals.

Going further, greater responsiveness by policy formulators to demands of the implementation process appears to be the only recipe offered by implementation research for improving policy design. Using the "top-down" approach, this means that policy must have a significant strategic component for coping with problems posed by interorganizational management. For the "bottom-up" approach on the other hand, policy formulation should remain tentative and establish only broad directions, in deference to the wisdom of prospective clients and implementers, although some versions would prefer an interactive process of feasibility testing and adjustment (Elmore, 1985; Hoppe, van de Graaf, & van Dijk, 1987). A perhaps more radical approach would argue for a better understanding at a cultural level of the characteristics of a policy area and policy community (Yanow, 1987) before any policymaking activities are undertaken.

In any case, deference is shown to the tastes and capabilities of the implementors and their prospective clients. To the extent that the design process is structured principally to accommodate these tastes and capabilities (bottom-up or top-down concerns, respectively), the design of policy is likely to be short-changed in two ways. First, the emphasis on accommodation can have a chilling effect on the incorporation of values that are neither consequentialist (i.e., readily reflected in material well-being) nor primarily responsive to client's tastes. Relying exclusively on mutual accommodation as a crucible for policy ideas tends to drive out claims that have no proven constituency, moral claims often being among them. Second, building designs around implementability and feasibility testing (Hoppe et al., 1987) elevates the "squeaky wheel" notion to a theory of policy development. This is not trial-and-error learning but an exercise in the anticipation of prospective complaints and their putative remedy through redesign—in other words, error without trial.

The second consequence of preoccupying our policy thinking with implementation issues is that definitions of success and failure become tautological. Once the product of the implementation phase of the process becomes defined a priori as policy—as is the case whenever sufficient conditions for policy development are assigned to implementation—external criteria for judging success and failure are displaced by internal, self-fulfilling ones. In the extreme, virtually any outcome can be taken to signify success. Failure, conversely, means no implementation, or perhaps an inconclusive process, and no product rather than an undesirable or inferior one. The process becomes the product, to paraphrase

Marshall McLuhan, and the success of one is thought to signify the success of the other. Accordingly, policy failure, in the sense of unanticipated or unacceptable outcomes (Sieber, 1981; Hogwood & Peters, 1985), becomes an anomaly.

Those who discover necessary but insufficient conditions for success in implementation—typically those adopting the top-down view—use an externally defined conception of success to avoid this tautology. In so doing, however, they sacrifice a flexible definition of the policy problem being addressed to a rigid one and exempt the basic ends of a given policy from scrutiny. Success in this perspective is akin to damage control; it involves a sufficiently detailed management plan to prevent mayhem from overwhelming implementing organizations, rather than a notion of an interactive or collaborative product. We appear to have something of a Goldilocks problem here. In one school, the concept of policy is too flexible to allow external (i.e., independent) assessment of success; in the other, a rigid concept of policy excludes many acceptable and reasonable outcomes from being labeled implementation successes. Nowhere does a reliance on implementation for judging policy designs allow decisions that are "just right."

If implementation is not alone at the center of analysis, these two views appear far more complementary. The bottom-up tradition is an effective counterweight to the top-down view abridgement of the role of politics in implementation. Conversely, the limitations of the bottom-up approach appear largely as by-products of its focus on the periphery rather than at the center of the policy delivery system: accountability to elected officials is weak, policy conceptions appear situationally determined, ends and means appear confounded, and so on. Changing to a top-down approach alters some normative assumptions that define what is observed and how it is interpreted, but has little effect on the perceptions of the process as a whole. To the extent that both implementation approaches share a focus on the implementation portion of policymaking, they are more similar than different. Regarding implementation as the primary source of either (or both) necessary or sufficient conditions for successful policy designs distinguishes both approaches from other orientations that define their focal points for success and failure differently.

Consider how shifting the analytic focus to formulation alters perceptions of design problems and interpretations of policy success and failure. Rather than implementation dictating necessary and sufficient conditions for success, that phase would serve either as a contextual constraint on the design of policy, or as a manipulable feature of policy governance. Design is then opened to the selection of different normative claims about governance and might frame the selection of implementation strategies in terms of top-down, bottom-up, or some trade-off between the virtues of centralization and decentralization. With a shift in the locus of design from implementation to formulation, the range of available design choices expands from those limited by the existing capabilities and sup-

portive climate in prospective implementing organizations to the full armamen-
tarium of government's policy instruments (Hood, 1986).

The relevant constraint from the formulation side is not an organizational one
but rather one of limited understanding and foresight (for a discussion in the
context of transaction costs see Calista, 1987). The design problem here calls
for good ideas about what the problem is and how best to deal with it. Similarly,
the uncertainty from the formulation side rests neither with the implementing
agency nor its prospective clients; it is concentrated around the choice of policy
instruments and the subsequent fit of instruments to the policy context (Elmore,
1987a). While the fit of any given instrument may be improved with successive
rounds of trial and error—this is where the implementation side comes in—the
initial choice and commitment to an instrument comes largely from ex ante
deliberations that may be systematic in nature or based purely on hunches and
instincts. Some recent work on policy design is intended to sort out whether
such deliberations actually occur and if they do, whether they are systematic or
not (Ingraham, 1987).

The formulation and implementation perspectives on design both attempt to
posit some form of design activity, whether by inference or by prescription, and
interpret its content and focus according to the dictates of its point of view.
From the formulation perspective, when design does occur it takes place in the
context of the larger task of formulating and appraising policy alternatives. The
process of designing is then akin to the process of planning and analysis that
underlies policy formulation. From the implementation perspective, design is a
product of the implementation process, either coming out of the center's strategic
needs, the periphery's accommodations, or some combination made in anticipation of each. Accordingly, the process of designing becomes synonymous with
the resolution of implementation issues (Elmore, 1987a). There is a third perspective on policy design, however, that effectively turns the design problem
inside out.

Rather than focusing on a selected stage in the policy process and considering it
as the locus of design activity, analysis can be concentrated on the designs themselves and on how individual stages of the policy process might accommodate, or
be made to accommodate, them. Instead of judging the pedigree of different policy means by a narrow reading of the requirements of the policy process, this perspective reverses the order, beginning with policy means and their preliminary
appraisal before allowing their prospects for survival at a particular stage to dominate. We refer to this preoccupation with instruments and their capabilities as a
"design perspective"; it differs from the process perspectives of implementation
and formulation primarily in the way it deals with process concerns. The design
perspective treats these concerns as features of the design context rather than as
arbiters of form and substance or determinants of success and failure.

While feasibility is important, it is but one of many possible bases on which
to formulate policy. When it serves as the primary basis, means and ends become

interchangeable and the purposes of policy become confused with the instruments needed to satisfy a certain class of constraints. Departing from conventional assumptions about goal-seeking or "rational" systems in management or economics (see Fox, 1987, on rational-comprehensive presuppositions), the implementation perspective transforms feasibility from a constraint on goal achievement into a separate, and at times competing, goal. In contrast, an emphasis on design logically separates the choice of means and from that of ends, requiring systematic analysis of each. Normative conclusions stem from the search for optimal designs (e.g., Marschak, 1965) rather than by inference from empirical regularities. Feasibility is handled in different ways by each perspective; it often forms a constraint on choice for the design perspective, but serves as a parameter defining choice in many versions of implementation perspective.

A design perspective imposes a heuristic separation between feasibility and other values in the normative appraisal of policies (Linder & Peters, 1984; 1986). The separation of feasibility from other evaluative criteria, although artificial, protects policy design from succumbing to the lure of "proven solutions" associated with the status quo, or the experience of an organization. Choices concerning governance and process are also separated analytically from the choice of instruments (Bobrow & Dryzek, 1987). In this case, however, the purpose of the separation is to uncouple these two fundamental elements of policy design to ensure balanced consideration of each. By contrast, the implementation perspective adopts one of several presumptions about governance— typically a bottom-up or top-down orientation—and derives design ingredients from its analysis of the implementation process. A priori choices about governance then effectively delimit the structure of the design process and its underlying premises. A design perspective is preoccupied with ways of achieving a more complete enumeration and evaluation of instruments and designs, while implementation and formulation perspectives can easily emphasize the conditions that circumscribe such an enumeration.

Whether the design perspective is (or can be) in some sense superior to the other two depends in part on one's point of view and, more specifically, on how one perceives the relationship between means and the policy process. If the process serves as both the principal source of policy ends and the crucible for testing policy means, conceptions of success and failure will be tied to how well a design meets process-based requirements. As a result, evaluations will tend to focus on the "goodness of fit," compatibility, or the feasibility of means relative to these requirements. Changing the process focus from, say, implementation to formulation changes the requirements and thus the definition of success and failure. Without an elaborate set of meta-criteria (Bobrow & Dryzek, 1987) that are independent of any given perspective, judgments about the relative advantage of these three for either the observation or prescription of policy designs remains inconclusive.

In part as a prelude to more systematic theorizing about policy design, the next section offers a scheme for examining the similarities and differences among these three perspectives on design. Besides the introduction of heuristic distinctions, the scheme pays special attention to identifying the logical origins of different conceptions of design as a policy-relevant activity. Consistent with the emphasis of this volume, we will continue to pay close attention to the implementation perspective and to the kinds of claims it makes for policy design.

AN EXCURSION INTO GENEOLOGY

Although there are many intellectual sources of difference among the perspectives on policy design, perhaps most fundamental is epistemological. In common with some fields in economics and with the management and policy sciences, the design perspective is concerned with analyzing the scope and improving the quality of public sector activity. From this point of view, empirical descriptions of policy actors and processes become relevant to design only as these contribute to our understanding of policy as a manipulable variable shaping that activity. Such descriptions not only clarify mechanisms of causality linking the manipulable and nonmanipulable features of the policy situation but also enhance our repertoire of workable policy instruments. In contrast to other areas of policy research, work on policy design tends to be both explicitly normative in emphasis and reformist in orientation.

Roots and Branches

To clarify how a design perspective might offer different insights into the normative aspects of policymaking, we trace the parallel, but separate, origins of the implementation, formulation, and design points of view in a highly selective and somewhat arbitrary survey of relevant lines of research. A tree serves as the organizing metaphor. Our survey focuses on only two of many roots supporting policy inquiry and admits only those branches considered useful for discriminating among approaches to policy design. Further, we will trace several distinctive conceptions of policy design that have led to some confusion in the policy literature and may introduce needless rivalry among their proponents. A diagrammatic survey of what follows appears in Figure 4.1.

Actors and Processes: The Process Perspective on Policy Design

The first major root, appearing at the far right of Figure 4.1, is the principal origin of implementation and formulation research and provides a footing for much of the policy literature within political science. (Note that references in this and subsequent sections are intended to be suggestive rather than inclusive.) The first major root itself splits into two branches, one supporting studies emphasizing interaction between governmental and nongovernmental actors (Schattsneider, 1960; Bauer, de Sola Pool, & Dexter, 1967) and the other studies that focus on government as the principal actor (Rourke, 1984; Wildavsky, 1964;

Figure 4.1
A Rudimentary Mapping of 'Design' Approaches

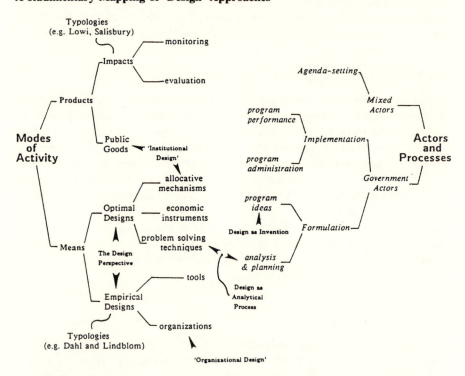

Seidman & Gilmour, 1986). The implementation perspective draws its sustenance from the latter branch and, in turn, supports more focused studies of program administration and performance.

The unique contribution of implementation to the study of government actors, however, was to cross over to another branch, that supporting impact evaluations, springing from a separate root (see below). Through hybridization of sorts, the implementation perspective surpasses the work of its immediate ancestors by introducing a novel set of questions that link the influence of government actors on policy to a policy's eventual impact.

Two distinct notions of design spring from this perspective. The first, "design as adaptation," is tied to an evolutionary notion of policy development, where policy design proceeds in a decentralized, iterative fashion involving successive rounds of trial, error, and adjustment (Browne & Wildavsky, 1985; Majone & Wildavsky, 1978; Yanow, 1987). Success in this instance represents convergence between internally defined expectations and observed outcomes. Despite the appeal to the biological metaphor, there is an inherent tendency toward conservation of administrative energy so long as any gap in performance remains a proprietary notion. Simon (1947) identified this tendency early on as one of lowering aspirations to meet performance rather than continually raising performance to meet expectations. Here, the impetus for engaging in design can be easily confounded with reflexive goals having more to do with health maintenance for the organization than improving outcomes for their clientele.

A second notion of design, "design as feasibility testing," can be viewed in part as an antidote to adaptation. Here, the design process moves back and forth between clientele interests and expectations defined, at least initially, outside the implementing agency (Elmore, 1985; Hoppe et al., 1987). Design ideas can also enter this process from outside and are then subjected to a regimen of anticipated challenges, each connected to the prospects of successful implementation. The strength of this approach lies in its attempt to bridge the conceptual gulf between the implementation and formulation perspectives. Unfortunately, it shares weaknesses from each perspective. From implementation, it effectively converts this perspective's preoccupation with implementability into a design criterion. From formulation, it remains ambiguous on both the origins of design ideas and the proper locus of design activity. Nonetheless, it remains perhaps the most coherent conception of a design process that falls entirely within the realm of the two process perspectives. A third notion of design ("design as analytic process"), introduced below, will bridge the formulation and design perspectives in a way that is intended to overcome the shortcomings of the "feasibility-testing" approach.

The study of policy formulation can be represented as a separate branch that splits into the critical appraisal of program ideas (Lynn, 1980) and the assessment of analysis and planning (Bobrow & Dryzek, 1987). These are largely meta-policy studies more attuned to studying ways that program ideas evolve and analysis is done than to developing programs or "doing analysis." Selecting these two kinds of studies from among the great variety that policy formulation has stimulated permits us to pinpoint several distinct notions of policy design. This helps clarify the logical origins of our idea of design as a perspective from which to view the interplay between formulation and implementation processes. In Lynn's case studies on policy ideas (1980) and Polsby's study of innovation (1984) we are treated to the notion that design is the creative element in governance, the combination of experience and intuition that gives rise to new ideas and recombinations of old ones. How this creative process occurs is not quite clear, but remains a shadowy mix of politics, sensitivity, and good sense with a rather large random component having something to do with timing. Design, then, is more art than science, more magic than technology.

Analysis and planning constitutes a second shoot from the formulation branch, sharing two different conceptions of designing (see Figure 4.1). As noted earlier, "design as invention" admits analysis and planning as means of stimulating creativity; "design as analytic process" changes that role from one of stimulating to that of structuring the design process. The emphasis here is on systematizing design activity in a way that makes it both external to the individual designer and amenable to analysis. We move from design as invention involving "right-brain'' thinking to a more methodical notion of design as analytical activity drawing mostly on ''left-brain'' patterns of thought. Most of the change can be attributed to the connection that ''design as analytic process'' makes between the analytical side of formulation (still essentially a process perspective) and the problem-solving orientation coming from a completely different intellectual root shown on the left side of Figure 4.1.

Science and technology offers a different conception of design based in techniques for expanding human information processing capabilities. Design according to C. Alexander (1964; 1965) and Simon (1972) is something to be programmed, a form of systematic analysis that expands our capacity for planning and innovation. The relevance of those conceptions to public policymaking were noted by Miller (1984b) and Linder and Peters (1984). The first attempt to examine whether or not the analysis and planning side of formulation was being turned toward design questions as an adaptation of systematic design techniques was made in several studies by E. Alexander (1982). Several recent studies of policy design as process and product follow this path, exploring whether design as an analytical process is occurring and what it should produce (Dryzek, 1983; Linder & Peters, 1985; Ingraham, 1987).

Modes of Activity: The Design Perspective

A design perspective, as we use it, can be traced to an altogether different root, one emphasizing modes of activity in the public sector, rather than particular actors or their interactions. The first branch considers policy means and supports the principal work on most forms of policy instruments. A second branch deals with policy products and serves as a bridge to the growing emphasis on institutional design (Kaufmann, Majone, & Ostrom, 1985).

Means. The first branch on policy means supports both normative and empirical studies. On the normative side, there is a search for optimal instruments, techniques, or mechanisms to meet a variety of needs, economic efficiency being perhaps the most prominent. This includes the general study of resource allocation problems (Koopmans, 1951) along with more explicit comparisons of centralized and decentralized modes of governance (Hayek, 1945; Lerner, 1944). The first group of studies concentrates on the role of incentive and information mechanisms in resource allocation (Hurwicz, 1960). This work focuses on evaluating the performance of different mixes of these two. The operational aspects of the ''mix'' problem (Arrow, Hurwicz, & Uzawa, 1958) are addressed by programming theory, attracting analysts in operations and decision research. A second group of studies considers the use of information alone as an instrument in mechanisms based on the economic theory of teams (Marschak & Radner, 1971). When the mechanisms of interest deal in public goods we move into the area of institutional design, combining the institutional concerns of public finance and administration with the criteria of applied welfare economics.

On a second shoot appears work on economic instruments of taxing and spending (Musgrave, 1959). Following Musgrave's convention, monetary and fiscal instruments are counted primary among them. Work on regulatory (Weitzman, 1974) and administrative (Williamson, 1975) instruments are tied logically to this early work on instruments of public finance. Efforts to refine each kind of instrument and to explain its use in particular settings follow, including work by Noll (1971) and Stigler (1971) on regulatory tools, Shavell (1980) and Posner (1972) on legal rules, and Goldberg (1976) on administrative forms.

While much of the work in this shoot focuses on the structure of particular instruments, like the design of an optimal tax or efficient legal rule, it serves as the foundation for interinstrument comparisons. Comparisons across policy instruments lie at the core of efforts to improve the process of designing policies (see Elmore, 1987). The basic idea is to extend the comparative appraisal of instruments to encompass a wider range of values as well as a larger set of prospective instruments. With this, one moves into the realm of "second-best" solutions and binding constraints. Difficulties in matching instrument to problem and of mixing instruments to serve multiple objectives become a primary concern. Here, the monumental work of Kirschen (1964), building on the ideas of Tinbergen, serves as a benchmark (at least in the domain of economic instruments) against which future works attempting to make such matches should be judged.

A third shoot from the optimal design branch supports the development of analytical methods for structuring the design process, typically in a formal way through an abstract model of a given set of requirements. This group of studies applies systems science to the task of designing (e.g., Sutherland, 1977; Ackoff, 1978). Such work has led to a number of techniques intended to show prospective designers how to fashion "designs" from lists of desired attributes or sets of assumptions (Kilman & Mitroff, 1977). From this view "designs" emerge as a product of certain logical processes called "designing," which can be not only programmed but made accessible to those without the creative spark that characterizes the "design as invention" view. This shoot on optimal design is one of the first areas where design emerges as a legitimate social scientific concern. Here design is seen either as a choice problem involving the refinement of certain instruments, or as a process problem with a programmable solution—both are amenable to formal analysis.

By comparison, work in organizational design (Lawrence & Lorsch, 1969; Nystrom & Starbuck, 1981), springing from the empirical design branch in Figure 4.1, views design not as a process but as a set of structural variables affecting the observable performance of organizations. More generally, the contingency approach to organizations, at the core of the "organizational design" literature, views structure as endogenous—determined by the nature of the task and task environment—and not as a choice parameter. This approach examines the etiology of empirical design forms rather than the more abstract normative problem of fashioning the best form. The analysis, hence, is both *ex post* and deterministic. Design, as an organizational response to perceived problems or opportunities, serves both as a basis of classification and a focal point for diagnosing performance problems. The process of constructing these responses and means of improving them remain unexplored within this segment of the design literature.

A second shoot of the "empirical design" studies inventories the tools available to government (Mosher, 1980; Salamon, 1981; Hood, 1983) and assesses their use. In this work, tools serve as a lens, superior to earlier impact based typologies, for viewing government activity. A focus on tools highlights the issue of substitution, directing attention toward alternative ways of doing things. Canadian political scientists (Atkinson & Chandler, 1983) have been far more active than their American counterparts in articulating and evaluating the tools that government uses for accomplishing its ends. Implicit in this line of inquiry is that tools are, in a sense, the "deep structure" (Levi-Strauss, 1963) latent in all that government does. The object of analysis, then, is to uncover these tools and to reveal their associated patterns. A "design perspective" goes one step further. Not only are there generic tools available to government, each disguised with a variety of surface features, but their selection and refinement represents a generic design problem (Linder & Peters, 1984). In particular, one hurdle for the would-be designer is to be able to map an array of tools into an array of problems. To date, there appears to be no fully satisfying conceptualization of either the nature of public functions or of the nature of "tools" to allow effective design choices to be made on other than an intuitive basis. These two premises form the basis of the design perspective's orientation toward both empirical and normative design. The first branch of the "Modes of Activity" root offers some prospect for developing designs as a problem-solving process; the second focuses on the development of a flexible tool kit consisting of policy instruments and organizational forms.

Products. The second branch of the "Modes of Activity" root supports inquiry into the nature of government's products. One shoot focuses on the character of these products as goods and services and implications for both the institutions providing the service and the people being served. As shown in Figure 4.1, the link between this shoot and the one on allocative mechanisms, springing from the "optimal design" branch, has supported the development of an "institutional design" approach associated with the work of Ostrom (1974) in public administration, Young and Nelson (1973) and Hirschman (1970) in economics, and the "Bielefeld Group" in Western Europe. In many ways, institutional design is the normative counterpart of organizational design with its emphasis on matching organization to product, task, or environment.

A second shoot of the "products" branch supports studies of impacts of government on society. Development of more precise ways of measuring changes in economic welfare (Hicks, 1946) and in social conditions (Bauer, 1966) invigorated the classical debate over the nature of government's impact on the economy, social institutions, and individuals. One result of this was raising standards of evidence behind claims of programmatic effectiveness. The expectation of careful monitoring and systematic assessment gradually undermined casual empiricism as a means of establishing impact. There are two principal offshoots from this one shoot.

One supports work on monitoring and process studies of administrative efficiency (Kaufman, 1977) and development of output measures of productivity (Levy, Meltzner, & Wildavsky, 1974). Studies of organizational effectiveness (Ackoff, 1974) also spring from this shoot. The administrative structure often is the central focus of performance monitoring, and failure is perceived to spring from administrative limitations. The problem then becomes improving coordination and control within and across organizations. Nonetheless, efforts at fashioning solutions typically have more in common with strategies of organizational and institutional design than with design recommendations coming from either process perspective. One key difference is the emphasis placed on structural determinants and their role in improving productivity and effectiveness.

A second shoot, paralleling "monitoring," deals with evaluation of programs either as public investments, through devices such as cost-benefit analysis (Mishan, 1971) or their stated objectives as benchmarks. The emphasis in the former is upon determining a program's social costs and benefits, before and after the fact. Accordingly, attention shifts from monitoring output to devising means of characterizing and then evaluating impact. Although the focus is typically on a single program, the criteria employed are societal and are expressed in terms independent of the stated objectives of any particular program.

For the latter mode of evaluation, criteria and performance norms are internally defined, and appraisal is restricted to the program at issue. Results are interpreted either as evidence for continuation, perhaps with modification, or against it. The existential question is why *this* approach, *these* objectives, and *this* program are ignored in favor of taking the program and its rationale as given. Here evaluation can only be *ex post*. Unfavorable evaluation results must contend with the political and organizational advantages enjoyed by an ongoing program, so that program termination or even modification is difficult. While evaluation of policy impact is crucial in any effort to enhance organizational effectiveness, emphasis on success and failure is too often infused with images of environmental antagonism. Together with an orientation toward *ex post* studies of single programs, this emphasis can rule out competing criteria and alternative policy means.

IMPLICATIONS FOR DESIGN PROBLEMS

The basic dilemma for research on policy design is that despite care taken to define and adhere to a boundary between empirical description and prescription, none can be established without adopting the normative premises associated with a given research perspective. One normative premise may be to trust either the stated objectives of a legislature (Mazmanian & Sabatier, 1983) or the product of a process of negotiation among diverse organizations (Barrett & Fudge, 1981) as a reference point for determining success and failure and, relatedly, the direction of redesign. In either case, the normative premise is taken a priori to represent virtue of some kind. Description then invariably begins with this premise as a point of departure; ignoring the normative underpinnings leads to confounding descriptive and prescriptive statements. The debate between top-down and bottom-up views within the implementation perspective, for example, is fundamentally a disagreement not over levels or units of analysis, but over an appropriate normative stance. Each such stance effectively supports the definition of manipulable and nonmanipulable elements in the system and entails a commitment to a corresponding notion of governance. Thus, one's perspective will not only determine who should be in control and how their control can best be exercised but also what will count as success and failure. Consequently, the direction of prescription appears largely preordained.

Returning to the basic question posed at the beginning, what are the design implications of these research perspectives? Within the implementation perspective looking from the top down the solution to the problem of designing successful policy lies in achieving the proper level of conformity to central direction. The design criterion invoked may be policy clarity (Nakamura & Smallwood, 1980). Instructions should be specific and unambiguous, and the design process focuses on refining the form and legal substance of policy. Looking from the bottom up, the key to design seems to lie in maintaining discretion and flexibility. The design criterion here is not clarity but simplicity (e.g., Bardach, 1977). The design focus shifts from substantive policy to the process of policymaking. The key is not to fashion policy alternatives with better prospects of implementation, but to simplify policymaking by decentralizing governance altogether.

Moving to the formulation side introduces an explicit role for analysis and planning, to use an old metaphor, replacing "interaction" with "cogitation" as the principal mechanism underlying the design process. The design criterion invoked is likely to place heavy emphasis on the reasonableness and cogency of the design idea, based on a large dose of analogy and historical precedent. The focus here is upon matching appealing solutions to problems and opportunities, an image not inconsistent with the "garbage can" metaphor (Dryzek, 1983). The two bridging views of design—design and feasibility testing falling between the formulation and implementation perspectives, and design as analytical process connecting the design perspective with formulation—represent more recent attempts to build design notions into existing conceptions of policy development. In some ways, the idea of a design process having something to do with formulation and yet promising more by way of better policy may raise suspicions of a resurgence of synoptic thinking in policy research. Prescriptions about designing are not so much synoptic as they are a plea for conscientiousness in fashioning policy means and awareness of at least how we tend to repeat our design mistakes. Building policy design in theorizing and research then offers an opportunity to merge the analysis of current practice with simple conceptions of how it might be improved. Since the implementation perspective has been widely embraced, it may serve as the portal through which the diffusion of design concerns will take place.

CONCLUSION: CHANGING THE COURSE OF INQUIRY

Our most basic critique of the implementation perspective on design has been its tendency, particularly manifest in the bottom-up approach, to conflate empirical and normative statements. In fact, most of the process literature does not deal clearly with normative statements, although the work certainly has normative implications for policy. As a consequence, empirical findings about details of formulating and difficulties of actually implementing policy in the manner intended quickly become statements that argue that we should concentrate on familiar problems and flexible processes if we want success. The concentration on the implementation process at the lowest organizational levels arguably moves away from the development of better mechanisms for designing implementation systems even if it enhances the feasibility assessment of policy instruments. This chapter, therefore, must be regarded as a plea for greater consideration of the application of carefully considered design criteria.

In short, the design of public policy may be too important to be left to the control of only one perspective. The literature on implementation, for example, has helped to remedy the apparent naiveté in much of the early policy analysis literature, which appeared to operate with the assumption that if we got the "right" solution, it would almost automatically happen. In bringing its needed dose of realism, however, implementation has come virtually to dominate thinking about what constitutes good policy—at least in political science circles. Implementability and feasibility, while important, are not the only factors that must be considered when attempting to develop a good policy design.

A design orientation, in contrast to both formulation and implementation perspectives, emphasizes the theoretical basis for selecting the instruments and targets in a program. Hence, such an orientation not only admits error (which at least one view of implementation does not) but it also helps to understand the error. Such a perspective makes it easier to identify sources of error that involve a misspecification of the proximate goals of a program or the selection of an inappropriate instrument to reach them. In either instance, remedying a defective design becomes something more than a trial-and-error process, whether informed by experience or not. Rather, remediation becomes a process that itself can be subjected to analysis, whether that be of the normative underpinnings of the policy or of the specific instruments selected.

The advantage of comparing perspectives on design problems is that it opens up questions of governance and policy means to a wider array of possibilities. Consistent with the top-down perspective, a concern for design is necessarily prospective; consistent with the bottom-up view, on the other hand, a design perspective admits the policymaking machinery into the calculus of reform. The design perspective requires the marrying of normative prescriptions with the mechanisms that will be used to reach goals, and then judging the appropriateness of that marriage. By limiting analysis to one perspective, however, we are logically compelled to anchor the design process and resulting prescriptions there. In contrast, design choices should range over alternative means as well as forms of formulation and implementation machinery, subject to the contingencies of different environments.

5

The Japan External Trade Organization and Import Promotion: A Case Study in the Implementation of Symbolic Policy Goals

Robert T. Nakamura

While the symbolic dimension of policies is often noted, the implementation of these elements is rarely discussed (Edelman, 1964; 1988; Elder & Cobb, 1983; Florig, 1986; Kowalewski, 1980; Ayres, 1986; Weiss, 1981, Molineu, 1980) because many political actors assume that the symbolic goals of policymaking are satisfied upon the adoption of a policy (see for example, Schlesinger, 1966). Appearing to act is thought to be enough when the demand was to appear to act. While there is in theory a clear distinction between symbolic policy goals and others, practice is not so easily differentiated. Appearing to do something, for example, often requires assembling the appropriate machinery and even making it run. And even goals adopted for symbolic reasons—such as the inclusion of women in the civil rights acts—may take on a policy life of their own during implementation.

Drawing a distinction between symbolic policies and more substantive ones is not easy because they are often mixed in practice. At some level most policies contain some mixture of substantive and symbolic goals. There is a continuum that stretches between policies that are little more than symbolic to those with a greater likelihood of producing substantive effects through behavioral change. I should, however, briefly sketch the characteristics of the ends of the continuum before proceeding, so that the subject matter of this chapter is clearer.

While all policies are intended to evoke some change in a target population (McDonnell & Elmore, 1988), that target population can range from an audience expected to change their minds about those adopting a policy to a set of people

This research was supported by the Institute for Policy Science of Saitama University, Urawa, Japan, and the State University of New York, Albany. Bong Hyoung Lee, my research assistant, aided in the preparation of the manuscript.

from whom behavioral changes in order to solve a problem are expected. Most of the implementation literature concerns substantive policies primarily intended to change behavior in a target population or populations: getting officials to register black voters, encouraging local firms to hire/train the hard-core unemployed, nudging local officials to adopt practices to make their schools more effective. Most symbolic policies, on the other hand, seem to be directed at changing people's attitudes or perceptions of those who are acting and the significance of what they are doing. So, for example, the Medical Waste Tracking Act of 1988 was intended to show that legislators were acting in response to public fears about dangerous medical wastes washing up on beaches despite the Environmental Protection Agency's (EPA) disclaimer that its successful implementation would have little effect on that problem.

How plausible is the link between the mechanisms envisioned by a policy and the problem to which it is directed? As Kingdon's (1984) work informs us, policies arise out of a concatenation of political demands for action and solution streams that may be only temporarily connected to the problems they ostensibly solve (Kingdon, 1984; Nakamura, 1987). The connection can, however, vary from tight to loose, and the expectation that some substantive outcome can be achieved will correspondingly vary. For example, the connection between Youth Employment and Demonstration Projects Act (YEDPA) and the problem of unemployed youth (see Levin & Ferman, 1986) is much tighter than the Medical Waste Policy Act of 1988 and beach washups (Church, Cooper, & Nakamura, 1989).

Thus while all policies have symbolic dimensions or serve as spectacles for audiences to watch (Edelman, 1988), more substantive policies usually involve, behavioral changes in the direction of solving the problem that prompts the policy. But even those policies that fall toward the symbolic end of this continuum—those with primary target populations from whom little behavioral change is expected, and with mechanisms only marginally connected to the problems to which the policy is addressed—face implementation problems. Even if we assume for a moment that such policies are intended more to produce "spectacles" (Edelman, 1988) than substantive outcomes, the quality and acceptance of the spectacle can be in doubt and requires affirmative efforts to pull it off.

The purpose of this chapter is to look at a policy adopted for symbolic reasons—the Japan External Trade Organization's responsibilities under their government's market-opening measures—and to draft a theoretical framework for understanding how symbolic goals may be implemented. For this latter task, I will adapt Goffman's analytic framework.

THE CASE

Since 1982 the Japanese government has been taking what it has termed "voluntary market-opening measures." Without going into detail, the policy was intended to open the Japanese domestic market by reducing tariffs, altering import procedures and regulations, raising or eliminating quotas, and other measures. As part of this general effort, the semi-governmental Japan External Trade Organization (JETRO) was to create and administer a system of "import promotion" (Nakamura, 1985; Patrick, 1982). JETRO's mission had been to promote exports from Japan through trade shows and encouraging cooperation among medium-size Japanese and foreign firms. The new policy directed JETRO to shift its activities to the promotion of imports into Japan.

Both Japanese and foreign sources recognize that the apparatus of formal barriers—tariffs, regulations, and so on—is now lower than those in most advanced nations. Thus, from the Japanese perspective on their external problem, improving relations has meant persuading others that their markets are indeed open. Foreigners, on the other hand, often see the problem in terms of testing the real level of Japanese receptivity to imports, and they argue that nontariff barriers work to keep their goods out. While termed voluntary, the impetus came from Japan's trading partners—primarily the United States—and the measures were undertaken under the threat of import restrictions on Japanese goods.

While the policy has many substantive goals, symbolic goals are an important subset: changing the way that the Japanese and their market are perceived by outsiders. While all saw reducing the trade deficit as being the most important long-term goal, my interviews with Japanese and American participants indicated that few of them expected the market-opening measures per se to produce any major change in the trade balance. Thus the proximate goal of many participants was to improve the climate of relations by taking these actions. One high Ministry of International Trade and Industry (MITI) official stated that the purpose of these measures was to "reassure the American Congress."

THE THEORETICAL FRAMEWORK

An important aspect of symbolic policies is that they have their effect by being seen in a particular light by a relevant audience. While there are undoubtedly many intentions behind symbolic policies—policies intended to reassure, to threaten, and so on—one common class would be policies intended to shape what some intended audience thinks of the actor or actors. Indeed, clientele satisfaction and responsiveness to constituencies have often been included among the criteria for evaluating policies (Nakamura & Smallwood, 1980, chap. 5 and 8).

While Edelman's most recent work on politics as spectacle is useful for its insights into the process, Goffman's earlier work deals directly with the management of impressions: how to affect how people think about one another (Goffman, 1959). Although devised to analyze face-to-face interactions, it has been applied more widely (Fenno, 1978; Nakamura, 1980).

A simple definition of symbolic politics, in the context of import promotion, would be activities conducted with the goal of altering people's perceptions about the openness of the Japanese market. The nominal goal of a given import promotion activity—such as holding a trade show to familiarize potential buyers with foreign products—does not describe all its intended effects, which may include altering people's perceptions about the governmental and private sector climate for importation. Symbolic actions achieve their effects indirectly through changes in audience attitudes rather than directly through the outputs of a given effort.

Such a goal, influencing attitudes through the manipulation of symbolic events, is clearly a consequential enterprise. It can have a number of consequences in shaping the governmental climate of trade relations, or in affecting the willingness of outside businessmen to invest in selling to Japan.

Goffman seeks to explain the dynamics of what he terms the presentation of self, a quasi-theatrical performance involving a team effort to present oneself in a way that defines an audience's response in an intended direction. His analysis applies to a class of situations with three attributes. First, participants recognize the possibility of a conflict between the presenter's goals and those of the audience. This sets up a relationship of distrust or skepticism. A presenter's efforts are not accepted in such settings at face value. Second, a presenter seeks to influence an audience's impressions through expressions given and given off. The former are messages under the control of the presenter, while the latter may be signs that are not. Third, the skeptical audience is particularly attentive to conflicts between expressions given and given off because such conflicts may signal the presenter's "real" character.

OPERATIONALIZING THE ANALYSIS

Does the framework fit the case? Is the theoretical problem close to the practical problem? Do participants think in terms of performances and audiences? Are there means for gauging the extent of impression formation on the part of the audience?

As indicated above, JETRO realizes that it is engaged in an effort to shape outsiders' views of its and the Japanese government's intentions. JETRO, like many other semi-governmental organizations, would not exist without governmental support; such organizations are often used to implement public policy goals in Japan (for a discussion of implementation in the Japanese context see Fukui, 1977; Pempel, 1982). MITI is the most important actor in JETRO's governmental environment, and it has taken on the mission in recent years of reducing trade tensions, a sharp modification of its traditionally protectionist character (Johnson, 1986; Winham & Kabashima, 1982). JETRO performed its historic mission of promoting Japanese exports by encouraging small and medium-size businesses to export goods by identifying opportunities and encouraging ventures. Its new mission is conceptualized in similar terms: affecting the impressions held by audiences about the openness of the Japanese market by identifying opportunities and reducing the information costs of joint ventures.

What is the audience, and what is its attitude? While there are a number of potential audiences for import promotion, my research has focused on the Americans. United States–Japan trade relations are the most important bilateral relationship for the Japanese. Easing United States–Japan trade tensions has been stressed by MITI, JETRO's bureaucratic superior (Destler & Sato, 1982, pp. 7–8). JETRO, too, recognized the importance of the United States in its placement of overseas offices, and the United States has the largest number of such JETRO offices. In addition, JETRO is involved in many activities specifically directed toward an American audience: sending trade delegations to the United States, participation in the United States–Japan Trade Study Group (Yamashita, 1983), holding shows of American goods in Japan, and offering English-language publications and providing services primarily consumed by American businessmen. Finally, the largest share of foreign business contacts by Japanese businessmen is with Americans, and this preponderance is felt through JETRO's old clientele of small and medium-size businesses involved in international trade.

If the Japanese effort is intended to win over Americans, loosely defined in terms of Congress and other American domestic audiences, then the first audience for these efforts has to come from those Americans already paying attention to what the Japanese are doing. What is the American audience's attitude toward these efforts? Interviewees—both American governmental agents and private businessmen—were almost uniformly skeptical about the seriousness with which market opening has been undertaken. Many of JETRO's efforts were characterized as half-hearted or token. In addition, American observers—embassy personnel, businessmen, representatives of American state governments—saw themselves as an audience sitting in judgment on Japanese efforts including those of JETRO (see for example the remarks of Ambassador Mansfield, reported in Japanese Trade and Industry, 1982). One American trade official described the Japanese task explicitly in terms of "turning around impressions" and "creating import visibility." It appears that the notion of the Japanese government and its agencies as performers and the Americans as an audience is comfortable for both sides. (See Destler & Sato, 1982). Americans, for their part, have also engaged in trade measures for symbolic reasons in domestic politics.

Without going into detail, these American audiences in Japan constitute highly differentiated groups: American government personnel, representatives of American business, the American Chamber of Commerce, middlemen, and consultants, each with different interests but all commonly concerned with gaining an overall impression of the openness of the market or the authenticity or depth of Japanese governmental claims that they are interested in promoting imports. Each member of this differentiated and specialized audience has personal experience with only a limited set of Japanese efforts. Yet they have an incentive to form an overall impression (for a discussion of fragmentation see Morse & Olson, 1983). The American politics literature on pluralistic ignorance in Washington gives us a clue about how that overall impression is formed (Huitt, 1969). They form their overall impression by trading gossip, drawing inferences from anecdotes gleaned from other's personal experiences and tested against their own sense of what is occurring. In this view, the overall impression of the attentive public is formed on the basis of an unsystematic process of individuals forming and testing opinions.

Students of symbolic politics have referred to such stories as myths, and for them myths have consequences for those who hold them. Cobb and Elder summarize much of this literature when they write:

Myths present culturally defined truths in the form of stories, parables, and aphorisms that simplify, highlight, or dramatize basic cultural premises and prescriptions. They offer socially constructed accounts of exemplary behavior and significant events. . . . Their primary purpose is to instruct. . . . They are instrumental in shaping the values and beliefs that come to define one's basic dispositional structure. Because myths are . . . couched in terms of or revolve around specific symbols, they not only give substantive content to one's political world view but also tend to define how that content is to be linked to specific political symbols. (Cobb & Elder, 1983, p. 54)

Such a world of impressions is driven by what students of Congress have called "exemplary anecdotes" (see also Cobb & Elder, 1983, p. 83, for discussion of condensational symbols). Such anecdotes are widely circulated stories that embody what amounts to an increasingly accepted view of some subject. Such stories, in United States–Japan relations, have included the "soybean shock," the "metal baseball bat controversy," the "China shock." Ethno-methodologists have recognized that such stories are both important sources of information for participants and a means for outsiders to understand the situation as it is understood in a given culture.

The assumption behind all this work is that events per se have little intrinsic meaning independent of the interpretations they evoke or are given. Barthes, in another context, observes:

the knowledge contained in a mythical concept is confused, made of yielding, shapeless associations. One must firmly stress this open character of the concept; it is not at all abstract, purified essence; it is a formless, unstable, nebulous condensation, whose unity and coherence are above all due to its function. (Barthes, 1972, p. 119)

Thus it is in the interpretation—the lessons drawn by observers—that events have their impact.

Often the most powerful interpretations, in the form of exemplary anecdotes, are those that reveal conflicts between an expression given and given off. From the Japanese perspective, the United States says that it is seeking Japanese markets but it subjected its biggest customer to the Nixon "soybean shock" by threatening to limit the export of this staple food item. Or, the Americans point out that the Japanese say that their market is open, but their baseball teams cannot buy American metal baseball bats because they are regarded as unsafe.

Let us now pause and take stock. We know that JETRO, and its governmental superiors, would like to have the Japanese market seen as open to Americans. The audience of Americans is diverse, the majority not paying much attention at all. Japanese efforts, then, are directed to those specialized audiences who are paying attention on the assumption that the message will have to reach the mass public through an indirect route. One way in which we might gauge the effectiveness of efforts is by tapping into the store of exemplary anecdotes traded within the attentive public of Americans. Among the most widely circulated of these anecdotes are those that point to some revealing inconsistency between what is said and a truer state of affairs.

THE IMPLEMENTATION MACHINE

Policy implementation involves the assembling of machines to achieve goals (Bardach, 1977). Policies also imply theories about what is supposed to happen and why (Pressman & Wildavsky, 1986). I have suggested that the machinery and theory in the JETRO case centered on items that are consistent with the conditions for Goffman's analytic tools. In this apparatus an actor makes a presentation for consumption by an outside audience in hopes that that audience will form an intended impression of actor intentions. The theory is simple; impressions are shaped by what people see and are told. The public policy goal of improved trade relations was to be achieved by JETRO efforts to change the mind of an audience through visible efforts.

The impression that the Japanese would like to convey is that their market is an open one. But no single member of the audience is in a position to testify to the openness of the whole market; indeed the degree of openness is a point of considerable controversy and there is little agreement on how to measure it (see discussion of the McKinsey Report in the *Far East Economic Review*, November 3, 1983). Instead, participants know only about those portions with which they deal personally and rely for their assessment of the whole market on stories and exemplary anecdotes that they trade with one another. These are the circumstances, then, in which JETRO's efforts occur. They hope to act in ways that affect the informal store of information on which impressions are based.

Expressions Given

JETRO, like others interested in shaping audience impressions, does things with the intent of making the correct impression. By their nature JETRO's actions are made before a limited subset of the audience with whom they are in direct contact. JETRO's actions are, in Goffman's terms, expressions given. Their hope is that these expressions given will be taken at face value by the part of the audience with whom they are dealing. Should the limited audience accept these acts, they may use the story (in the form of exemplary anecdotes) to convey the hoped-for impression onto others.

Expressions Given Off

As the previous section indicates, the audience may be skeptical. They want to establish the authenticity of the presenters expressions given before they act upon them or spread the story to others. As the initial discussion of Goffman indicated, one way of authenticating the validity of an expression given is to check it against expressions given off. The latter are actions that are thought to be less under the direct control of the presenter. Goffman gives the example of a host who hears a guest say that he likes his meal (an expression given) but watches how much the guest eats (an expression given off).

Clashes between expressions given and given off are particularly relished by critical audiences. Americans in Japan, as indicated above, are such a critical audience, and often such a clash itself becomes the basis for an exemplary anecdote told to others. In that sense, then, making a presentation poses the risk that efforts will backfire.

A Clash Between Expressions Given and Given Off

Let me give two examples of how specific presentations by JETRO might have produced a clash between expressions given and given off and how these acts, then, might have proven counterproductive in making the intended impression. JETRO, like most organizations, finds it easier to announce changes than to put them into effect. Sometimes there is a perception gap between how important an announcement seems and the actual activity it describes.

For example, take the Task Forces on Import Promotion. JETRO announced the creation of import task forces through the press. An official handout, ''JETRO's Import Promotion Activities'' (undated), also refers to this event.

Special Task Force for Import Promotion. A special JETRO task force has been formed, in cooperation with government and trade-related bodies in Europe and the United States, for the exchange of opinions and discussion of prospects regarding the promotion of exports to Japan, which also offers advice and personal consultation. Such task forces are working so far in London, Paris, Milan, Hamburg, Dublin, Vienna, New York and Los Angeles.

One JETRO member of this task force described it in far more modest terms.

Task Force? [We are] seven persons who coordinate [in the Tokyo office]. . . . The main work of the Task Force is to coordinate with other departments. [Example?] We are going to have a catalog exhibition of consumer goods at the end of this month in coordination with the information service department. [history?] New. We have just started last year. August or September. Why? Just to promote imports. We have many activities, so we had to coordinate them.

The explanation of the task force member, in this case, was far less imposing than the announcement of the apparatus, a clash between the expression given—

in the formal announcement—implying a large and important apparatus for import promotion and the reality of a number of small, scattered efforts that are just starting up.

Another conflict between how JETRO would like to be seen and things that it does that contradict this image was related to me by an American who heads a state commerce promotion office:

My thinking is that JETRO comes in with two and a half strikes against them. Everyone thinks they are not for real. OTO (the Office of the Trade Ombudsman) has been raked over the coals. . . . JETRO came out with a new service, the import corner. They said that, in their Japanese publication, they were willing to accept import enquiries, publish descriptions and photos of products and contacts. It is an excellent idea. I sent the information back to my state and the JETRO office there had not heard of it yet. I complained to the office here. And they called their office in the states, and a few days later my office went back again. Even then, my office was skeptical. There was a memo from my guy in [state]. But they put out a notice and they were inundated with requests. JETRO published every one of them. They were willing to put out a special issue [for his state].

In Goffman's terms, there are implicit "rules of conduct," in this case the claim to be helping to open the market—an expression given—calls forth behavior that is consistent with that claim. And the expression given off in this case by inaction, also conveys a message: The rules of conduct transform both action and inaction into expression, and whether the individual abides by the rules or breaks them, something significant is likely to be communicated (Goffman, 1967, p. 65).

THE CASE OF THE HOUSEWIVES' SHOW

JETRO, in short, is trying to achieve a symbolic policy goal whose purpose is to convince outsiders that the Japanese market is open. JETRO is presenting itself—through expressions given and given off—to a skeptical audience of Americans in hopes of making the intended impression gauged by the effects on the store of exemplary anecdotes told by the audience. The enterprise is difficult, and its success depends upon keeping expressions given and given off from clashing in a way that hurts the impression formed. I will now explore one instance in which JETRO tried to achieve its symbolic policy goals during its implementation effort.

Ultimately changing people's impressions involves doing things that they can see and evaluate. One of the most visible things that JETRO does is to put on trade shows. Basically, such shows exhibit goods as a way of getting sellers and buyers together. Most interviewees in JETRO and outside mentioned these shows as one of the ways that they have seen JETRO's work. In short, these shows are one source of information about what the Japanese government is doing in the area of trade.

By their nature, trade shows are usually cooperative events coordinated by JETRO or by some other organization in conjunction with JETRO. Cooperation takes place at several levels. JETRO sometimes takes the initiative in seeking joint sponsors as a means of either sharing expenses or building legitimacy for the show itself. When other organizations initiate shows, JETRO is often asked to lend its name. Cooperation is required at other levels as well. The exhibitions themselves, for example, come from private parties, and enough of them have to be interested to make it worthwhile.

One trade show that JETRO personnel were particularly proud of was a show of household goods held in the MIPRO (an affiliate of JETRO specializing in manufactured products) Exhibition Hall at the Sunshine City Building in Tokyo. The show was held in October 1984.

It would be an exaggeration to think of this show as a major event, but it was important for JETRO. A brochure was published, showing the goods exhibited. JETRO personnel repeatedly and often spontaneously referred to it in interviews, indicating that they thought the show was a good example of what their organization could do. This show, then, became part of the store of stories that JETRO people wanted told of their efforts. Many Americans, for their part, also mentioned the show spontaneously. Again, they did not think it important in itself. Rather, like the JETRO people, they thought of it as illustrating something about JETRO and about the Japanese government. The perceptions, however, differed between JETRO personnel and many in the American audience.

How the Japanese Saw the Show

The Japanese view of this particular trade show will be presented from the bureaucratic top down: how it was seen at MITI, by the leadership of JETRO, and down through the JETRO ranks.

JETRO operates in a bureaucratic environment defined by MITI. One senior MITI official put the housewares show in the context of his overall analysis of the trade problem and what to do about it.

There may be many useful manufactured items [from all over the world that would be attractive to the Japanese]. . . . Because of ignorance and hurdles, those manufactured items may not be coming into the Japanese market. We would like to change this. [There are many] likely areas for import expansion . . . hospitals (for example) are showing interest in medical equipment. . . . Habitat furniture has been well received in Seibu [department] stores. . . . Japanese department stores are looking for something new in conception. JETRO carried [in their show] about 86 household items identified by Japanese housewives (married to JETRO personnel who had been stationed in the United States) who found those items convenient.

This official went on to identify other aspects of the government's program of import promotion.

The importance assigned to the show—in the context of JETRO's overall mission—was repeated by Naoichi Akazawa, JETRO's president:

Comparing the Japanese market to a high mountain, Akazawa said: "If they say they want to climb this mountain, we have very good guidebooks. If they really want to reach the top or go deep into the mountain, we are ready to provide a guide. If they complain about roadblocks in the mountain path, we will try to remove those obstacles [through the government's trade ombudsman office system which JETRO helps to run at its overseas trade centers, hearing foreign companies' complaints]. We want to strengthen our capacity to provide such assistance to foreign companies and businessmen wishing to export their products to Japan. But the more basic problem is that what JETRO is doing to encourage Japan's imports is not yet known very well in the U.S. and elsewhere in the world. . . .

This month, JETRO is sponsoring many American fairs displaying American consumer goods such as kitchen and housekeeping utensils, recommended by the wives of Japanese businessmen and officials living in the U.S. The exhibitions were held at Tokyo's JETRO and MIPRO exhibition halls as well as department stores. . . . JETRO has compiled a list and catalog of 84 such useful American goods, the names of the makers and where to buy or import, on the basis of its questionnaires to Japanese housewives living in five big U.S. cities, and its own research. If these goods prove to be popular with Japanese consumers, as JETRO hopes, Japanese importers will be encouraged to import them. (*Japan Times*, November 8, 1983).

These are only the first steps to help Americans gain better access to the Japanese market. These plans will not instantly improve or reverse the two countries' trade imbalance situation. But we hope they will help ease frustration of Americans who say they cannot sell their products to Japan, and thus we hope to create a better, smoother environment for Japan–United States Economic relations. A similar view was expressed by another high JETRO official in the International Communications Department who also mentioned the housewares show. This view of the show seemed to penetrate all levels of JETRO. One member of JETRO's seven-person import promotion task force discussed the role of this same show in context:

[Effect on trade imbalance?] It is rather difficult to [reduce] through our activities in. . . . import promotion. We are not the organization that has direct control. . . . We are not the government. We cannot dissolve barriers [to] trade. Only through import promotion activities we can try to make foreign businessmen understand the Japanese market. . . . [successes?] The American consumer goods selected by Japanese housewives stationed abroad. Some of these have been taken up by a Japanese department store. . . . As a result of this exhibition [the housewares show], Takashimaya [a department store chain] has purchased products from the Sunshine City Fair. They have done this directly from US companies. Other examples? There was a hot water baby feeding dish that is now being taken by the Meiji Company. A famous company for Japanese baby food. They did not deal with these products but since this exhibition they started to import more goods. Of the 84 products [exhibited] about 42 were not then imported.

In short, JETRO personnel saw their show as important enough in their overall efforts to mention explicitly. Since these remarks were made after the show, it is reasonable to assume that they thought the show succeeded well enough to be worth taking credit for.

How the Americans Saw It

The Japanese, at MITI and JETRO, seemed to think their housewares show was a success. The Americans with whom I talked had little good to say about it. Their impressions were uniformly negative. It would be useful to analyze what they said about it and the reasons they gave.

A representative of an American state put his impressions of the show in the context of his general views on Japanese government sponsored trade shows:

A general consumer goods show is not a good vehicle. . . . It was a flop. They claimed thousands of people, the figures were ludicrous. We were promised one day for the trade [limited to wholesale buyers]. . . . The ACCJ also demanded it. I went the first day and it was crawling with kids. I was furious, they ignored the promise. Trade shows cannot be completely horizontal. . . . I think the vertical trade show is the better vehicle. If you are going to sell medical equipment you invite buyers and not the general public. Consumer goods even, if they are not available there is no point in having consumers look at them. Only those companies actually selling in Japan would benefit. [what would you like to see?] It depends on what you want to sell. [Names his state] is interested in selling machinery, medical, and scientific rather than consumer goods.

In short, he did not like the kind of show that the housewares exhibit represented. His indicator of success was selling things rather than attendance figures. (JETRO is, of course, more concerned with attendance figures because it is one of the few hard indicators they can point to to show their activities are having an impact. In addition, JETRO wanted to have products not yet available in Japan precisely to interest potential buyers.)

Another American, an official of a U.S. government organization promoting American goods, was also critical of the show. He brought up the housewares show along with other efforts in his response to a question about JETRO's import promotion efforts.

[concept of promotion?] Very superficial. They can't get away from a consumer goods interpretation of promotion. For example, we had a medical technology exhibit which they co-located with flying devices for hobbyists and a women's exhibit. That was a weird mixture of products and not effective promotion.

His criticism was also directed toward the apparently diffuse nature of JETRO's efforts. To him, the potpourri quality of the several exhibits—the general audiences that attended—were all indications of a lack of seriousness and focus on JETRO's part. He went on to note that his main interests were in "big ticket" sales of high technology equipment rather than in consumer goods. To him consumer goods were high in visibility but relatively low in their ability to make a dent in the trade imbalance.

In part, this official's perception of the Japanese efforts—directly toward high visibility consumer goods—reflects the stress of other American officials. Ambassador Michael Mansfield, for example, cited the area in which American products have been doing less than they should in an interview. These were commercial jets, petrochemicals, and agriculture. He did not mention general consumer goods.

Other American officials were also critical of what they saw as a stress on high visibility but purely symbolic items. Consumer goods—particularly expensive novelty items—are one case of the exotic.

This view was also reflected by an official of the American Foreign Commercial Service. He was concerned that the Americans might be coopted into symbolic activities intended by the Japanese to give the impression that everything was all right.

[Symbolic?] Example, we were approached by MITI and JETRO to lend the Embassy name for an American products exhibition to be displayed during the Reagan visit. JETRO and MITI were appalled when we said no, . . . [We had participated in] extravaganzas in the past, a whole series of them. This was the first time we said no.

The problem as we saw it was that we did not want to distract attention from the policy issues. From high technology, energy, depressed industries. We did not want to distract by putting attention on consumer goods. By implying that things were better, and the Japanese market was really open. We did not buy into this good public relations overture.

Clash of Expressions Given and Given Off

By itself, the show was not a significant event, but it apparently symbolized different things for different participants. The show worked its way into the store of exemplary anecdotes that the Japanese told about themselves. In that sense, the show tells us something about the relationship between the organization presenting itself and the impressions it made on the audience.

For the Japanese, their housewares show represented one way they have gone about helping the Americans. In Goffman's terms, JETRO—and by extension the Japanese government—presented themselves as making formal trade concessions (in the form of the official market-opening measures) and as showing a willingness to promote goods (expression given) by holding a trade show that actually identified goods likely to be attractive to the Japanese public.

For the Americans, the same and similar shows represented one set of things wrong with Japanese efforts. Expressions given clashed with their view of expressions given off. The smallness of the items symbolized an extremely limited conception of what the government wanted the Japanese to buy. Furthermore, some Americans seemed insulted with the implicit message that such things represented the best that they had to sell.

In short, this attempt to implement the market-opening measures symbolic goals was not a success. Expressions given clashed, in the minds of some, with expressions given off. As a result the impression made was not that which was intended by the presenting organization.

Why, then, did the Japanese do what they did? After all, one agreed that the implicit purpose of the show was to give Americans a more favorable impression of the authenticity and depth of Japanese governmental efforts to increase imports and to show that the Japanese market was open. American reservations about such vehicles had been expressed earlier, so that the Japanese should have been forewarned.

The answer lies in the differing initial beliefs of both sides about the problem they are dealing with, and in JETRO's response to the legal, bureaucratic, and consensual imperatives that it is facing (Rein & Rabinovitz, 1978). Actions and responses varied according to beliefs and to the situations in which actors found themselves.

At one level, Japanese and American participants were dealing with a common problem: encouraging American business to be more active in Japan. But at another level, each was advancing its analysis of political positions whose acceptance or rejection would have other consequences in future negotiations or for the future state of their power within their respective political environments. Edelman notes:

The "career" of an explanation . . . manifestly hinges in part on the acceptability of the ideological premise it implies. Because a social problem is not a verifiable entity but a construction that furthers ideological interests, its explanation is bound to be part of the process of construction rather than a set of falsifiable propositions. (Edelman, 1988, p. 18)

Indeed, Edelman suggests that in the area of chronic problems, explanations are offered both for the purpose of soliciting acceptance and rejection and in order to sustain polarization around an issue.

In the above sense, then, neither the Japanese nor the American participants were evaluating the housewares show entirely as an event per se. Rather they were responding to a more complex set of constraints shaping their impressions about what had occurred. In this case, the requirements of these and other constraints clashed with the nominal task of putting on a show that would make participants happy. These other sets of constraints, rather than the requirements of the immediate task, determined what people did and how they reacted.

Japanese Beliefs and Their Functions

JETRO's actions can be understood in terms of the beliefs they held and the role of those beliefs in meeting the demands placed upon it. JETRO is an old organization with a new mission and operating under the demand to act quickly and effectively.

Japanese officials—from MITI and JETRO—maintained the same analysis of the openness of the market and the nature of American opportunities in it. Beginning with the premise that their market is open, they see foreigners as lacking knowledge about how and what to sell in Japan. Furthermore, these officials see the Japanese market as nearly saturated with goods, making large-scale foreign gains difficult. Finally, the archaic Japanese distribution system and other unique practices are difficult for foreigners to understand and deal with.

Trade shows like this one perform several functions: identifying the kinds of goods appealing to the Japanese, providing a chance for Japanese businessmen to see what is available and offering a chance for joint activity (providing knowledge about how to do business in Japan), and steering foreigners toward selling goods that are not in direct competition with items already available in Japan.

The beliefs described above indicate why a trade show like the housewares exhibit might be considered a creative and effective act. It showed goods that were both already and not yet available in Japan. The former indicated that businesses were already successful and the latter indicated other opportunities.

JETRO's own bureaucratic interests were also served by the show strategy adopted. First, it already knew how to hold export shows, and holding an import show used those same bureaucratic talents. JETRO operating under the demand that it act quickly would naturally select to perform in areas where it had organizational capabilities. Second, JETRO's traditional domestic clientele is small and medium-size Japanese businesses, and consumer goods can be handled more easily than complex commercial equipment by such firms. Thus such a show would allow them to try once again to serve a clientele group with whom they had had good relations in the past and on whom they depended for financial and other support. Third, trade shows are highly visible events and answer the need to appear to be acting. Such an appearance would, of course, be most easily seen by their bureaucratic superiors. The remarks of MITI people seem to confirm the efficacy of this strategy for building support within the Japanese government. Fourth, and finally, opening the show to the general public—to look at many things they currently could not buy—would increase the show's visibility and attendance figures, which would be useful in justifying JETRO's activities to other audiences.

Insofar as the problem of increasing imports into Japan was conceptualized as one of creating opportunities for the Japanese to investigate specific American goods, JETRO's special competence would give it favorable standing with MITI. Edelman (1988) discusses this point: "The language that constructs a problem and provides an origin for it is also a rationale for vesting authority in people who claim some kind of competence" (p. 22).

In short, the housewares show made sense for JETRO as an organization responding to new legal, bureaucratic, and conventual imperatives. It chose the vehicle and chose to emphasize it, not out of miscalculation but as a rational response to the situation in which it found itself.

In retrospect, this strategy seems better adapted to meeting its own needs for internal and external support than it does for altering the impressions of the American audience. In a guessing game, where it is not clear what strategies will achieve the symbolic goal, the answer that does political service to the organization may be the natural one to select despite its shortcomings for other purposes.

American Beliefs and Their Functions

This reasoning explains why JETRO did what it did. While the effort was— by estimates on both sides—modest, it did make sense as a step toward greater imports. Why, then, did the Americans react as they did? The answer again lies, in part, in beliefs and their functions. In this case, American attitudes— specifically those of government officials—toward the show were shaped by other considerations.

The general analysis of the Americans is similar to that of the Japanese. Few informed observers dispute that the formal barriers are lower now than they have been, or that residual bureaucratic resistance is slowing down the actual pace of market opening. Furthermore, the Americans concede that part of the problem has been the reluctance of American businesses to move into the Japanese market in a serious way. After that, however, American and Japanese views differ. Probably the most important point of difference is in perceptions about the nature of opportunities in the Japanese market. While the viewpoint represented in the show stressed consumer goods, many Americans interviewed stressed manufactured goods.

This view was particularly strong among American government officials who stressed "big ticket" sales of high technology items. This stress may have had many roots. U.S. officials prefer to think of themselves as representing a nation that is capable of producing sophisticated goods (and may be insulted at the implication that their country was competitive only in small consumer items); trade negotiations had recently stressed "big ticket" items because they would have a greater effect on the trade imbalance; and U.S. trade officials were sensitive to the charge that they were too sympathetic to the Japanese and too willing to participate in symbolic events that took the pressure off the Japanese government.

American beliefs, like those of their Japanese counterparts, also perform functions for the believers. There is, on both sides, some bargaining advantage to be derived from being satisfied or dissatisfied with Japanese efforts at market opening. The American view, that efforts have been inadequate, enhances the effectiveness of their demands for greater efforts. Expressing satisfaction with existing efforts, then, diminishes bargaining leverage. The Japanese, for the opposite reasons, have an incentive to present their efforts as effective.

In addition, the American position is not particularly consistent. There are many examples in which the signs of Japanese bad intentions were put in terms of the very class of luxury or consumer goods promoted by trade shows. Stories of Japanese bad faith have included those about the restriction of access for American metal baseball bats, Johnny Walker scotch, luxury cars, and other such items. The standards for evidence of bad faith and evidence of good faith are not the same. We change our mind about what is important in these small ways and in larger ways as well. The American trade agenda has changed considerably over time, often driven by particular hot issues—citrus, textiles, autos, and so on—on the American domestic agenda. This poses a moving target for the Japanese in seeking to alter American impressions in areas that the Americans identify as important. In turn, if a Japanese bureaucracy is asked to incur costs—loss of domestic clientele support or alienation of important political groups—the willingness to pay those costs to hit an ephemeral target may be lacking.

CONCLUSION

This case shows the implementation of policies to be no easier for the Japanese than for the Americans. More specifically, the implementation of symbolic policy goals is, as the analysis indicates, always tricky because both the presenting organization and the audience make and respond to presentations based on beliefs originating outside the actual interaction underway. While symbolic actions are easy to undertake, symbolic goals are harder to achieve in the face of a skeptical audience.

At the risk of finding the world in a grain of sand, I will now deal with the question of what, if any, conclusions can be drawn from this case study. Several points can be made. Symbolic goals are not necessarily self-implementing, and their achievement often requires an explanation. The Goffman framework and its implied machinery does seem to be an appropriate approach for analyzing how symbolic policy goals might be implemented; it identifies the central problem of such efforts in terms of clashes between expressions given and given off, it identifies pitfalls, and it directs our attention to the conditions for successful implementation in cases such as this.

The symbolic goals of a policy may require implementation for their achievement. While some of the symbolic goals of a policy may be achieved by taking any action, by appearing to act, action alone may not be enough. In this case the Japanese government did respond to American demands by undertaking a program of import promotion. But as the interviews make clear, there was an expectation that subsequent actions were to authenticate the seriousness with which the Japanese government approached the problems posed by the trade imbalance. The American demand was for both immediate action and reassurance. On the latter point, the audience expectation centered on what the Japanese efforts were supposed to communicate rather than on any substantive effect they were intended to achieve. While a given trade promotion effort could do little to redress the trade imbalance, it could serve as a benchmark against which to judge the authenticity of Japanese commitment. And since the Japanese themselves wanted the same message conveyed, the quality of the implementation did have a direct impact on the achievement of this symbolic goal of altering the audience's perceptions about their motivations.

One problem posed in analyzing symbolic policies is the absence of guidance on how a symbolic goal is to be achieved. Since "symbolic" is often equated with "inconsequential," policy framers are usually not very forthcoming about the connection between what they are proposing to do and what they hope will happen. In one class of situations—those in which the goal is to change people's minds about an actor—the Goffman framework provides us with a generic conception of the anticipated mechanisms. It differentiates actor roles, lays out significant activities, and provides indicators as to the success or failure of enterprises in achieving their intent. And the framework provides some guidance for the conditions under which it can be used effectively: when the presenter and audience roles are accepted by participants, when actors are skeptical about one another's intentions, and when definitive indicators of a true state of affairs is absent. While the case material in this instance is far from definitive, the fit between these categories and what actors said lends credence to the notion that such a framework underlies behavior in this instance.

If the goal is to alter the impressions that one set of actors holds of another, the analysis suggests that the central problem of implementing symbolic goals of this type lies in controlling conflicts between expressions given and given off. It is the principal thing that can go wrong, and thus keeping the two consistent ought to be the task around which implementation is organized. While this might seem intuitive and obvious, most implementer attention is directed at expressions given with less attention by any organization to expressions given off.

The case material indicates that internal concerns played a very large role in determining JETRO's behavior. It chose to act in an area where it had bureaucratic competence, where its former clients were likely to be involved, and in ways that confirmed its worth to governmental superiors. Each of these factors directed JETRO attention to what it did to express itself, and none in these environments were concerned with the expressions given off by such activities. And it was in this area that the outside audience would set the great store in assessing the authenticity of message being sent.

Ultimately such a presentational effort depends for its success on both the presenter and the audience. It is in that sense a cooperative enterprise engaged in by actors with differing interests. Both parties have something at stake.

While the analysis to date has centered on Japanese miscalculations, the Americans too missed some opportunities. Both sets of actors want better trade relations and have some incentive to cooperate, at the same time that each wants bargaining, behavioral, and attitudinal advantage surrendered by the other. Recognizing that actions are intended to please and possibly mislead an audience is a first step. But this and other audiences also have incentives to get the presenter to act in particular ways that advance the audience's interests. The presenter's need to perform is also a tool for audience influence. The audience can, under the right circumstances, get things from the presenter. Some obvious American strategies might include: being clearer and more consistent about what it wants, and increasing the frequency of feedback about impressions to steer presentational efforts better.

From the Japanese side, the decision rule (of maintaining bureaucratic peace discussed above) might be less effective than a more conflictful strategy in achieving the desired change in audience attitude. Recall that an audience seeks signs of the authenticity of a commitment. One such sign might be the willingness to pay high costs to do something. In this case there might be some gain for the Japanese, in the eyes of the Americans, when they suffer some conflict in the pursuit of market-opening goals. Take, for example, trade concessions in agriculture. The very costs to Japanese politicians, in rural hostility, increase the value of such concessions to the Americans. Americans, used to some level of conflict, take such suffering as a sign that their trading partners are serious in their concessions. Similarly, the very smoothness of implementation of new goals—valued by Japanese organizations in this case—may be a sign that the activities are not sufficiently seriously motivated. This is, of course, "political logic," but it makes sense to participants.

The foregoing suggests that the task of implementing the symbolic goals of a given policy may be different from implementing its manifest goals. If, as the analysis suggests, outcomes in "impressions" formed may depend as much on exemplary anecdotes—built on previously held positions and an unsystematic sampling of events—as upon the broader impacts of a policy, then the success or failure of a policy in achieving its symbolic goals is also independent of the degree of formal implementation achieved. In short, you cannot assume that just because a policy is formally implemented, it will also achieve its symbolic goals. Trade shows were held, but the intended impressions were not formed. That means that the achievement of symbolic goals requires as much explicit attention as is devoted to the formal implementation of a policy. At a minimum, then, the same kind of scenario writing advocated by implementation analysts for formal implementation (see for example Bardach, 1977; Levin & Ferman, 1985; Nakamura & Smallwood, 1980) needs to be done for a policy's symbolic goals. As the previous analysis suggests, symbolic goals are often not self-executing and require efforts specifically tailored to the audiences to which they are directed.

APPENDIX

Thirty-one persons selected by several informants were interviewed. The composition of the set of interviewees is as follows: MITI (4); The American embassy (5); American Chamber of Commerce (2); private persons working on trade issues (4); JETRO personnel (in Tokyo, Los Angeles, New York offices) (8); the research staff of the Diet library (3); members of the Diet (2); private foundations and business organizations (3).

These interviews lasted from one to two hours. In addition, a number of other informants—American and Japanese scholars—were interviewed to test guesses and to develop leads.

In addition, I attended a three-day seminar on business opportunities for Americans sponsored by an American group and JETRO. Here, lawyers, business people, and others described the formal and informal characteristics of the Japanese market from the point of view of foreign businessmen. I also attended several trade shows sponsored by JETRO.

I drew on written materials from the JETRO library (in Tokyo), the Foreign Commercial Library (of the American embassy), the Japan Foundation Library (for English-language periodicals), and the International House Library (which keeps current business newsletters and other publications).

PART II

Implementation Politics and the Organizational Context

6

Implementation and Managerial Creativity: A Study of the Development of Client-Centered Units in Human Service Programs

Glenn W. Rainey, Jr.

Organizational design and management may be both instrument and goal in public policy, and are therefore of dual importance in the study of policy implementation. Experimentation with organizational form is ongoing, and the analysis of new forms is of continuing academic and practical interest for those concerned with program implementation. The field of implementation research, however, has advanced to a frontier of broad epistemological and ontological uncertainty. Theoretical underpinnings and research methods are subjects of review, debate, and doubt.

This chapter focuses on a recurring variation in the design of service delivery components for human service programs; it examines small, functionally comprehensive, or client-centered service units, and the environmental conditions that favor them. At present, such forms appear to be recessive traits in public programs, but they also appear to have emergent potential and may have wide application if certain favorable environmental changes were to occur. A review of their use may provide insights into specific options for organizational design and into the broader linkages between top and bottom in the development of public policies. Before proceeding, however, an analytical framework must be established within a complex, sophisticated, and therefore ambiguous theoretical discourse.

This chapter is based on a secondary analysis of material originally presented in Glenn W. Rainey, Jr., ''Reassessing Organizational Modeling for Human Services Administration: Lessons from the Effective Use of Functionally Integrated Small Groups,'' a paper presented at the meeting of the American Society for Public Administration, Portland, Oregon, April 17–20, 1988. The author wishes to express particular thanks to Sally Snyder, executive director, and to Henry Benlolo and April Manning on the staff of WORKFORCE for their assistance in developing the description of this case.

SEEKING STRUCTURE IN IMPLEMENTATION RESEARCH

Out of ferment, frustration, and growing insight, students of implementation have entered upon a search both for theoretical models which will adequately encompass the complexity of their subject and for methodological approaches to research that will adequately support the development and testing for such models. Motivating this search is a recognition that criteria for evaluating implementation have been highly relativistic, in both "top-down" and "bottom-up" approaches (Linder & Peters, 1987), and that implementation processes include significant creative and entrepreneurial dimensions whose outcomes are probabilistic rather than determinate. Thus reality may, to some extent, be created by the participants—but how much may be created, under what circumstances, and by what means remain crucial and unanswered questions.

Methodologically, the perspectives shaping the search are associated with multiplism (Cook, 1985) and increased emphasis on design science (Miller, 1984). A strong reaction has developed against the trappings of logical positivism in research on implementation. Experimentalist and nonmentalist epistemology, applied to cross-sectional studies and case studies, are seen to reinforce simplistic conceptions of implementation processes as subordinated and substantially pathological routines which may be portrayed in static terms, rather than as interactive and dynamic encounters among actors and institutions, which have evolutionary potential. Solutions are seen in more comparative and diachronic analysis (Lester et al., 1987), presumably to be applied to more complex models using multiple hypotheses and measures by multiple analysts (Cook, 1985).

Resolution of the ambiguities in implementation studies, and escape from what Cook has called "mindless relativism" (p. 57), therefore requires simultaneous development of better theory, better measures (i.e., more "functionally relevant"), and better data (i.e., more "reliable"). A paradigm to guide this effort has not been systematically formulated, and the development of a paradigm must surmount certain paradoxes, beyond the classic paradox of science—that the demonstration of theoretical validity requires valid measurement, and valid measurement requires valid theoretical constructs. Some general directions which the development is taking may be discerned.

In the first place, there are calls for the reconciliation and merger of top-down and bottom-up frameworks of analysis (Lester et al., 1987; Sabatier, 1986; Linder & Peters, 1987). The means remain largely ambiguous, but a number of suggestions have been made, generally in the form of arguments for conceptual refinement. For example, Lester and associates argue for more definitive specification of implementation activities, identification of crucial variables, and a focus on the actor rather than the policy.

A number of students of implementation are prepared to assume that the subject matter itself is multidimensional—that we must study not implementation but implementations. Myrtle (1983) sees the implementation process as unique to each policy, organization, and implementer. Lester et al. assert that the implementation "process may vary according to policy type" (p. 209) and suggest the need of an implementation typology. And Miller (1984, p. 264) has suggested that unique methods may be appropriate for the analysis and evaluation of each policy. These assumptions have not been reconciled with the major advances that have been made in the study of macro-implementation and with the equally plausible assumption that macro-implementation follows general rules (Palumbo, 1987). An interim assumption with intuitive appeal is that implementation processes reflect both general and policy-specific phenomena, and that a complete explanation will require an understanding of both. By inference, implementation research cannot be divorced from mainstream social sciences and their strengths and weaknesses; a complete theory of implementation is a theory of all social behavior, as it makes no more sense to develop a theory of adult illiteracy alleviation than to develop a theory of state bird selection.

A potentially unifying theme is also evident in a shared interest in instrumentation. Linder and Peters (1987b) call for "broader conceptualization of success and failure, based more on design criteria" (p. 126), and also suggest the possibility of a "policy in implementation" paradigm (p. 122), which seeks to identify a compromise or balance between the policy formulator's intentions and the implementer's routines. Salamon (1981) calls for the identification and analysis of generic tools of implementation. Myrtle (1983) suggests the analysis of specifically targeted change strategies. And Sabatier (1986) suggests the utility of focusing on linkages between policy problems and implementational strategies. These suggestions have arisen out of varied conceptual lines of reasoning, and communality among them is by imputation rather than the intention of their proponents. But they do appear to share an interest in the study of instrument-goal linkages in specified environments.

Absent a theoretical paradigm, empirical inquiry must perforce adopt a relatively inductive posture—that is, replicating structures are more likely to be identified through processes akin to natural history. In this sense, the discovery of order in implementational phenomena may follow processes more analogous to the descriptive and taxonomic work of primitive biology than to relativistic modeling characteristic of computer science, nuclear physics, or genetics, which afford prototypes of design science (Miller, 1984b, pp. 253–254). The biological analogy is further appropriate in that it allows for probabilistic and opportunistic influences, within dynamic and evolutionary processes.

The remainder of this chapter, therefore, seeks to advance the identification and assessment of useful instruments, together with comparative observation and systematic taxonomical development, in the subfield of organizational implementation. "Instrument" in this context is not restricted to tangible phenomena or institutional structures; it includes replicable patterns of social interaction and influence. The object of inquiry is the functionally comprehensive small service unit in human service programs. Continued experimentation and experience with this organizational form provides a modest basis for examination of its viability and utility in given environmental contexts through a comparison of case histories. A preliminary effort will be made to identify its distinguishing features, explain its development (in a nonpredictive sense—see McKelvey, 1982), and define, in a preliminary way, the environments in which it seems to thrive. The subject has timely implications for policy; recent years have seen increasing reexamination of the lengthy experimentation with decentralization and integration in human service programs, which began with a series of pilot projects of the Department of Health, Education and Welfare in 1969 (Gans & Horton, 1975; Austin, 1978; 1983; Imershein et al. 1983; Martin et al., 1983; Calista, 1986a; Chi, 1987), and small functionally integrated units represent a transferable tool for delivering client-centered services of the sort presumably targeted by the experimentation.

The analytical approach is primarily inductive and intuitive, and is influenced by but loosely coupled with McKelvey's tentative modeling for organizational systematics—that is, the application of taxonomical science to organizations. Functionally integrated small units being encompassed within organizations, they are more appropriately defined as "characters" (i.e., observable attributes) than as taxonomical units. As we shall see, however, they are characters of potentially great significance, as they are associated with extensive adaptations of both technical processes and managerial skills and strategies—the fundamental components of the "dominant competence" which McKelvey uses as the central quasi-genetic dimension distinguishing organizational species. In the process, we shall ignore McKelvey's advice to formulate species concepts first, and simply observe for comparable attributes (although a gesture toward conventionalism and legitimacy is easily available in McKelvey's own avowedly tentative classification schema which lumps all public agencies, federal, state, and local, into one genus within one class within one subdivision in the "normatives kingdom"—p. 262).

While the methodology falls far short of the ideals of multiplism, design science, and systematics, it has certain advantages: it is comparative; it provides substantial opportunities to consider longitudinal dimensions; it focuses on actors and strategies; and it incorporates at least some of the ideals of the design science perspective in that the particular form to be examined has been modeled in the abstract, and the modeling has played a direct role in the dissemination of the instrument. It is, moreover, an affordable strategy for advancing in small steps a new research agenda which is, from the perspectives of multiplism, design science, and systematics alike, quite massive. And while generalization from a few field observations may entail some of the intellectual arrogance of alchemy, even alchemists sometimes produced valid observations and useful information for the prince.

THE FUNCTIONALLY INTEGRATED SMALL UNIT

Under certain specific conditions, models incorporating simultaneous application of decentralization and integration to production processes have been used

Figure 6.1
Traditional and Alternative Production Structures*

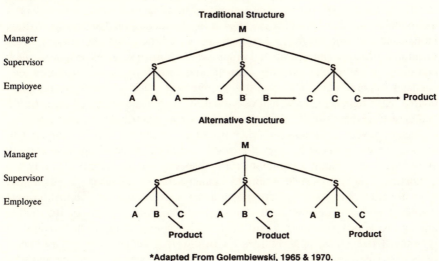

Adapted From Golembiewski, 1965 & 1970.

for specific effect in both public and private sector organizations. As early mechanistic theories of organizational behavior were succeeded by research and theory placing greater emphasis on the broad capabilities and complex social relationships of ordinary employees, a vision emerged of a managerial strategy in which the downward movement of authority and the merging of specialized functions could be systematically linked to serve both humanitarian and performance goals. A model of organizational structure which accommodates this vision was first graphically and abstractly portrayed by Golembiewki in 1965, as shown in Figure 6.1. The "alternative" model envisions small but complete production or service units arrayed in such a way that any competition between them may be relatively easily channeled to serve productive goals, rather than the disruption of a delicate and extended functional division of labor. The decentralization of authority and integration of functions are directly represented in the model, but two other features are equally essential: (1) The integrated subunits must achieve productive closure, and whatever they are created to produce—be it carefully crafted rules, procedures, and policies or a completed service for a client—will become the primary focus of effort of the members of the units; and (2) The model's benefits are further predicated upon the assumption that the integrated units will be socially compact—small, and with close communication among members. Otherwise, they will fragment, formally or informally, into self-defined work groups, straining intragroup communications. An upper size limit has not been determined. Fifty members can establish a cohesive group identity. Several hundred would almost certainly subdivide.

The alternative model, which will be called the functionally integrated small

unit (FISU) model, thus represents the confluence of four factors: social compactness, unified supervision at the intended production level, merged production
functions, and output closure. The synergy of these factors sharply distinguishes
the model from other, coordinative approaches to integration that attempt to draw
human services into heightened cooperation with little or no alteration in organizational structure and operational processes. In human services programs, such
coordinative approaches include consolidated governing boards and umbrella
agencies; coordinating and facilitating agencies such as intergovernmental
boards, case representatives, and coordinating councils; and shared information
and case tracking systems. Such mechanisms may contribute to more intensive
linkages between programs or functions (e.g., Agranoff, 1985), but tend to
accomplish this purpose by imposing additional layers of administrative activity
and/or without creating a common, service-specific group identity. County coordinating boards and state umbrella human services agencies, for example,
typically attempt to integrate action over a vast social space through institutional
mandates and oversight without changing fundamental patterns of interaction
among operations personnel. Co-located services under multiple supervision, on
the other hand, create opportunities for face-to-face cooperation among operations personnel, but deny decentralized control over operations policy and procedures. The differences between such approaches and a fully integrative model
such as the FISU are therefore related to processes and constraints of fundamental
importance for understanding and influencing the orchestration of cooperative
human activity, yet little has been done to identify the circumstances under which
experiments with organizational arrangements do and do not result in effective
emulations of a FISU model.

Approximations to this model have long been in use, an example being the
historical practice of providing multiple health services through small localized
centers. The comparison of cases that follows suggests that use of the form may
be spreading, haltingly, and that recent adoptions approach quite closely the
attributes that define the model in the abstract, including social compactness,
unified supervision, merged production functions, and output closure. It is therefore assumed for the sake of the inquiry that extensive use of this model may
be treated as a taxonomical attribute or "character" of organizational form,
clearly distinguished from reliance on other, noncomprehensive integrative and
coordinative arrangements. This assumption is not entirely gratuitous: use of
small, comprehensively integrated units imposes on operations supervisors and
employees, perforce, a comprehensive responsibility and expertise for overall
production that is not found in functionally and spatially differentiated arrangements. In this sense, it would appear to alter what McKelvey has called the
"dominant competence" of the organization (1982, pp. 169–192).

COMPARING IMPLEMENTATIONS OF THE FISU

To explore these circumstances, and the variations in form that may occur
with effective use of such a model, a small number of empirical approximations

to the model were identified in the literature and through field interviews and used to support judgments about comparable and noncomparable aspects of the circumstances in which they developed. The objective was to highlight organizational and environmental factors essential to understanding the successful use of the model in given contexts. To simplify the presentation, three illustrative mini-cases will be referred to in the analysis. They concern specific instances of reorganizations moving in the direction of the FISU. Each reorganization, however, involved significant differences in both environmental and historical context. One occurred in a large, classic formal bureaucracy, another in a municipal health department's community health services programs, and another in the jointure of services between a nonprofit job-training agency and a state job services bureau.

FISU Integration Within Formal Structure—Social Security Modules

The first example is the use of comprehensive case processing modules, developed for adjudication of Retirement and Survivors Insurance claims by the Social Security Administration (SSA) during the 1970s, and subsequently adopted with design variations in other components of SSA (Rainey & Rainey, 1984; 1986a; 1986b). In this instance, performance problems in the processing of retirement and survivors' claims in six regional "Payment Centers" (now called "Program Service Centers" or "PSCs") of about 2,000 employees each were addressed by reassigning a respected and energetic bureau director to the bureau administering the centers and inviting him to seek solutions. The result was a regeneration and reorganization project lasting eight years. The most prominent feature of this effort was a newly developed administrative structure in which large functional divisions housing claims authorization, payment determination, and support functions (e.g., payment processing and records maintenance) were consolidated into small, functionally comprehensive "modules" averaging about forty-eight employees each. These modules now house the files for a specified subgroup of beneficiaries, together with the claims, payment, and support staff necessary to carry out complete service on most actions brought to the modules. Small group interaction among functional specialities occurs under the supervision of a single module manager, responsible for the entire work flow, and the results have included substantial, empirically demonstrated improvements in speed and accuracy of service. Variations on this form have subsequently been adopted by units handling disability claims and record keeping operations within SSA, and by claims processing units of the U.S. Railroad Retirement Board in Chicago.

FISU Integration Within Formal Structure—Health Centers

Another example, approximating the alternative model but blending more central control into organizationally decentralized units, would be the district health centers described in Robinson's (1967) case study of the reorganization of the Philadelphia Department of Public Health. Over a period of approximately eleven years, from 1948 to 1959, the department pursued a program of general professionalization and enhancement of service, a part of which was the development of ten consolidated district health centers. Key elements in the progression included: initial intervention by the city government in favor of decentralized over centralized services; subsequent strong support by a progressive mayor; appointment of a strong, progressive department head; professionalization through enhanced salaries and recruitment of progressive divisional managers; creation of a director of health services and appointment of a strong leader to the position; construction of new district health centers followed by enhancement of the organizational status of their directors and, eventually, a preemptive maneuver that accorded them significant control personnel and field activities in their districts. Through a combination of technical necessity and resistance by professionalized divisional leadership, much of the health services activity remained under the direct control of headquarters staff. The district centers did not achieve a complete integration of function and identity analogous to the SSA modules, but they did achieve primary control over such activities as maternal and child health programs, a large portion of health education, a large portion of the public health nursing service, and certain other services related to sanitation. Robinson (1967) reports that most of the staff of the department felt the reorganization had improved the general performance of the agency.

FISU Integration via Diplomacy and Treaty—WORKFORCE

Both of the preceding cases involve formal restructuring and might be taken to imply that such restructuring unification of authority are essential features of FISU development. A case that has not been previously presented in the implementation literature provides an example of the creation of systematically unified action at the operations level through diplomatic arrangements between formally autonomous agencies. This is the WORKFORCE concept in Florida, in which state job services units and Job Training Partnership Act (JTPA) staffs are co-located in integrated client service teams under shared advertising and recruitment activities, and publicly represented under a single agency name. Because the case has not received much prior attention in the academic literature, it will be summarized in more detail than the previous two.

When planning for the 1986–1987 program year began in Florida, the local job services and JTPA training agencies faced a mandate from the U.S. Department of Labor and the state to generate joint service plans. Beginning in February 1986, the state's twenty-four JTPA Service Delivery Areas (SDAs) and twenty-three district job services units were forced to sit together to plan their programs. In Pinellas County, a management committee was formed of representatives from the job services staff and the Pinellas County Business and Industry Employment Development Council (the JTPA PIC). The relationship between managers from the two sides became close enough that a new joint service delivery concept began to emerge. The executive director of the PIC was particularly interested in a joint arrangement, as were a couple of other managers.

The managers were attracted by the prospect of shared operating centers and maximized staff use. Their planning began with the concept of co-located services and was extended to encompass a concept of team services. An idea for joining different JTPA services under a single name had emerged earlier in discussions between the executive director and PIC contractors, and the reorganization was further extended to encompass the development of a common logo by which the public would know and contact the integrated employment and training office.

Circumstances were favorable for rapid co-location: a lease for space at a PIC center in St. Petersburg was expiring, and the Clearwater office was to be restructured. Some new space was acquired, some existing space was expanded, and five joint centers emerged in St. Petersburg, Pinellas Park, and Clearwater, housing a total staff of about eighty-five people.

By July 1986 a team concept was emerging in the centers. To create the client service teams, the job services staff contributed an assessment specialist, a counselor, and a Job Club representative, while the PIC staff contributed a job developer and a team leader. A client could now deal with one team, which would focus its combined skills simultaneously on the client's needs, performing an assessment, recommending a specific program of training and placement, and helping to implement that program.

The managers knew, however, that implementation of a joint concept would require staff acceptance and that both sides had familiar ways of doing things. The job services units, being in operation much longer, had many long-time employees with time-honored approaches to their work. To create the opportunity for a meeting of minds, a task force of staff from different levels and specialties was created early in the process of integration. A marketing specialist from the JTPA staff was appointed by the executive director to serve as liaison to both the managers' committee and the task force and to design the joint concept and its representation to the public.

The task force was deliberately staffed with some of the most resistant and doubtful individuals who were also, if possible, opinion leaders in their own work settings. Initially, resistance was strong, but as discussions proceeded, members who were moderately resistant began to pressure those who were outspoken and unbending to listen and consider the options.

Eventually, the managers made it clear that they intended to move in the direction of unification, with clear implications that those who could not accept this might not be able to remain comfortably in the new joint program. In the end, the task force not only accepted the decision, but moved proactively to implement it. The task force itself developed three days of implementation training, and the persuasive advocates of the new approach included some of the job services people who had been most strongly opposed at the beginning.

The services of the combined units are now advertised and marketed under a common trademark, "WORKFORCE." Marketing strategies can be adjusted to specific types of programs. Employers and participants focus on one phone number and one administrative unit, instead of being hit from both sides. Service districts are assigned across the county to facilitate orderly public contact. Phone calls tripled in response to the advertising strategies. In April 1988 the Pinellas County PIC won the first presidential award for Private Industry Council of the Year for the program year 1987.

The joint arrangements were not legally mandated and could be disbanded by changes in priorities at higher levels. The marriage of the two programs was essentially voluntary and could dissolve in the face of internal dissension or change in priorities from higher levels. It is held together by mutual benefits and concessions. Jobs have been redesigned for the shared centers and client service teams to facilitate interfunctional cooperation. Choices of recruitment, assessment, training, and placement procedures must be worked out together, and the ideas or goals of one side may not be immediately or fully shared by the other. JTPA funds paid the costs of merging into common centers and developing the marketing programs, and even paid for contract services by existing job services staff. But the WORKFORCE concept has been trademarked and marketed, and the JTPA staff continue to pursue contracts and funding on an entrepreneurial basis. In addition to programs of their own, they have assumed a brokerage role, developing cooperative grant programs with other service agencies in the community in return for administrative costs. Not being state employees, they can enjoy salaries above the levels mandated by the state for job services employees, and they can earn bonuses.

A few other SDAs in Florida have either adopted the WORKFORCE concept directly or made other types of energetic efforts to establish or maintain effective joint relationships. After the concept had been implemented, the state JTPA Council developed interest in putting more momentum behind joint arrangements and approved funds to develop a statewide joint marketing program. The WORKFORCE staff submitted an application for the contract to develop the program. The contract was awarded instead to an advertising firm, and it appears as this is written that the statewide effort will focus on joint program advertising without the emphasis on joint planning and co-location of staff. In most areas, job services and JPTA remain administratively separated, and apparently will remain so.

WORKFORCE staff members have been pleased with the results of the joint program, but warned that the co-location and joint program effort are most appropriately regarded as the aftereffect of having worked out problems in cooperation. Co-location per se, in their view, would not necessarily guarantee cooperation. They expressed the belief, however, that strong cooperative arrangements might be established between units at opposite ends of a county if the participants in the relationship first developed the appropriate mind set.

CONDITIONS FOR IMPLEMENTATION OF "ALTERNATIVE FORMS"

A review of experiences with the implementation of FISU models provides some tentative clues to requisite conditions for effectiveness. These conditions overlap with the more general requirements for effective social change intervention. But repeated experience with the form suggests, even more tentatively, that the conditions are probably interlocked, so that most or all must be met for effective implementation. Six conditions seem to hold, with permutations, in a variety of settings.

Entrepreneurial Leadership

A common feature in the development of FISU models at the service delivery level is leadership by an entrepreneurial manager or political leader—an "instrumental person," as one social services manager put it. The leader usually requires active and creative staff support, but despite the participatory and job enrichment ideals that lie in the background of the "alternative organization" concept, implementation seems to follow a pattern: initial discussion and experimentation followed at some point by an authoritative decision to adopt a new approach. It appears that to exert the necessary force, the instrumental person must, either formally or informally, exercise independent control over the affected units. In SSA, a new bureau director was appointed and given, effectively, carte blanche. In Philadelphia, the principal movement to delegate real authority to district health directors occurred when a reform mayor appointed a new health commissioner who, in turn, appointed a new director of public health services who emphasized bringing people into physical contact and direct communication with each other. In the case of WORKFORCE, the executive director of the PIC had no formal authority over the job services staff but was supported in a unification effort by a central policy mandate for joint planning and apparently by a fortunate meeting of minds with other managers involved in the planning process.

It is tempting to draw parallels to concepts of "bureaucratic entrepreneurship" as they have been applied to policymaking and executive positions (e.g., Levin & Ferman, 1985; Ferman & Levin, 1986). Concepts such as "action bias" and situational opportunity clearly have applications to policymakers, program executives, and agency managers alike. But each has unique concerns as well. Agency managers, for example, will tend to have the preponderant share of responsibility and expertise for the design of production flows and the generation of internal organizational support for change. The circumstances with which leaders at each level must contend are therefore summatively unique.

Slack Resources

The development of an FISU is not a cost-saving strategy but a service improvement strategy requiring an initial infusion of risk capital. The needs contributing to the initial costs include changes in work space, new or improved equipment or communications and information systems, training, and improved salaries or other rewards for "enriched" jobs. Since the FISU model is predicated upon a small, face-to-face work team, spatial rearrangements seem a prerequisite. The creation of the Social Security modules was facilitated by the implementation of a massive program to provide previously promised new space to the Program Service Centers. Implementation of the WORKFORCE co-location was eased because spatial arrangements were open to reexamination and change (through expiration of a lease). District health centers in Philadelphia were encouraged by surges in political commitment to improved public health, reflected first in the acquisition of old space in service districts (under a specific mandate from a city council oriented to accessible services) and later in the construction of new facilities (with the support of a reform administration).

The creation of umbrella agencies, and other merged administrative arrangements, may result in the development of new spatial facilities based on an idealism as powerful as any that might motivate co-location of services at the operating level. But it is difficult to trace tangible benefits in improved services or reduced costs to the development of these facilities.

An Encapsulable Service or Product

In the three cases we have reviewed, priority was placed on creation of interfunctional linkages to achieve a specified service objective. In the Social Security Administration, claims processing modules produce finished actions resulting in a service decision rendered to the client, and under WORKFORCE a complete training and placement routine is provided to a client by a team. In the Philadelphia health centers, a service routine apparently could not be completely isolated for autonomous administration in district centers because a substantial range of functions had to remain centralized for professional, technical, and political reasons. But the district centers did achieve sufficient control over certain functions to be able to arrange comprehensive service packages if they desired. For example, they controlled maternal and child health programs, community nursing services, and a substantial portion of health education.

By contrast, such arrangements as umbrella departments or coordinating bodies serve varied, often with competing or even mutually exclusive objectives. The continued use of functional subdivisions places a priority on intrafunctional linkages such as professional specialization and identity.

Exceeding a Support Threshold

Management of the transition from traditional to fully integrated production units seems from situation to situation to follow a comparable process, which may be described as guided participation. The method of involving staff and building receptivity begins with some form of inquiry and constructive encounter, for example, creation of investigative committees or task forces, conferences, team-building or training, and/or informal consultation and discussions. Planning processes are used to signal reassurances about such concerns as job security or managerial status. But at some point—after several years in the case of SSA and the Philadelphia Health Department and a few months in the much more compact WORKFORCE reorganization—a signal is transmitted conveying to the unpersuaded, with as little direct confrontation as possible, that the change has become the "thing to do." In SSA, after several PSCs had adopted modular organizations, headquarters staff were simply sent to yet uncommitted centers to explain to them that the agency was on its way to the new form and to help them plan their reorganizations. In Philadelphia, a decision was reached at a staff meeting to appoint a committee to plan decentralization of functions to district offices. In the WORKFORCE case, study and discussion were used to help foster insight and understanding, and build a climate supportive of change, but at a certain point the managers apparently simply announced a decision to complete unification.

Long Time Frames

The amount of time required to install the FISU model in a traditionally organized hierarchy seems to vary with the scope and complexity of the requirements for transition, but it is always substantial. In the case of the Social Security modules, the prior team building and experimentation, discovery and testing of the alternative model, and its dissemination throughout the centers took about eight years. In Philadelphia, approval of a decentralization plan was accomplished about eleven months after John Hanlon became director of public health services, but the groundwork of developing integrated facilities and staff actually began nine years earlier. In WORKFORCE, all major elements of unification were essentially accomplished in about five months, but were no less patiently pursued, given that the total staff involved numbered less than a hundred, community-based spatial facilities were already in use, and no major rewriting of position descriptions or chains of command were necessary for what was, on its surface, simply a variation on co-location.

In sum, reported experiences confirm what common sense suggests: the greater the degree of adjustment to be made in command structures, job assignments, support systems, and spatial arrangements, the longer it will take to build sufficient consensus to support a change and to plan and execute it carefully. This constraint is not uniquely a requirement of large agencies implementing fully integrated production units. Any specifically targeted change effort, such as integration of social services in a county or the development of an integrative management information system, may need several years to be done with the necessary support and administrative systems to meet its performance expectations (e.g., Vander Schie et al., 1987; Mutschler & Cnaan, 1985).

A Political Window of Opportunity

Finally, reorganization efforts in a human service agency must contend with the political environment, which poses both static and dynamic supports and constraints. Modularization of Social Security claims processing was carried out against the backdrop of relative indifference to administrative details by congressional and executive policymakers—an indifference encouraged by SSA's reputation for efficient and economical operation. This gave the SSA leadership free field of play, which they had the talent and motivation to exploit. In contrast, WORKFORCE benefited from the active intervention in interagency relationships by state policy makers, that is, the mandate for joint planning by job services units and PICs, which created the opportunity for entrepreneurial action in a local setting. And in Philadelphia, creation of integrated community health centers was the outgrowth of a larger political contest over the nature and role of health services in the community. The final decision to delegate significant independent authority to center directors apparently held little interest for political leaders but could be implemented by a top administrator as a preferred management strategy because prior political attention had focused strongly on the expansion and professionalization of health services, and provision of health services through arrangements emphasizing community identification and client access.

The relationship between decentralization and integration efforts and the political opportunity structure is thus quite complex and rich with research potential. The available experience suggests that active political support may facilitate integrative reorganizations, but is neither necessary nor sufficient. If needed resources and authority are available from other sources, such reorganizations may be pursued by entrepreneurial administrators through their own initiative under conditions of political neutrality. Indeed, this tentative analysis suggests that such reorganizations can be successfully implemented only by managers with the requisite talent and interest at or near the operational level. Attempts to impose such changes by political officials at exalted levels seem likely to fail, since the approach is only appropriate for a limited range of situations under the policymaker's oversight and since managers and employees are not likely to understand or accept an imposed arrangement. On the other hand, concerted opposition to integrative reorganization by political leaders is very likely to kill it.

SUMMARY—THE FISU-ENVIRONMENT INTERFACE

This lengthy list of conditions surrounding the emergence of the FISU would seem to imply that the form is something of a hothouse flower, and certainly such comprehensive units are not as commonly used as traditional, functionally differentiated work processes. But the case studies themselves confirm that the form is propagable, the most fertile ground apparently being the kind of environment provided by the Social Security Administration, that is, a large formal structure with numerous separable, multifunction service objectives, whose internal managerial processes are strongly buffered against external processes of political oversight and accommodation. The relative success of SSA in spreading and maintaining use of the form may, however, be a matter of historical accident. Had interest in joint job services/job training planning and cooperation been maintained in Florida, the concept might have spread more widely there, and the change of priorities appears to have been linked to certain changes in personalities and interests among political officials. Similarly, the use of area team concepts in health and other social services has waxed and waned with variations in professional and political priorities. We are willing to venture a tentative conclusion concerning the greater favorability of the formal bureaucratic environment because changes in priorities and personalities at the elective and appointive level are so common.

Moreover, the review of experience with the form suggests that it is more hearty than its theoretical origins might imply. In all three of the cases we have reviewed, the redesign of jobs needed to make the functionally integrated units work was relatively limited in scope and could be described as "democratization" or "job enrichment" only in a relatively narrow sense. The gains achieved by adopting the form are thus as easily attributed to technological and social effects, that is, enhanced interfunctional communication and interpersonal contact and cooperation, as to motivational effects related to job redesign. This is an important finding for use of the model in human service programs. Human service work forces tend to be extensively professionalized and would presumably tend to respond to job enrichment strategies. Available research supports this view only in part. Glisson and Durick recently found very low relative levels of job satisfaction combined with average levels of organizational commitment but did find that job satisfaction responded strongly and negatively to role loss (i.e., reduction in skill variety). A larger body of research argues that mainstream social service employees are not especially dissatisfied with their jobs in an absolute sense or, in particular, with the challenge or self-fulfillment properties of their work; nor do they necessarily consider themselves overly "bureaucratized" (Barber, 1986; Jayaratne & Chess, 1983; McNeely et al., 1986; York & Henley, 1986). Thus, both practical applications and research on employee attitudes imply that decisions about whether to adopt models such as the FISU in human service agencies may readily hinge on the cybernetic and social considerations. Work forces with strong needs for enriched work are not essential.

IMPLICATIONS FOR THE STUDY AND PRACTICE OF IMPLEMENTATION

The case histories on the FISU also imply some more general conclusions and priorities for future inquiry. They illustrate the creative powers that can be exercised at the operating level, that is, the potential for change *from* the bottom, at least insofar as organizational implementation is concerned. If implementation is to be understood as an interactive, evolutionary, and emergent process, the need to understand the conditions under which, and the means by which such creative initiatives from the bottom develop and propagate is obvious. They afford an avenue to the increased emphasis on equity, participation, and backward mapping of options in implementation which critics of top-down thinking see as an antidote to the tendency of "functionally determined centralized organizations" to compel their members to accept narrowed interests and engage in distrustful and opportunistic behavior (Calista, 1987; Elmore, 1987).

The development of such understanding must, of course, be tied closely to progress in mainstream organization studies. The opportunity to systematically study organizational implementation hinges directly on progress in the development of the clearer taxonomies that are so badly needed in mainstream organization studies (e.g., Perry & Rainey, 1988). And the linkage between policy goals and organizational options will not be fully understood until the critical role of symbolic and expressive behavior in the policy process is incorporated into theory (Yanow, 1987).

Yet implementation research affords opportunities to force issues and make advances in the understanding of organizational phenomena. The study of change initiatives at the operating level, for example, must address a number of questions relevant to both implementational and organizational theory. To what extent do such initiatives reflect natural systematic evolution in management practice or represent "a social reality . . . constructed by free-thinking humans" (Miller, 1984b, p. 253)? By what means and under what circumstances might such initiatives be encouraged, controlled, channelled, and supported? What is the range of utility of such initiatives, in other words, what kinds of social and administrative goals may they and may they not reasonably be expected to address?

Taxonomical Development in Organizational Implementation

Absent a comprehensive theoretical paradigm to guide such inquiry, methodological and conceptual refinement must be developed in tandem, and this will require students of implementation to pursue their own lines of taxonomical development. The foregoing analysis further highlights, however, the need for *multiple* taxonomical development. Organizational options, set in particular contexts to serve certain goals, interact with environmental conditions which foster or impede them. In the study of organizational implementation, complete explanation therefore requires a simultaneous focus on taxonomies of options, goals, and settings.

The development of these taxonomies must build on available experience, much of which is derived from topical studies. In the area of human services, for example, experiments with organizational structures and oversight processes during the last two decades provide points of departure for classifying options, goals, and environments, while reemphasizing the breadth of the remaining task. A range of organizing options has been developed—umbrella departments versus programmatic bureaus at oversight levels; coordinating boards versus case coordinating systems versus functionally specialized subunits versus FISU's at service provision levels—but the comparative advantages and disadvantages of these forms remains to be fully explored. Points of departure for the study of goals and contexts are evident in such schemas as Austin's (1978) proposed framework for clustering state programs into seven groups (protection and emergencies; personal development and socialization; social interaction and recreation; community development and housing; financial assistance and basic necessities provision; employment and employment support; remedial/treatment/ care services). Yet such work remains preliminary in that service goals and environmental conditions appropriate to specific organizational options may cluster more cohesively across such programmatic divisions than within them. Investigation of specific types of integration within these clusters might, however, clarify the degree of overlap and differentiation between them.

The investigation of goals and environmental conditions is complicated by the multiple time dimensions and levels of interaction through which implementation processes weave. In his critique of the "top-down" perspective, Elmore (1987b) has noted the importance of prior development of implementation capacity, the dangers of overemphasizing change for its own sake, and the apparent importance of prior political coalition building as a condition for effective change. These caveats are fully appropriate for organizational change strategies directed at operations components. But prior development of capacity and support typically represent prior implementation problems in their own right.

In the human services arena, for example, some research suggests that social work supervisors tend toward relatively inert managerial styles, and would benefit from strategies to promote more adaptive, active leadership (e.g., Russell et al., 1984). Traditional strategies for change would include management development programs, recruitment programs, or incentive and appraisal programs, all of which are as easily subverted to serve defensive purposes as other initiatives from the top. The study of options must therefore not be construed narrowly to structure alone but must include methods and processes of change and the conditions appropriate to their emergence. Thus students of implementation have a particular opportunity and duty to contribute to improved understanding of the development of entrepreneurial leadership, slack resources, internal support for organizational change, insularity and permeability of managerial control, separability of service goals and measurement of goal attainment, and political windows of opportunity for change initiatives.

7

Implementation as Policy Politics

Evelyn Z. Brodkin

The conceptual foundations of implementation analysis are showing serious signs of wear and tear. Essays in this volume and elsewhere indicate discomfort with—even dissent from—research frameworks that treat implementation simply as a phase of the policy process in which mandates are converted into action. These essays represent part of a growing effort to stretch the boundaries of conventional analysis by taking into account a rich empirical literature that repeatedly demonstrates the slipperiness of policy "mandates" and "objectives" and indicates a wide range of policymaking opportunities beyond formal legislative or regulatory processes. These efforts have generated considerable disagreement about how to bridge the "politics-administration dichotomy" and whether the superior position for implementation analysis is from the "top down" or the "bottom up."

The conceptual framework here seeks to respond to these issues and move beyond them. The approach integrates the study of implementation with the study of social politics, viewing implementation *as* policy politics—a continuation of conflicts to define social policy.[1] It is an approach that "brings the politics back in" from the periphery to the center of implementation research by framing it as a quest to explain social politics. This stands in contrast to conventional approaches that treat politics as a variable in the quest to explain implementation.

The framework is based on the proposition that policy politics (the contest to determine what policy should be) is ubiquitous; it neither begins with the formulation of a policy proposal nor ends with its enactment or defeat. Although this may seem obvious—and is certainly recognized in studies of agenda setting—it is not well incorporated into the study of implementation, which commonly regards formal policy as the fixed point for assessing the activities that are presumed to follow it.

There are several conditions under which it is misleading to use formal policy as the fixed point for analysis. One condition exists when lower-level discretion is intrinsic to implementation, as is the case in most social programs. Under these circumstances, policy may effectively be made by street-level bureaucrats closest to the point of policy delivery (Lipsky, 1978). Second, policy lacks fixed meaning when legislation is vague or internally inconsistent as numerous studies of legislative policymaking have demonstrated. Ambiguous policy is produced when politicians seek to avoid thorny political issues and, effectively, "pass the buck" to the bureaucracy (Bullock & Lamb, 1984; de Haven-Smith & Van Horn, 1984; Rein & Rabinovitz, 1978; Thompson, 1982; Van Horn & Baumer, 1985). This strategy (whether consciously intended or not) enables politicians to claim credit for grand policy objectives while reserving the opportunity to blame the bureaucracy later for policy interpretations that generate political heat. A third condition under which the notion of a policy "mandate" is highly problematic occurs when legislation is largely symbolic, at times intentionally so. In studies of various types of civil rights legislation, analysts have argued that, at times, statutes are best understood as symbolic gestures (Ingram & Mann, 1980; Wade, 1972). From this perspective, subsequent "implementation failures" should constitute an unsurprising result.[2]

To complicate matters further, even issues that appear to have been clearly resolved in legislation are later subject to redefinition under new conditions and in a new arena. Under such conditions, it is appropriate to treat implementation as a continuation of multilayered contests to define social policy. Implementation, analyzed as policy politics, can be used to investigate why, when, and how policies are defined and redefined.

This approach potentially enhances the study of social politics, in part, by distinguishing analytically between the state's policy promises and the state's policy products. Additionally, it opens to empirical examination elements of social politics that occur within administrative institutions, largely outside of formal policymaking channels. Reciprocally, the analysis of social politics contributes to implementation research by directing attention to policy delivery institutions as vehicles for policy politics and to the structural opportunities and constraints that animate policymaking and implementation processes.

The conceptual framework described here builds on a variety of studies of social policy that suggest, but do not explicitly elaborate, the interrelationship between social politics and implementation. This chapter begins to elaborate this relationship, first by examining the political foundations of implementation problems—or the influence of social politics on implementation. It then considers the structural boundaries of social politics—or the influence of implementing institutions on social policy possibilities. It concludes with observations about the implications of this perspective for future implementation research.

THE POLITICAL FOUNDATIONS OF IMPLEMENTATION PROBLEMS

Although rarely treated as such, implementation analysis in its broadest sense is fundamentally concerned with the capacity of the state to act in pursuit of its social objectives. Such analysis emerged, in large part, out of puzzlement and disillusionment at the perceived failure of many Great Society programs. In their influential book, *Implementation*, Pressman and Wildavsky (1986) posed the analytical problem as one of understanding "how great expectations in Washington are dashed in Oakland; or, why it's amazing that federal programs work at all." Their objective, they said, was "to build morals on a foundation of ruined hopes."

Simply stated, implementation research focused on the gap between legislative intent and bureaucratic action. It suggested that the hopes of policymakers were ruined by their inadequate understanding of the specific steps necessary to convert their expectations into reality. The creative thinking by academics and politicians that shaped the social policies of the Great Society too often neglected the practical realities of local-level politics and a decentralized policy delivery system. Implementation analysis hopefully leapt into the breach.

Conventional implementation analysis proceeded from the normative assumption that the bureaucracy should serve as production agent for social policies established by authoritative policymaking institutions, namely the Congress or, in some instances, the president. The problem was to understand why implementation deviated from the expressed purposes of these policies. Detailed case studies of specific social programs revealed a daunting multiplicity of implementation obstacles, among them: policies requiring complex joint action, inadequate incentives for local-level compliance, a mismatch between bureaucratic resources and policy tasks, and inadequate upper-level control over lower-level discretion.[3]

In general, explanations for the gap between intent and action that followed from these analyses focused on the exercise of bureaucratic discretion and on the technical feasibility of policy designs. These factors were incorporated into sophisticated models of the implementation process that sought to account for external influences, such as policy design or political incentives, and internal influences, such as technical knowledge or bureaucratic resources and interests.[4]

Bureaucratic Discretion and Policy Production

Critics of this approach to implementation argued that analysis was distorted by its normative allegiance to the assumption of a policy hierarchy. For example, Rein and Rabinovitz (1978) suggested that formal policy statutes did not necessarily determine the shape of policy as implemented, but only generally established its boundaries. Extending that argument further, Lipsky (1978) argued that under certain circumstances, lower-level bureaucrats actually made policy by giving it concrete meaning through their actions. This was most likely to occur when implementation involved the substantial exercise of discretion by street-level bureaucrats such as social workers, teachers, and others who deal directly with social program clients. In these circumstances, Lipsky contended that analysis should be "turned on its head" and directed toward understanding, first, how lower-level bureaucrats exercised discretion in policy delivery and second, what they produced as policy through their activities.

In an application of this "bottom up" approach, Weatherly and Lipsky (1977) examined how a state special education law manifestly intended to extend appropriate schooling to handicapped children was translated into a program of massive relabeling of special needs children but only modest recasting of the educational programs serving them. One might interpret this, from a conventional perspective, as yet another example of undesirable bureaucratic autonomy sabotaging social objectives. In contrast, Weatherly and Lipsky interpret the bureaucratic response as a rational adaptation to overwhelming and conflicting policy requirements.

But this case illustrates more than the power of bureaucratic discretion to give meaning to policy. It also illuminates how statutes that embrace multiple and conflicting objectives tacitly delegate policymaking discretion to the bureaucracy. The asserted intent of the special education law was to widen participation in special education decisions, use professional expertise to make individual assessments of children's needs, and rapidly extend special services to students needing them. Without an enormous commitment of new resources (or arguably even with it), educators could not simultaneously satisfy requirements for expansion of service, rapid implementation, detailed expert evaluation, and expanded parental participation. Under the circumstances, it should come as no surprise that trade-offs were made in the process of implementation and that these trade-offs gave policy a specific meaning more limited than its rhetoric implied.

Legislation that is ambiguous, contains competing objectives, or is not adequately supported with resources to fulfill its requirements represents a more symbolic than real political victory. Under such circumstances, bureaucrats responsible for implementation necessarily interpret policy and make trade-offs among competing objectives. Interpretations and trade-offs are compelled by the policy itself—and by the social politics that produced it. To label as "unanticipated consequences" bureaucratic practices that fail to satisfy ambiguous or conflicting policy promises conveniently, but unfairly, blames bureaucrats for the deficiencies of policymakers.[5]

The implementation as politics perspective builds on and extends the insights of "bottom-up" analysis, which accepts policy as problematic and seeks to understand how bureaucrats give specific meaning to policy in the course of implementation. Bureaucratic analysis provides a means of exploring what happens when social politics continues under the rubric of policy delivery.

Political Capacity and Policymaking

In order to understand more fully how social politics influences implementation, it is necessary to consider both the essentially contested character of the issues involved in social policymaking and weaknesses in the political institutions charged with resolving them. Social policymaking raises questions of the appropriate size and scope of the state, the degree of government intervention in private affairs, the distribution of power and material goods, relations among competing interests, even questions of morality and values. These latent issues are potential axes of conflict over issues as diverse as employment policy, welfare, health care, housing, support for the old and infirm, disability insurance, workplace safety, environmental health, and so on.

One of the striking peculiarities of the American welfare state is that it has grown despite the absence of any clear political resolution of its basic premises.[6] Irving Howe (1982, p. 4) explains: "It is something, this welfare state, that is constantly being undermined, reconstructed, patched together. It is a result of social compromise and improvisation; certainly here in the United States it cannot be considered a planned construct. The model we advance for it may suggest an inner equilibrium, but the reality has frequent difficulties, conflicts, breakdowns."

Not only are the issues raised by social politics contentious ones, but the capacity of political institutions to resolve them is weak. These weaknesses have been the subject of considerable scholarly discussion that variously attributes these weaknesses to the atrophied party system, a Lockean liberal heritage of decentralized power and antipathy toward a strong state, inherent contradictions in democratic capitalism, and other factors.[7]

More proximate sources of policy irresolution identified by observers of congressional policymaking include the electoral-maximizing strategies of politicians that lead them to avoid difficult policy choices, take symbolic action when possible, and otherwise delegate to the bureaucracy the hard task of giving specific meaning to vague or contradictory statements of legislative policy intent (Dodd & Schott, 1979; Fiorena, 1977; Lowi, 1969; Mayhew, 1974). As Nakamura and Smallwood (1980, p. 39) have observed: "Two kinds of policy vagueness can result from the need for policymakers to build coalitions. Coalitions can be built around vague goals that sound good to participants for a variety of reasons. And coalitions can be built by offering to address many diverse and even conflicting goals, each of which is attractive to particular actors. . . . Thus, the grounds for future interpretive conflicts during implementation are often laid by the ambiguous directions of policymaking majorities that are profoundly divided, transient, unaware of the ultimate consequences of their actions, or a combination of all these things." Suffice it to say that contentious issues coupled with weak institutional mechanism of conflict resolution make it likely that social politics often will be irresolute.

There is a rich and growing body of empirical studies that is beginning to illuminate—although it may not explicitly acknowledge—the political foundations of bureaucratic discretion and the political products of that discretion. For example, Frank Thompson's (1982) detailed study of the implementation of the Emergency Health Personnel Act of 1970 provides a classic illustration of manifestly purposive, but, ultimately, ambiguous legislation. The ostensible purpose of the act was to improve access to medical care for people living in so-called "underserved" areas of the country. Yet, Congress did not specify what it meant by "critical shortage areas," criteria for identifying them, or the means that should be used to assist them.

By avoiding these "implementation details" Congress also avoided a confrontation between rural and urban legislators over the geographical distribution of assistance and between public health professionals and private physicians over the system that would be used to deliver medical care. The act, in effect, delegated to the implementing bureaucracies the task of choosing between a health system based on the provision of incentives to private physicians in fee-for-service practice versus a public medical corps that could be sent to serve clients in poor neighborhoods.

Thompson's microscopic analysis reveals that choices made in implementing the act just after its enactment shaped it into a program for recruiting private physicians to work in rural areas where residents could afford medical services. However, subsequent implementation decisions, made under the auspices of a new administrator in a different political and bureaucratic context, revised the program into one dedicated to the development of a public medical corps for poor, mostly urban neighborhoods.

The implementation activities that produced these disparate "policies" reflected two possible (in this case sequential) interpretations of legislative "intent." According to Thompson, these implementation choices were influenced only modestly by congressional pork-barrel politics or interest-group lobbying. Implementation choices—and indirectly policy—were primarily influenced by the biases of the program director and by the adaptive responses of lower-level bureaucrats who coped with implementation pressures by trading the difficult task of recruiting private physicians for the easier task of placing public medical corps enrollees in poor neighborhoods.

From a conventional perspective, one might regard this as an example of policy effects deriving from bureaucratic coping behaviors. Alternatively, from a social politics perspective, one may regard this case as an example of how contentious distributive questions that were not resolved legislatively then slipped underground only to reemerge in relatively nonpolitical form as implementation issues.

INSTITUTIONAL STRUCTURE AND POLICY POLITICS

Social politics influences implementation, not only by producing vague and ambiguous policy statements, but also by channeling policies through decentralized and discretionary delivery systems that provide numerous opportunities for the continuation of policy politics. To a certain extent, discretion is intrinsic in social policy delivery. The provision of social services, education, and health care, for example, requires that experts exercise discretion to meet individual needs.

But beyond that, the extent and character of discretion are more politically determined than is generally acknowledged. The choice of discretionary, intergovernmental programs over more automatic, centralized programs is a political one, as a comparative perspective makes apparent. For example, American social politics has produced health care policies that emphasize public and private insurance schemes rather than a national health service; welfare policy delivered through discretionary, state-level bureaucracies rather than a centralized tax-based transfer system; and housing policies that rely heavily on subsidies to private contractors and individuals.

The American approach of channeling policy delivery through multiple public and private intermediaries, each of which must receive some "payoff" in return for policy support, has been aptly characterized as one of "passive intervention" in contrast to the arguably more efficient "active intervention" (involving direct state provision) that is more commonly (although not exclusively) used in advanced social welfare states (Starr & Esping-Anderson, 1979).

Forms of intervention are politically significant because social policy delivery systems, like the policies they administer, reflect a social politics infused with conflicting interests that are not fully resolved in legislative policy politics. As Norton Long (1986, p. 453) astutely observed: "Administrative organizations, however much they may appear the creations of art, are institutions produced in history and woven in the web of social relationships that give them life and being. They present the same refractory material to the hand of the political artist as the rest of society of which they form a part."

The reciprocal relationship between politics and structure that Long described has implications for implementation, noted earlier, in creating difficulties in achieving coordination, efficiency and accountability. The fragmented structure of implementing institutions also has implications for social politics, significantly affecting the range and feasibility of policy possibilities in at least three ways. First, institutional competition over policy may restrict policy options. For example, Skocpol and Ikenberry (1983) have argued that New Dealers were able to develop a national social security system, because pension policies had not been preempted by state government. But they were discouraged from pursuing other national-level social policies, similar to European health, education, and welfare policies, because such proposals intruded on state government programs.

Second, institutional arrangements influence the identification, articulation, and aggregation of potential policy issues. Skocpol (1985, p. 21) asserts that analysis of state structures is critical to understanding social politics because they "affect political culture, encourage some kinds of group formation and collective political actions (but not others), and make possible the raising of certain political issues (but not others)." If agenda formation and promotion are advanced by institutions that have a stake in a policy issue, they are impeded when no single institution (or influential group of institutions) has a compelling interest in claiming an issue as its own. For example, Sosin (1988) describes the issue of homelessness as one that was perceived to be tangential to the primary mission of most government and nonprofit agencies. Consequently, as homelessness began to emerge as a serious problem, its scope and significance received relatively little recognition as a public policy problem. Sosin's analysis suggests that policy responses were fragmented and inadequate, in part, because there was no conspicuous institutional "home" for those seeking to place the issue on the public agenda.

Third, the institutions that deliver social policy influence the agendas and strategies of policy entrepreneurs. As noted, competition among institutions may preempt policy options or make them costly to policy entrepreneurs. However, policy development is also affected by intraorganizational factors. The efforts of public executives to press their own agendas on organizations are frequently exercises in frustration (Califano, 1981; Lynn, 1981; 1986). The strategic executive assesses policy options for their political and organizational feasibility and for the opportunities they offer to build personal capital (Heclo, 1984; Lynn, 1980; 1986). This interaction between executive entrepreneurs, other public officials, and their institutional environments effectively constitutes a third dimension of social politics.

Implementation as a Channel for Policy Politics

The institutions that deliver policy, at times, provide an alternative to legislative institutions as channels for social politics. For example, the expansion and contraction of social entitlements is an obviously political matter. But, as documented in the cases of welfare and disability insurance (Brodkin, 1986; Stone, 1984), changes in the provision of benefits, at times, have depended little on legislative activity and largely on bureaucratic activities.

For example, in the case of public welfare, administrative reforms implemented in the 1970s accomplished what legislative reform could not. While attempts to respond legislatively to the "crisis" provoked by surging welfare rolls failed repeatedly, administrative reforms responded to that crisis by indirectly restricting the distribution of welfare. Implementation analysis reveals how the meaning of public assistance was transformed as street-level caseworkers coped with the manifestly nonpolitical demands of administrative reform by raising new procedural obstacles for their clients. These obstacles created barriers to assistance for certain types of poor families, irrespective of their substantive eligibility. In a sense, implementation became a strategic vehicle of social politics (Brodkin, 1986).

A similar pattern is evident in Stone's (1984) research on disability policy, which indicates that the provision of benefits to the disabled has expanded and contracted over time through indirect bureaucratic means, rather than through formal policymaking. In this case, physicians acted as the gatekeepers of public benefits, indirectly altering their distribution by changing medical criteria for determining disability. In both the welfare and disability cases, policy responses to changing conditions in the political economy, at least initially, occurred through obscure bureaucratic means rather than more visible and overtly contentious legislative means.

These examples should alert researchers to the dangers of adopting a view of implementation that disconnects the apparently technical or procedural activities of policy deliverers from social politics. These activities, in the aggregate, may have significant distributive implications that make them the appropriate concerns of social politics. It is only by linking the analysis of politics and policy delivery that one is led to question the conventional wisdom that "the issues that become politicized almost always are value issues, not technical questions that can be answered definitively" (Nathan, 1984, p. 377). There is undoubtedly an element of truth in this axiom. However, an alternative proposition is that when questions of value are not resolved politically, they may reappear in the form of technical or administrative questions during the implementation process. The bureaucratic responses to these questions (as illustrated in the examples of welfare and disability) are infused with political content because they effectively give new meaning to policy.

The conceptual framework advanced here directs attention to implementation as a vehicle for policy politics, that is, as a vehicle for defining and redefining social policy. It also directs attention to ways in which policy politics in implementation differs from legislative policy politics in both its terms and structure. This is significant because, to paraphrase E. E. Schattschneider (1960), it is the terms and rules of the game that determine who can get into the game. Consequently, changes in the terms and arena of conflict have important political consequences for the mobilization of bias and, ultimately, for political outcomes.[8] The implications of a form of policy politics that would appear to limit the scope of social conflict by depoliticizing its terms and obscuring the role of administrative agencies in determining its outcome have yet to be fully explored.[9]

THE CHALLENGE FOR FUTURE RESEARCH

The study of policy implementation has pushed beyond its early conceptual foundations. Scholars writing here and elsewhere are engaged in redefining and extending those foundations in recognition of growing criticism that it is inappropriate to regard implementation as a distinct phase of the policy process that can be adequately understood on its own terms (see Burke, 1987; Nakamura, 1987; Yanow, 1987). This chapter, in part, constitutes a response to that criticism. It also responds, albeit in a partial and preliminary way, to the challenge issued by Douglas Ashford (1977, p. 576) that scholars initiate a "reformulation of *how* policy relates to politics" and to the institutions of the state.

The policy politics perspective offered here links the analysis of policy delivery activities and institutions to the analysis of social politics. It is based on the premise that inquiry into politics or institutional process alone may mislead analysis. But when these inquiries are joined, they can illuminate dimensions of both politics and process that are not otherwise evident. In this first cut at explicating some of these linkages, several issues have emerged that merit attention in future implementation research.

First, when social policy is unclear or open to interpretation, social politics continues in the implementation processes that give policy specific meaning. If implementation analysis were to take into account the sources of legislative ambiguity, fewer studies would be apt to conclude with prescriptions for more specificity as a "solution" to implementation difficulties. Ultimately, policies can be no more resolute and precise than the political processes that produce them. Research aimed at improving strategies for policy design and implementation needs to contend with this fundamental problem.

Second, under certain circumstances, implementation is a vehicle for social politics, at times even an alternative to more visible processes of policymaking. It is premature to evaluate whether policymaking advanced by implementation bureaucracies constitutes "benign adaptation" as some scholars have suggested or whether such "adaptations" could as well be "malign."[10] The prior analytical task is to assess the terms and rules of the game under which implementation policy politics are played and their implications for the scope of conflict and outcomes of the battle. It is also important to examine the extent to which outcomes are contextually, not structurally, determined.

Third, research only briefly summarized here indicates that policy agendas and opportunities are influenced by the general structure of implementing institutions (their fragmentation, decentralization, and so on) and by organizational dynamics within these institutions. The construction of theories of social politics and the development of innovative policy strategies both require greater understanding of these structural opportunities and constraints. It is important for scholars to reach into these institutions in order to identify structural precedents for policy entrepreneurialism and to explore how executives can recognize and seize opportunities. A related line of inquiry that merits equal attention concerns the normative questions of political authority and democratic accountability raised by executive and bureaucratic discretion in policymaking and implementation (Burke, 1988).

Fourth, inquiry into state capacity needs to consider not only the state's ability to make policy promises, but also its ability to deliver what it promises. The conceptual framework advanced here suggests the utility of implementation analysis in illuminating and assessing policy products. It also emphasizes the importance of making those assessments in the context of a broader understanding of social politics. Policy outcomes that appear as random or as "unanticipated consequences'' from a conventional implementation perspective may appear systematic or even predictable from a policy politics perspective.

The conceptual framework advanced in this chapter offers a basis for analyzing the reciprocal relationship between social politics and implementation. This essay also indicates, more suggestively than in detail, the potential for adding ''peripheral vision''[11] to implementation analysis by examining bureaucratic processes and institutions as channels for social policy conflicts, that is, by linking macroscopic and microscopic perspectives. The issues raised here pose a challenge for the next generation of implementation research but also present an opportunity to build on its rich foundations.

NOTES

1. Pressman & Wildavsky (1986, p. 304) distinguishes policy politics, ''the politics of what policy should be,'' from partisan (electoral) and system (decision structures) politics.

2. Ingram and Mann (1980, p. 20) comment that ''language in legislation is sometimes targeted toward making people feel better rather than causing events to occur.'' For a discussion of the symbolic function of the legislative process, see Edelman (1964).

3. In addition to Pressman and Wildavsky, see Berman and McLaughlin (1976), McLaughlin (1976), Bardach (1977), Ingram (1977), and Murphy (1971).

4. Major examples of this approach include Sabatier and Mazmanian (1979) and Van Meter and Van Horn (1975).

5. Van Horn and Baumer (1985, p. 45) describe a strategy familiar to observers of legislative politics—a strategy of credit-claiming and scapegoating. As they explain, ''Members of Congress are . . . rewarded or punished for their issue *positions*, not according to whether the laws they adopt solve or ameliorate public problems. If laws are subsequently judged ineffective, then Congress can easily blame the bureaucracy and obtain additional rewards from those seeking corrective action. In short, members of Congress may ignore important policy design issues, not because they don't know better, but because it is in their interests to do so.''

6. In the United States, there is nothing resembling the Butskellist consensus in Britain or the social compact with labor in Sweden that formed political bases for welfare state development. For varied perspectives on the ''reluctant'' American welfare state, see, for example, Hartz (1955), Patterson (1981), Rimlinger (1971), Flora and Heidenheimer (1981), Skocpol and Ikenberry (1983), and Wilensky (1975).

7. Explanations for weaknesses in the political institutions of governance have been exhaustively debated. It is not possible to do justice to this discussion within the modest scope of this essay. For various viewpoints, see Huntington (1975), Burnham (1980), Lowi (1979), King (1975), and Offe (1984).

8. Ironically, the strategic possibilities of advancing policy objectives through relatively inconspicuous bureaucratic means have been well appreciated by politicians. The ''administrative presidency'' strategies of the Nixon and Reagan administrations were largely built on the premise that ''operations is policy'' and that policy objectives too contentious to achieve legislatively could be pursued bureaucratically. See Brodkin (1976, chaps. 1–3), Lynn (1984), Nathan (1983), and Vig (1984).

9. See Brodkin (1987, Chap. 7), for a discussion of these points.

10. There are some who argue that bureaucratic discretion is desirable because it permits "benign" adaptations to be made to policy without becoming mired in legislative disputes. For example, Thompson (1982, p. 439) argues that adaptation is benign when "the implementing agency shapes the program so that it fosters the achievement of broadly supported social goals without doing serious damage to such widely accepted values as political accountability." In effect, he seems to argue that discretion is benign when the policy outcomes it produces are desirable (perhaps to the analyst).

Alternatively, Stone (1984) argues from a systems perspective that bureaucratic discretion in the provision of disability benefits was benign, because it permitted adaptation to changing political and economic conditions. Although this form of adaptiveness may be benign from a regime perspective, it is arguably malign in its implications for democratic accountability (and certainly for the losers in the game of implementation policy politics).

In a similar vein, Musheno et al. (1989) attribute "retrospective rationality" to street-level bureaucracies, through which policy purposes and strategies "bubble up from ongoing practice" but are "sensitive to power relationships." However, they do not presume that these processes or their products are necessarily "benign" and instead seek to identify the factors that contribute to adaptive or maladaptive outcomes.

11. I borrow this term from Heclo (1984) who contends that the appropriate unit of analysis for the study of policy and social politics is "the cluster of interrelated parts that produces the results by which we are governed" (p. 374).

Female Executives in Public and Private Universities: Differences in Implementation Styles

Bryna Sanger and Martin A. Levin _____

THE CONSERVATIVE BIAS

Two major criticisms of implementation research focus on its biases. One of these is the conservative bias of the research. As Palumbo put it in his introductory essay for an implementation symposium, "The large number of 'implementation failures' described in early research have unwittingly produced a conservative bias in which the conclusion seems to be that government can't do anything right" (Palumbo, 1987, p. 95). Others explain this bias as being a product of the researchers' use of an unrealistic rational comprehensive model (Dror, 1984) and methods derived from now discredited positivist epistemology (Fox, 1987).

It is true that much of the early implementation research found a pattern of what it called failure. It is also true that many researchers drew conservative policy implications from these findings. And this conclusion was supported by political leaders from George Wallace to Ronald Reagan, who suggested that "government is the problem, not the solution." However, we will suggest that there have been other reactions, especially among practitioners, to these findings and to implementation obstacles in general. Those who direct large organizations are so frustrated about getting things done that they have developed a backlash of admiration and even uncritical acclaim for action-oriented approaches to implementation.

For example, the Great Society's familiar legacy of dashed expectations, unmet promises, and failed programs was followed by the less familiar domestic policies of conservative Republican administrations, often with rather modest goals, which also foundered at the implementation stage. This was true for the swine flu vaccination program and the Community Development Bloc Grant program. The moderate Democratic Jimmy Carter administration fared no better. One of the most notable implementation failures of the past decade occurred in 1980 during his administration: the failed mission to rescue the hostages in Iran.

The pattern continued in the Reagan administration. For instance, its War on Drugs was plagued by the typical implementation problems of poor interagency coordination. Despite the seeming society-wide agreement on the desirability of this "war," the Reagan administration efforts faced delay, disagreement, and sometimes even resistance. We learned that even under a conservative administration, the essence of implementation is a complicated program assembly process. It involves numerous (usually independent) actors and decision points in an interactive process of bargaining. It is not a process of hierarchical command.

Levin and Ferman make this argument about policy implementation more generally: Implementation obstacles are generic; they plague conservative as well as liberal administrations. Bright ideas are often distorted and delayed in the process of implementation. It seems that more is needed to achieve effective policies than good intentions or even good program designs. For most public programs, the allegedly simple, basically technical details of implementation actually are quite difficult to accomplish effectively. In fact, in the last two decades, implementation has become the single most problematic aspect of policymaking. It is the stage at which most domestic policies have foundered (Levin & Ferman, 1985).

All this has not, as some have feared, led to a conservative bias. Rather, it seems to have led to a backlash of admiration for action and getting things done. In California, for example, a group of state-level administrators recently sponsored a weekend workshop called "Management by Guts."

THE TOP-DOWN BIAS

Another bias of implementation research is said to be its "top-down" approach. As Palumbo critically observed,

this approach assumes the goals and perspectives of those at the top of an organization are the only legitimate ones, and deviations from these goals are considered to be dysfunctional even if they do contribute to some social good. Such an analysis ignores the fact that implementation takes place in a multiorganizational network where official goals are vague, where each actor is responsible for a number of programs that may be conflicting, and where they are pursuing different goals. (Palumbo, 1987, p. 93)

In response to this bias, Elmore, Lipsky, and others have developed the bottom-up or backward-mapping view (Elmore, 1979; Lipsky, 1980). Lipsky, for example, argues that street-level bureaucrats are more sensitive to the problems encountered in program implementation and they should therefore have a large role in policymaking (Lipsky, 1980). But as Palumbo and others argue, "field-level personnel can also be wrong, so it is dangerous to take the descriptive reality which points out that street-level bureaucrats make policy and turn it into a prescription for action'' (Palumbo, 1987, p. 94). In short, these views represent quite different perspectives on implementation and have largely remained unresolved.

We will suggest another perspective and a way to resolve these differences. As organizations experience the limits of rules based on command, they should adopt more interactive and market-like processes. A study that we conducted of effective women university executives found that they successfully used these approaches. Their approaches to implementation are interactive and indirect rather than based on command and rules. They use the skills of social interaction, as in the decisions of political arenas, or economic markets, or university decisions. These decisions are the results of individual actions and interactions without anyone centrally controlling either the decisions or the individual interactions. Wisdom enters into these decisions through exchange.

But which approach is preferable? We suggest this depends on the organizational context. The bias toward action approach is preferable in the context of top-down organizations, where the norms are command and control—whatever the actual behaviors. By contrast, the social interaction approach probably is preferable in the context of more diffuse organizations, where norms of collegiality are important and where the hierarchy is shallow and power tends to be shared.

MACHO MANAGERS: ONE APPROACH TO IMPLEMENTATION FAILURE

The Kennedy School case management series focuses on effective managers such as Gordon Chase, Ira Jackson, and William Ruckelshaus. The dominant pattern in all these successful cases is what we will call, with some poetic license, the "macho manager." They have a bias toward action. They meet obstacles with energy and confidence. They inspire their subordinates to get quick results in the face of lethargic and incompetent bureaucracies. They move to short-circuit the numerous clearance points and formal rules. They tend to take a top-down approach to implementation.

These macho managers, such as Chase, often tried to get their programs off the ground even before they received formal budget authorization. One told his staff to carry their very ambitious proposal through the legislature by "hold[ing] it together. The only offense is a totally concerted, straight, nose-guarded, up the middle with this thing. Don't allow anyone to touch it in any of its parts" (Behn, 1986, p. 42).

In the public sector these action-oriented executives worked to develop constituent support to be used to influence decision makers, deflect critics, and defeat opposition. They sought action, not analysis. They wanted to tackle the whole problem, not a pilot study.

As head of New York City's Health Services Administration during the early

1970s, Chase repeatedly developed and implemented innovative health programs in problem areas that were not only technically complex but were also politically sensitive. In response to the lead poisoning problem he instituted mass screening and treatment programs; in response to the crisis-stage heroin epidemic, Chase successfully implemented a very large methadone maintenance program; and as an answer to the equally explosive riots in the city's jails he developed and effectively implemented a new prison health program. In these and in all his other programs he successfully insisted on delivering services, not just at a few "pilot" or "demonstration" sites, but to massive numbers of clients (Levin & Hausman, 1985, p. 28).

When a budget analyst for the city suggested that his proposed program to deal with rat bites needed more study and analysis because "maybe there are other and better ways of cleaning up rats," Chase replied, "the point is not to study the problem of death or develop a pilot program. We need something that will deal with the entire universe of the problem. Not a pilot for one or two neighborhoods. We need action." A colleague of Chase's said, "Gordon's vision of achievement was not cluttered by reality" (Levin & Hausman, 1985).

Chase took a project management approach. Once he selected a problem area and a programmatic response, he divided the program into discrete projects. Project managers pushed the programs to completion by operating outside the normal bureaucratic chain of command. The managers were tightly controlled from Chase's office by detailed and frequent reporting systems (Morris, 1980).

Ira Jackson became commissioner of the Massachusetts Department of Revenue (DOR) in 1983. He developed and implemented several innovative programs and made creative use of existing tools to improve tax enforcement. In 1982 DOR had been seriously marred by a major scandal that had led to one suicide, major investigations and indictments, negative public reactions, and low employee morale. As a result of neglect and prior incompetence, the department was operating in a highly inefficient manner, which cost the state millions of dollars in lost revenue. Jackson agreed to head this agency that he knew nothing about in a policy area in which he had no experience. His colleagues at Harvard's Kennedy School almost unanimously advised against taking the commissioner's job. They said it was a job without any policy content and merely involved organizational routines, with little outside visibility and high probability that "corruption will come home to bite you in the ass; it's a no win job" (Behn, 1986, p. 5).

But Jackson's ambitious efforts resulted in a significant increase in the amount of revenue collected by the state. Through an aggressive enforcement policy, which included commercial property seizures, Jackson and DOR recouped more than $200 million in unpaid taxes. One of Jackson's programs—a three month amnesty on penalties in order to encourage payment of back taxes—served as a model for other states.

Jackson's early enforcement program, which involved a vigorous pursuit of major tax evaders, was very effective in molding public support for the Department of Revenue. Symbolic actions, like going after one of the biggest restaurant chains in Massachusetts (Callahan's) with civil and criminal charges, were especially effective in enhancing DOR's visibility. And these policy initiatives were implemented in the context of a media campaign.

In 1970 William Ruckelshaus was appointed administrator of the newly created Environmental Protection Agency (EPA). Richard Nixon's creation of EPA was an attempt to consolidate environmental protection efforts. EPA brought together fifteen separate agencies and almost 6,000 personnel.

As administrator, Ruckelshaus faced several challenges. Primary among them were coordinating the various agencies within EPA and establishing goals for the agency. Ruckelshaus did mold the various divisions into one agency, though coordination problems still remained. Most of his energies went into goal development. He selected pollution abatement as EPA's initial goal and embarked on a vigorous legalistic enforcement policy (Bowers & Mills, 1981). Ruckelshaus's decision to "litigate as quickly as possible" was inspired by the need to develop public support for EPA. By going after major polluters, including bringing suit against several cities, Ruckelshaus achieved significant visibility for EPA and established an activist image for the agency (Bowers & Mills, 1981).

THE LIMITS AND COSTS OF ACTION-ORIENTED EXECUTIVES

The behavior of these action-oriented executives is a striking reaction to the frustrations and obstacles confronted during the implementation process. More importantly, these action-oriented executives effectively got things done. However, their approaches also have some limits and costs. One is that contemplation and analysis become secondary to action. With an overriding emphasis on action and a concern for implementation, these executives gave limited attention to policy analysis. One cost of such an approach is that sometimes there is insufficient consideration of alternatives. This may lead to excessive opportunity costs, as well as direct costs. Indeed, these action-oriented executives, as part of their conscious disregard for bureaucratic obstacles, operated as if theirs were a world without opportunity costs.

For example, the opportunity cost of the programs that Gordon Chase pursued so vigorously and with such ample funds was the foregoing of alternative approaches and programs. Yet, whenever his staff sought to raise questions about the large expenditures for new programs or about alternative programs, Chase would "disarm" them by responding: "It's only money. And if you want money for some other projects, don't worry: I'll go to the mayor and get it. You know my record on getting money is damn good." And it was "damn good"; he regularly got what he wanted from the mayor. But the fact was that he did not go to the mayor about all the possible alternative policies. He could not; there was a limit to how many times he could propose new things and a limit to the amount of money he could ask for. This limit reflects the opportunity cost of the programs that he did pursue.

These executives' disregard for obstacles and the apparent confidence it produces tend to obscure the issue of opportunity costs. In the Callahan Restaurant case, for example, Jackson had one of his "most substantial victories" (Behn, 1986, p. 72). However, there is no evidence whether it was worth the time invested. Jackson's victory took "a year and a half to create" compared to resources that could have been devoted to other alternatives such as increased efforts in routine tax-compliance areas.

The current implementation literature, in its efforts to uncover the winning formula, is understandably taken with these models of action-oriented implementors; single-handedly, they appear to impose their wills on recalcitrant bureaucracies and political opponents. This view, however, ignores several critical dimensions of reality. As Palumbo and Calista have persuasively argued, current thinking ignores the fact that policy is often made during the implementation process (Palumbo & Calista, 1987). If the significance of the policymaking role for implementors were more generally understood, more attention might be directed to the character of the implementation process. Consensual and interactive processes produce wiser results rather than macho implementation, actions that are informed by collective scrutiny. A participatory and interactive approach would be more highly valued were implementation seen as an essential policymaking activity. When we see implementors more as policymakers, involved at every step in learning, in error-correction, and in shaping public policy, then the biases of the literature appear obvious. In our next section some alternative models are identified that emphasize alternative approaches to getting things done. These are approaches that are less dependent on the top-down authority of command control and more on the skills of social interaction and consensus.

DILEMMAS OF ACTION-ORIENTED EXECUTIVES: THE TENSION BETWEEN MANAGEMENT AND VISION

Generally, the approaches of these action-oriented executives are characterized by a tension between management and vision, between effective implementation and considered policy analysis, between getting things done and choosing the right things to do. Chase's development of the prison mental health program illustrates this tension. Most of his staff felt that the effort to establish an expensive therapy-oriented mental health program in the city's prisons was ill advised because it could not survive the prison environment. The general feeling was that at worst the funds were being wasted, and at best the program had only a marginal chance of success. The comments of one staff person are typical: "It was not always great that Gordon didn't see the other side—the other ways of doing what he wanted to get done. . . . He just didn't analyze the prison mental health situation carefully."

THE HIDDEN HAND EXECUTIVE

There is an alternative to the bias toward action implementation, but it is not discussed in the implementation literature. It flows from a dominant strand in the American political culture, our anti-power ethic. It is that of the "hidden hand executive." Because of the American anti-power ethic, those who wish to build power must, in the words of Samuel Huntington *"create a force that can be felt but not seen. Power remains strong when it remains in the dark; exposed to the sunlight it begins to evaporate. . . .* Effective power is unnoticed power; power observed is power devalued" in our political culture (1981, p. 75). The awareness of power creates suspicion and hostility and thus in effect reduces power. In European countries, for example, individuals and groups often go to great lengths to call attention to their power. Awareness of their power creates respect, fear, awe: power breeds power. But in this country, Huntington persuasively argues, often there is the paradox that *"hidden power is more effective"* (Huntington, 1981, p. 75). It becomes necessary to deny the facts of power in order to preserve power in fact. We will discuss three instances of this leadership style: two from existing literature and one from the beginning stages of our own research project.

The operation of this paradox in practice can be seen in the behavior of hidden hand executives. They appear to have less political power and knowledge of political and governmental details than they in fact do—a hidden hand. They do this to maximize their actual power in our anti-politics political culture. We will elaborate on this pattern with three cases of hidden hand executives. First, Dwight Eisenhower, according to Fred Greenstein's analysis, acted as if he were only the head of state, so that he could be, in fact, both head of state and head of government. Ike, as supreme allied commander in Europe, was a political general with the task of coordinating a complicated allied political and military coalition. He had reached this position by leapfrogging from the middle ranks on the strengths of his strategic successes in war-game maneuvers. But as president, he shrewdly sensed the need to mask both his political acumen and his power in order to exercise it in fact, albeit with a hidden hand (Greenstein, 1981).

Second, Landy and Levin argue that in part President Reagan has used this hidden hand strategy. Ironically the Tower Commission's blurred conclusions are an indication of Reagan's effective use of this strategy. The commission's emphasis upon the failure of Reagan's management style, especially his inability to grasp the details of government, missed the essence of his approach to governance. His lapses are genuine, but they also support his hidden hand strategy of appearing to have less political power and knowledge of governmental details than he does. In the process, he maximizes his actual power. Like Ike, he acts as if he were only the head of state in order to in fact be both the head of state and head of government. Former President Reagan joined the rest of us in learning the facts from the Tower Commission. He appeared to be unable to fire Donald Regan when he was actually using him as a lightning rod for the criticism that would have come his way. The Tower Commission report itself is a testament to the success of this approach: Unacceptable policy judgments were transformed into unpleasant but palatable implementation mistakes.

SUCCESSFUL WOMEN UNIVERSITY EXECUTIVES

Our own hypothesis is that many successful women executives exercise leadership and shape outcomes in ways more typical of hidden hand executives than of the macho variety. While they share many of their goals with their male counterparts, they employ an effectively different implementation style. Our own research does not seek to explain the reasons for these different implementation styles, but there is considerable academic controversy about this. Others have argued that successful managers use similar approaches regardless of gender (Donnel & Hill, 1980). But others point to the importance of biological, sociological, and/or psychological explanations in perceived gender-based differences in choice and action. Early socialization, it has recently been argued (Chodorow, 1978), through infant-maternal relationships results in men achieving identity and self-definition through separation or autonomy. Interpersonal relations are conceived in hierarchical terms. For women, self-definition is acquired through connection. Women, therefore, are most comfortable in the center of a web of interpersonal attachments rather than at the head of a highly structured hierarchy (Brown, 1983). Incorporating this view in organizations as we now know them may serve, however, to legitimate existing gender hierarchies. Women come to be seen as better at human relations and men as better in positions that require autonomy.[1] Carol Gilligan's study, *In a Different Voice*, suggests that women bring a special approach to management—an interactive, consensus approach—because they are women (Gilligan, 1982). While our research did not attempt to resolve the reasons for the differences in men's and women's managerial "voice," it is critical to understand the potential importance of how these differences may function politically and how different organizational cultures create, support, or suppress them.

Our own research sought, among other things, to identify cases of successful senior executive performance by female university officials and to describe their managerial styles.[2] The absence of women from the ranks of publicly acknowledged action-oriented managers suggested both that their success might not be as visible (even if just as real) and that their approaches might be different.

Our findings strongly support this position. Most of the successful women university executives described approaches to management that were distinctly nonhierarchical. They were also more likely to have emphasized process-oriented accomplishments. They described efforts to solve problems collaboratively and or to seek relationships with institutional actors in ways that would permit the development of solutions around which consensuses could be built. This approach often indicated a willingness on their part to tease out a compromise or an accommodation and, as such, to abandon a personal solution for one collectively derived.

Most of these university executives saw themselves as process-oriented executives concerned with how decisions were made. Unlike the qualities normally associated with the management-by-guts types, these women were far more likely to use hidden hand approaches because they seemed more generally to be less interested in the appearance of power. Some even described their roles as facilitators acting to provide the conditions under which organizational objectives internally defined can be realized.

Executives who see their roles as enablers—to promote participation, group ownership of organizational solutions, and a collective vision—are more likely to be oriented toward developing the capacity to choose the right things to do than they are toward merely getting things done. Many did not point to the measurable and objective results of their leadership such as the improvement of the fiscal outlook or increased growth and development (although some certainly mentioned these things). Rather they pointed to qualitative changes in the character of institutional relationships such as between and among divisions and between the faculty and administration. In many cases they pointed to an improved environment for the faculty, an increase in trust and perceptions of fairness and most importantly from many of the women executives' point of view, an improvement in the faculty's perception of the administration's responsiveness to their concerns.

Many mentioned the development of internal institutional capacity to govern and to achieve in a collective way a broad set of institutional goals. Very often these were qualitative improvements in such areas as academic programs or appointments. These accomplishments would show up on a balance sheet only indirectly and reveal an orientation to process and to the character of individual participation in it.

For instance, one president mentioned the need, in many cases, to wait—to let the process work to achieve consensus—before moving ahead. Action-oriented managers concerned primarily with getting the thing done would be less likely either to spend institutional resources to develop improved processes for collective decision making and participation, or to wait until there was a consensus about what ought to be done. Many of these women executives simultaneously developed the processes and assisted in fashioning the solution around which a consensus could be developed.

In preferring less bureaucratic means to manage, these executives depend most heavily on their human processing skills. Because they depend upon the participation of large numbers of actors for problem solving and decision making, they rely on their own abilities to listen to and understand the needs and fears of different constituencies, to see relationships between the interests of competing constituencies, and to see ways to fashion solutions that can appeal to those interests or negotiate and bargain to bring about a reconciliation among them.

This must often be achieved in very subtle ways that are not so much dependent on cultivating personal relationships as on knowing how to bring people together. One dean of a professional school revealed her success at program development in the absence of explicit financial support from the central administration by seeing common interests among her faculty and those in departments outside the school, thus creating a pattern of interest convergence. Cultivating relationships among other university departments revealed enormous opportunities for joint teaching and research ventures and brought together individuals who might not otherwise have seen themselves as natural allies.

The dean of a small women's undergraduate college in a larger university system developed multiple program initiatives university-wide in the area of women's studies by continually linking people with potentially common interests but whose organizational affiliations might not have brought them together. In the face of disorganized interests (a pattern in which there was a latent convergence of interests), she helped to develop an actual convergence of interests. Often these women pointed to their ability to see linkages between people that provide opportunities for shared interests. Their special managerial skills here seemed to have been their ability to ignore formal organizational or disciplinary distinctions and depend upon the opportunity that interpersonal contact provides for building understanding and opportunities to see common goals.

Finally, as we noted earlier, the hidden hand approach is especially effective and even necessary in democratic contexts where there is suspicion of power. Thus, it should not be surprising that it is used by university executives. Universities are very shallow hierarchically. Power is shared by tradition and necessity. Faculty constitute the largest layer of the organization below the administration, and they are highly autonomous with respect to the means of production.

Moreover, interactive, participatory, and nonhierarchical approaches to management have virtues beyond their necessity in or suitability for particular institutional settings. Considerable evidence shows that real participation in the decision-making process by those who will be affected by it increases their investment in the decision (Cohen et al., 1970). Implementation, therefore, meets less resistance, and solutions can be more lasting. Inclusiveness of the process serves to reduce recalcitrance and eliminate the forms of internal sabotage that losers in a top-down system often carry out.

THE POTENTIAL AND LIMITS OF INTERACTIVE EXECUTIVES

The implementation literature, with its current emphasis on action-oriented leaders, often ignores the benefits of interactive and consensual approaches. In so doing it may also ignore the very real success that women are having as program and policy implementors.

While our research explored successful senior executives in a single institutional setting, observers of organizational change throughout American culture are arguing that organizations may be developing along the decentralized lines where women have figured prominently (Pinchot, 1985, p. 315). In settings where we have observed participatory and interactive approaches to leadership and problem solving develop, women may very well continue to emerge, and their prominence may be more appropriately recognized. These are likely to be settings where rigid hierarchy and top-down command and control are eschewed. In these settings the pendulum will shift and the tension reoriented between action and analysis, between getting things done and choosing the right thing to do. As a consequence of these organizational changes and the management approaches they support, we predict wiser results, results where action is scrutinized by an interactive process and informed by more considered analysis.

And the skills of these university executives—interactive and indirect rather than those based on command and rules—are transferable, and thus they may have generic significance. We are arguing for the skills of social interaction, similar to what occurs in the decisions of political arenas, economic markets, and universities. In this pattern of decision making, decisions about office holders, prices, or teaching and research are the results of individual actions and interactions without anyone centrally controlling either the decisions or the individual actions or interactions. Wisdom enters into these decisions through exchange.

However, just as the behavior of effective action-oriented executives has its limits, these interactive approaches have their costs. Individual and departmental faculty decisions about teaching, research, and hiring and firing are not always perfect. But on the whole, we suggest that they probably are preferable to the decisions in these areas that a central decision maker, like a dean or president, would make for each department.

On the other hand, as Calista and others have suggested, there often are significant inefficiencies in these decentralized decisions. For example, a dean or president in an outstanding university usually cannot intervene in departmental affairs to reverse a pattern of a weak department situated in a fine university. Conversely, the dean or president in a weak university has the same inability to reverse the tendency of a single outstanding department to carry on at a high level.

While these interactive approaches are advantageous for decisions about the faculty, research, and hiring and firing, they have serious disadvantages elsewhere in these institutions. Decisions for universities as a whole often are not well made by individual faculty and by departments. Indeed, they often are not made at all. Stalemate and extremely slow decisions often characterize faculty decision-making processes, especially because of their interactive style.

DILEMMAS OF IMPLEMENTATION AND POLICY ANALYSIS

The more reflective and analytical approaches to implementation also have their costs. Earlier we indicated the potential costs involved in the action-oriented executives' lack of consideration of alternative policies and of analysis generally. But analysis also has opportunity costs. Time and energy spent on analysis is time *not* spent on getting things done. Thus there is a strong tension between considered policy analysis and implementation, between choosing the right thing to do and getting things done. Chase's development of the New York City prison mental health program illustrates this tension. Most of his staff felt that the effort to establish an expensive therapy-oriented mental health program in the city's prisons was ill advised because it could not survive the prison environment. The general feeling was that at worst the funds were being wasted, and at best the program had only a marginal chance of success.

More generally, under Chase these tensions were always resolved in the direction of efforts at implementation rather than policy analysis, alternatives were not considered. There was little effort to aggregate the direct costs of programs, or even the total thrust of the agency's policies. However, it probably would have been neither necessary nor wise for Chase to perform the function of considered policy analysis. If he had, he probably would have been much less successful at implementing his many innovative programs. Consideration of opportunity costs and alternatives, in practice, can easily lead to the "paralysis of analysis."

Similarly, Jackson's tax amnesty program represented a major investment of resources (e.g., large overtime costs). Time spent on the tax amnesty program was time not spent on regular collection and compliance work, and the Massachusetts Department of Revenue fell behind in its 1985 compliance collections. But it is not so clear that an alternative approach might have yielded similar revenue outcomes, but it probably would have met with negative coverage when it began targeting ordinary taxpayers. A crackdown also would have defeated DOR's efforts to improve its image and to create an impression of fair tax.

CONCLUSION

Which approach is preferable? As we suggested at the outset, this depends on the organizational context. The macho manager bias toward action approach is preferable in the context of top-down organizations, where the norms are command and control, whatever the actual behaviors. The bias toward the action approach also is preferable in organizations where "credit" is given for getting a job done rather than holding an organization together. That is the context of an organization facing crisis or an agency trying to ameliorate a serious social problem. Indeed, that was the context confronting several of the macho managers analyzed here.

By contrast, the social interaction approach probably is preferable in the context of more diffuse organizations, where norms of collegiality are crucial, where the hierarchy is shallow, and where power tends to be shared. The social interaction approach also is preferable when holding the organization together for future use is at least as important as performing any given task. And that was the context that the hidden hand executives analyzed here faced, from Eisenhower to the university executives. And perhaps most importantly, more organizations are coming to resemble the pattern of shared power and shallower hierarchy. This may mean that for the organizations of the future, there will be significant limits to the command and control approach and increasing emphasis on the more interactive approach. The appropriate implementation approach depends a great deal on context. But as organizations seem to change, the context is changing.

NOTES

1. One critical political question that has not been adequately considered is whether listening to women's different voice asks us to work to eliminate or maintain the current sex/gender system that produces such differences (Auerback, 1985).

2. To analyze executives who might take an alternative approach to macho managers, we examined *women* university executives. And to develop a better sense of effective management approaches, we focused on *successful* university women executives.

Specifically, in an effort to determine how they manage and to compare their methods to the approaches of those prominently featured in the action-oriented literature, we undertook an exploratory study of successful university women executives. We generated a preliminary list of about twenty-five names of women generally recognized to be successful senior university executives by polling a range of opinion leaders in the field (both male and female) of academia. These women constituted the preliminary sample. Of these, fourteen women were interviewed. The selection process tried to get a cross section of different types and sizes of universities, academic disciplines, and locations. We also were careful not to limit the analysis to presidents and deans of women's colleges, institutions where senior women are obviously most likely to be found.

This yielded a wide range of different cases (e.g., five came from large state universities, three from women's colleges; three were presidents or chancellors; four were provosts or deans of faculty; four were deans of colleges or professional schools; and three were associate deans).

There are limits to our data. They represent only a first step toward filling the gap in our knowledge about these particular types of executives. This studies' data are illustrative of the conclusions of this larger chapter. But in themselves they cannot definitively demonstrate these conclusions. Despite these limitations, because these are primary data, this study should help get going the next stage of research.

9

Policy Implementation and the Responsible Exercise of Discretion

John P. Burke

This chapter examines the normative issues that arise when bureaucrats exercise discretion in the implementation of public policy. At an earlier point in the history of public administration, discussion of the proper role of discretion in the policy process was relatively simple: any exercise of discretion must be authorized by formally empowered political authorities and tightly regulated by formal rules, procedures, and administrative processes.

As a body of empirical research on policy implementation has developed, however, it became clear that the formal legalists' neat, simple view of the proper role of discretion within the policy process could not be maintained.[1] There is well-substantiated evidence that the exercise of discretion can positively contribute to the policy process, not only in more effectively attaining policy goals defined by formal political authorities, but also in the way policy implementors can play an active part in defining the very policies they implement. Advocates of "bottom-up" approaches (see, for example, Johnson & O'Connor, 1979), "backward-mapping" strategies (see, for example, Elmore, 1979; 1985), "adaptive" evolution of policy (Orfield, 1975; Baum, 1976; Berman, 1980), and norms of "selective relativism" and "limited contingency" (Linder & Peters, 1987a) all testify to the positive benefits of bureaucratic discretion both in defining policy ends as well as in enhancing the means for attaining them.

Despite the evidence that those involved in policy implementation exercise a significant role in this process, the prescriptive question of how to evaluate bureaucratic discretion has not been adequately analyzed. It is one matter to understand more fully—from an empirical perspective—the "fact" that bureaucrats exercise discretion, but it is another matter to determine whether that discretion "ought" to have been exercised; that is, whether an exercise of discretion is good or bad in a normative sense.

The need for such prescriptive analysis is compelling for a number of reasons. First, there are still some lessons to be learned from formal legalism, especially in the scope of its analytic concerns. Its shortcomings notwithstanding, the formal-legal approach embodied both empirical and normative concerns: empirically, politics was thought to be separate from administration, while normatively, the rule of law and political control by higher authorities was thought to define the proper relation of bureaucracy to democratic government. In contrast, contemporary analysis of policy implementation goes only halfway: advancement on the empirical front but little normative insight about what to make of its heightened descriptive understanding.

One could simply argue that discretion always serves the implementation process well.[2] But to make such a claim skirts some questions that allegiance to democratic rule, however defined, might raise. Does a particular exercise of discretion result in the fair treatment of client and other affected groups? Does a particular exercise of discretion protect individual rights? Does a particular exercise of discretion serve the public interest? Just as the formal-legal approach has been faulted for assuming that discretion threatened democratic rule, to suggest that all exercises of discretion serve public policy is equally suspect. Such a suggestion either reduces the normative import of discretion to one of simple effectiveness in attaining policy implementation or is naive about the prescriptive consequences of discretion. Neither is justified for obvious reasons.

Further prescriptive analysis is especially in order, given that there seems to be little agreement in the literature about whether exercises of discretion aid or hinder policy implementation. One might argue that it is perhaps unfair to criticize ostensibly empirical research for failing to reach adequate prescriptive judgments, but most studies do draw implicit—even quite explicit in some instances—conclusions about bureaucratic behavior and its effects on the policy process and policy outcomes. Some scholars (Lindblom, 1959, 1977; Pressman & Wildavsky, 1973; Van Meter & Van Horn, 1975; McLaughlin, 1976; Johnson & O'Connor, 1979) are optimistic in their assessments of the role of discretion in the implementation process. Other studies—Bailey and Mosher's (1968) analysis of Title III of the Elementary and Secondary Education Act of 1965, Moynihan's (1969) reflections on community action programs, Bardach's (1977) discussion of implementation "games," and Bullock and Lamb's (1984) study of civil rights policy—present a more negative view. Still others (Hargrove, 1975; Nakamura & Smallwood, 1980) fall somewhere in the middle (for a fuller discussion, see Lester et al., 1987). Clearly, some exercises of discretion are more or less beneficial to the policy process than others.

TOWARD AN ALTERNATIVE

Given these difficulties in evaluating implementation from a purely empirical perspective, a normative analysis of discretion is clearly needed in order to complement empirical observation. As Yates has noted, policy implementors make valuative choices based on a "substantive public philosophy" when they exercise discretion (1981, p. 50). If so, then just as formal-legal approaches were incorrect to assume that discretion was an unwarranted intrusion into the policy process, more contemporary observers cannot assume that discretion always serves that process well; they must take up the question that Yates poses of what "substantive public philosophy" is involved when discretion is exercised.

In determining what substantive public philosophy should justify discretion the tension between the formal-legal perspective and more recent literature remains. On the one hand, although formal legalists were wrong to insist that discretion must be limited if not eliminated, they were right in suggesting that justification of discretion must be politically grounded. That is, it requires analysis of the *political* standing and legitimacy of exercises of discretion. In democracies, exercises of public authority, the discretion of bureaucrats included, must ultimately stem from the consent of the governed and the workings of the institutions legitimized by that consent.

On the other hand, however, it must also be recognized that policy implementors frequently take an active role in exercising discretion, often in defining the very policy ends that those "higher authorities" are thought to have set. This is the essential insight that runs through much of the recent literature on policy implementation. Thus, to say that discretion must be grounded in the consent of the governed and the workings of political institutions seems to contradict the view of policy implementation as a more interactive process.

How can these seemingly opposed perspectives be reconciled? Two concepts, responsibility and accountability, may be useful in resolving this dilemma. Attention to responsibility addresses an important facet of discretion that emerges in many of the studies of the implementation process: the sense that policy implementors exercise discretion because in doing so they feel they are acting responsibly or according to what they deem to be their proper responsibilities.

Although the concept of responsibility is often confused with accountability,[3] responsibility generally involves a conception of duty and obligation that focuses on what state of affairs an individual attempts to bring about or fails to bring about. It is thus concerned largely with the question of "What?" officials should or should not do. A concern for responsibility is useful, in turn, since its focus on the content of an official's actions and directs attention to evaluation of the public and philosophical import of that exercise of discretion.

Accountability, too, speaks to the issue of the substantive public and philosophical import of discretion, but from the perspective of answerability for one's actions. In contrast to the "What?" question that a concern for responsibility posits, accountability raises the question of "To whom?" one is answerable.

The "To whom?" question is important, given the frequent absence of a clearly defined role for bureaucracy within a democratic system of government. If bureaucratic tasks are ill defined and implementors find they must exercise discretion, accountability for that exercise may serve as an important—perhaps in some cases the only—check on their actions. The obvious mode of accountability involves answerability to some higher authority, but accountability may also be present if officials are accountable to themselves, their peers, or the clients they serve.[4] As Romzek and Dubnick (1987) point out, accountability does not just mean "answerability" nor does its exercise need to be confined to "mere formalistic" responses. It more broadly involves how "public agencies and workers manage the diverse expectations within and outside the organization" (1987, p. 228). Managing diverse expectations—whether one's own or those of others—would seem to figure strongly in determining when officials should exercise discretion.

An emphasis on responsibility and accountability thus need not simply mean that the policy views and positions of those with "formal" authority or those "higher up" in the administrative chain of command should always prevail. In fact, if we turn to one of the seminal points in the origins of the general debate over bureaucratic discretion—the classic exchange between Finer (1941) and Friedrich (1940)—we can see, in Friedrich's position, a nonformalistic view, one combining professional mores and expertise, that in the last fifty years has gained as much allegiance as the formal-legal approach once possessed.

Dimension I: Responsibility

We can also find in this early debate the emergence of two distinct views of responsibility—counsel about "What?" implementors should or should not do—that are useful in discriminating among types of discretion. The first, following Finer's lead, occurs when the direction over the implementation process is largely defined by institutions, processes, and persons (e.g., higher political authorities or the public) who are external to those actually engaged in implementing policy. Here responsibilities for implementation are largely spelled out beforehand, and from the perspective of those external agents, the exercise of discretion should be highly constrained. (Although as I shall argue, some exercises of discretion may still be needed even when responsibilities are seemingly clearly defined.)

Alternatively, following from (but not confined to) Friedrich's position, different norms govern the exercise of discretion when the direction over what officials should or should not do largely originates directly from those involved in implementation. In this case, responsibility for policy implementation is internal in character. Policy implementors possess greater authority to make substantive decisions; discretion is given a wider role.

Dimension II: Accountability

In addition to distinguishing the norms governing the exercise of discretion, whether those originating from the implementor or some external entity, the ability of different sources, in Dimension I, to elicit accountability for what transpires in the implementation process should be differentiated. Here descrip-

Figure 9.1
Responsibility: Nature of Source Governing the Exercise of Discretion

Strong	External Sources	Internal Norms
	I	II
Accountability: Degree of Answerability for Discretionary Actions	[e.g. Formal-Legal]	[e.g. Professional]
	III	IV
	[e.g. Fragmented Implementation]	[e.g. Personal Political and Moral Views]

tive studies of implementation are especially useful in providing information about the degree of accountability present when discretion is exercised. Put most simply, we need to explore whether accountability is *strong* or *weak*. Strong appeals to formal-legal dictates or to expertise, generally speaking, seem to justify discretion; in contrast, an inability to frame convincing accounts for acts of discretion offer weaker justification for it.

A TYPOLOGICAL APPROACH

Together, these two dimensions generate a typology useful in distinguishing different situations where discretion might be exercised as shown in Figure 9.1.

The typology allows us to classify and understand the vast differences in situations where the exercise of discretion arises. Different kinds of bureaucratic conduct—and thus different degrees and types of bureaucratic discretion—are present in each of the four cells. For example, the conditions posited in Cell I typify the formal-legal view of bureaucratic conduct: higher authorities define the norms governing the exercise of discretion and strong mechanisms of accountability are in place to ensure compliance. In Cell II, the professional expertise of those involved in the implementation process govern their responsibilities, but there is also a strong sense of accountability, for example to the professional community or that following from the demands of professional expertise. In Cell III, external authorities attempt to define responsibilities but accountability is weak, as is often the case, for example, where implementation is highly fragmented (i.e., policy decisions must be made at lower levels in the bureaucracy without adequate guidance from those above). In Cell IV, implementors attempt to exercise discretion based on their own personal political or moral views but often with weak accountability for their actions.

The typology enables us to begin to make sense of the normative import of bureaucratic discretion, especially in answering the critical prescriptive question: When should officials exercise discretion. For example, the justification for discretion under the conditions typical of Cell I is probably weaker in most instances than under conditions of Cell II. In the former, the argument for discretion must weigh strongly against rules, procedures and processes that seek to limit it; in the latter, discretion is necessary to carry out professional expertise. Discretion permitted under the conditions of Cell III differs from that of Cell IV. In Cell III, fragmentation of the implementation process calls for different kinds of discretionary activity (for example, implementation that attempts to cope with vague policy mandates) than does discretion that involves the expression of personal political and moral views, which are present within Cell IV.

As further discussion of the different types of discretion within the bounds of each cell will indicate, the analysis in each instance is more complex than this brief discussion of differences. But by determining the descriptive facts about particular acts of implementation and understanding differences in the situations when implementors exercise discretion (i.e., properly classifying each case in its right cell), we can begin to arrive at some prescriptive understanding of times when discretion is or is not justified. Let us consider each cell in turn.

I. External Sources Determine Responsibilities—Strong Accountability

In this cell, we can locate cases of policy implementation that occur when external agents (1) define bureaucratic responsibilities, and (2) can exercise strong control over bureaucratic activity in the implementation process. In these situations the typical formal-legal view of accountability is at its strongest; situations where a respect for formal hierarchy within the organization—obedience to superiors—and deference to the dictates of political authorities outside the bureaucracy are both possible and feasible. These conditions are likely to obtain when: (1) policies are implemented within one agency or department (the organizational "distance" between policy formulation and policy implementation is relatively short); (2) the implementing organization itself is relatively non-complex; and (3) implementation tasks are relatively simple.

Where these conditions for formal-legal control of the implementation process are met, the need, and hence justification, for discretion lessens. If higher political authorities are attentive to the implementation process (responsibilities are clearly defined), possess the means to control what individuals farther down in the organization and further on in the implementation process are doing (accountability is high), and each of the three organizational characteristics conducive to formal, external control are at their highest, then the case against the exercise of discretion is generally strong.

The difficulty with Cell I, of course, is that in many instances one or more of these conditions will not be met. Few cases of policy implementation probably fall within this cell. Lipsky's (1980) discussion of the organizational conditions within which street-level bureaucrats operate, for example, illustrates a set of common situations where the need to exercise discretion may be more legitimate precisely because it does not fall within the combination of highly defined responsibilities and strong accountability characteristic of Cell I. According to Lipsky (1980, pp. 27–28) street-level bureaucrats "experience the following conditions in their work":

1. Resources are chronically inadequate relative to the task workers are asked to perform.
2. The demand for services tends to increase to meet the supply.
3. Goal expectations for the agencies in which they work tend to be ambiguous, vague, or conflicting.
4. Performance oriented toward goal achievement tends to be difficult if not impossible to measure.
5. Clients are typically nonvoluntary; partly, as a result, clients for the most part do not serve as primary bureaucratic reference groups.

Lipsky's first and third points indicate difficulties in defining the responsibilities of street-level bureaucrats; points two and four reflect weak modes of accountability, while point five—the inability of clients to serve as bureaucratic reference groups—reflects problems in both defining responsibilities and serving as a mechanism for accountability when street-level bureaucrats turn to client groups as a mode of coping with the demands of their jobs.

Cases where these conditions of accountability and responsibility exist belong under Cell IV and raise different issues about the proper exercise of discretion than those found in Cell I. But Lipsky also notes that some street-level bureaucrats do operate under conditions of more delimited responsibilities, more effective mechanisms of accountability, and in more conducive organizational contexts. Thus even in what is usually taken as one of the prime scholarly works suggesting the need for greater bureaucratic discretion, we find at least implicit arguments about when the exercise of discretion should be limited:

These [his five points] conditions of work may not always prevail. For example, it may be that the welfare department in a small city with a stable, homogeneous, white population is large enough to provide a relatively full range of social services to recipients and perform with relatively full objectives derived from the relatively homogeneous political culture of the city. . . . In such a situation one might expect social workers in that office to behave quite differently from the social workers in a large, more heterogeneous central city. (Lipsky, 1980, p. 28)

Lipsky, in turn, implies that discretion may be less necessary in such instances: "The analysis presented here depends upon the presence of the aforementioned working conditions. If for some reason these characteristics are not present, the analysis is less likely to be appropriate" (1980, p. 28).

Although discretion is often taken by observers of the policy implementation to be endemic to the process, some studies substantiate Lipsky's contention that discretion may not always be necessary for effective implementation. Rodgers and Bullock (1972, pp. 164–169), Sabatier and Mazmanian (1980, p. 545), Van Horn and Van Meter (1976), and Wirt (1970, pp. 286–288) all emphasize the importance of having policies clearly stated as a prerequisite for effective implementation, hence reducing the need for implementors to exercise discretion. In their study of implementation of civil rights policies, Bullock and Lamb (1984, p. 16) explicitly list ten factors conducive to enforcement of civil rights legislation, eight of which (1 through 6, 8, and 10) imply tighter control over the process, hence strong accountability to higher political authorities, clearly defined responsibilities, and, thus, significant limits on the exercise of discretion by implementors:

We may expect that changes in the direction of equality in the treatment of minorities are more likely to occur when

1. policy goals have been clearly stated;
2. precise standards for measuring compliance have been specified;
3. a mechanism for monitoring compliance has been created;
4. an agency responsible for implementing policy has been set up;
5. personnel responsible for implementation are committed to promoting civil rights;
6. those enforcing policy enjoy the support of their superiors;
7. the policy beneficiaries are organized and cohesively support implementation;
8. efforts by various agencies responsible for achieving a policy goal are administratively coordinated;
9. the cost-benefit ratio of the situation favors compliance; and
10. the federal government is an active participant on behalf of minorities.

Some exercise of discretion, however, may still be needed, even when external authorities can exercise control and direction over policy implementation. The limits of formal-legal and related approaches need to be recognized, and these limits may call for some forms of discretion. Singular reliance upon the dictates of formal political authorities, for example, could lead to an overly strict adherence to laws, rules, and regulations. Taken to the extreme, formal adherence can become formalistic adherence: officials lose sight of general policy goals and become overly scrupulous in the interpretation of their authority and duties.

Higher political authorities also can err. Rules and procedures, for example, may violate law and legislative intent. Constitutional principles may also be violated by the dicta of formal authorities. Bureaucratic discretion, such as whistle-blowing or disobedience of superiors, would clearly be justified in such instances.

Exercises of discretion that fall short of substantive policymaking, but which might make positive contributions to the policy process nonetheless, also may be justified. In particular, discretion may be in order if it is directed at enhancing the effectiveness of policy implementation.

Here the literature on implementation might be helpful in identifying conditions where policy implementation has proven ineffective but where discretionary steps by implementors might conceivably have provided remedy. Thus, there is a need for further analysis of cases of policy implementation that fall into Cell I but call for exercise of discretion that enhances the mission and mandate set by external authorities, where that mission and mandate do legitimately constrain the actions of those called on to implement public policy.

II. Internal Norms Determine Responsibilities—Strong Accountability

In this cell we can place exercise of discretion when the norms governing an official's responsibilities are internal, that is, it is generally the implementor who essentially defines his/her contribution to the policy process, and the ability to control that contribution is strong, that is, accountability is high. Such is the case, typically, when matters of technical expertise and professional competence call for the exercise of discretion. Professionals operating in the policy process often are delegated authority to exercise significant amounts of discretion, but at the same time there is generally strong accountability for their actions, either through the norms governing the professional's own knowledge and expertise, the control exercised by the professional community or through political oversight of the professional's role in the policy process.

The place of professional expertise in the bureaucracy, especially the role of professional autonomy, raises complex issues that have been the subject of extensive discussion elsewhere (see, for example, Friedrich, 1940; Price, 1965; Mosher, 1968; Burke, 1986, pp. 24–37, 142–160), and cannot be discussed here with the attention they deserve. But, at least generally speaking, where professionals and other technical experts have been granted license to act on the basis of their own skills and judgment, deference to discretionary actions that may result is obviously in order.

However, as in the case of formal-legal approaches in Cell I, the limits of professional expertise must also be recognized. Following from those limits, further responsibilities of professionals in the policy process may arise. The fact that officials possess professional skills or knowledge to which others involved in or affected by the policy process might defer does not necessarily imply, however, that discretion should be exercised in all cases or that professionally based reasons for exercising discretion are the only reasons that count.

Sometimes the judgments of professionals are biased or in error. For example, one study of the role of professionals engaged in regional development planning in Appalachia found rampant paternalism in the experts' assessments of the region's economic and social conditions. This paternalism was in part based on the notion that "time stood still," a view "locked into romantic or negative stereotypes in a static image of Appalachian time and history." Thus a seemingly "professional" perspective "deflect[ed] or obscur[ed] comprehension of the region's particular form of modernization" (Reid, 1980–1981, p. 622).

With respect to the abilities of professional expertise to define an official's responsibilities, it must be recognized that professional expertise can be mis-applied or not be applicable in some cases. For example, in 1970, Congress passed a number of amendments to the Clean Air Act. This legislation satisfied public demands for pollution control, but it did not adequately specify ways to achieve policy goals, particularly with respect to the costs and technology of implementation. The bill set strict standards and deadlines but, according to one study, "the technology was not presently available for meeting them," a point that Senator Edmund Muskie of Maine had pointed out in debate on the Senate floor (Jones, 1974, p. 459). Since the required technical expertise did not exist, experts involved in implementing the policy would clearly be remiss in acting as if it did.

With respect to accountability, which is assumed to be high in Cell II, since experts can generally give good accounts for their discretionary actions, the professional community's own interests can sometimes predominate, often at the expense of the public's interest. The forms that this pursuit of self-serving professional interests can take are varied. Professions can seek to enhance their own "turf" and organizational mission within agencies and departments; they can develop exclusionary communications networks, biased agendas, rigid problem-defining and problem-solving methods, and hostility to innovation and external control (see, for example, Friedson, 1970; Johnson, 1972; Bledstein, 1976; Barber, 1978). In instances where professional interests intrude in a self-interested way, deference to professional expertise must be tempered by a recognition of the contestable and often problematic character of professional judgment and practice.

III. External Sources Determine Responsibilities—Weak Accountability

In this cell, implementation takes place in a context where external authorities try but cannot exercise strong control and direction over the implementor's activities. Such cases are likely to arise when conditions for strong external control outlined above (Cell I) are weakest: the distance between policy formulation and implementation is great, the implementing organization is complex, and policy tasks are difficult to achieve. The exercise of discretion is especially problematic in such instances—there are no strong "internal" reasons for it (e.g., it is not a matter of professional expertise)—yet external direction provides no ready substitute. As Ianello (1987) suggests, policy implementation is fragmented in such cases: "critical policy is made at lower levels . . . without guidance from upper levels."

What policy implementors might do in such cases clearly calls for further thought and research. Of all the situations in each of the four cells where discretion might be exercised, the normative justification for exercising discretion under the circumstances of Cell III has not been adequately examined.

Three possibilities, however, do come to mind. First, exercises of discretion under these circumstances should be remedial in character. Conditions of fragmentation are not generally ones suitable for effective policy implementation. Officials caught in those conditions should try to get themselves out of them, either by requesting more formal direction where possible (in effect, approximating the conditions of Cell I) or developing their own expertise (moving toward the conditions of Cell II).

Second, if discretion is exercised, it should be incremental and pragmatic: moving forward in small steps based on experience and practical results. Exercise of discretion that leads to long-range commitments or that is grounded in rational, comprehensive planning seems especially unsuitable in such circumstances. Where long-range commitments result, implementors may set policy on a course that makes future corrections and changes difficult. Where exercise of discretion stems from what implementors might consider their own abilities to plan rationally (or to borrow from Lindblom, to engage in "synoptic" planning), the difficulty lies in their failure, as rational planners, to possess the needed expertise.

Finally, implementors might take a cue from cases where policy implementation in contexts of decentralized participation has been successful. Decentralized participation often takes place in situations where policy goals are unclear and the political environment or hierarchical chain of command from which officials are expected to take their cue is fluid and ill defined. Exercises of discretion that have positively contributed to policy outcomes in such situations might yield useful lessons for implementation that takes place under conditions of more general fragmentation.

IV. Internal Norms Determine Responsibilities—Weak Accountability

In this cell, discretion is exercised essentially on the basis of the official's own judgment. Unlike Cells I and III, there are few if any formal guidelines for officials to follow, and, unlike Cell II, implementors do not possess expert knowledge or professional expertise as a justification for their actions.

One argument for the exercise of discretion under the conditions of Cell IV—the notion that officials should do whatever they feel justified in doing—can be dismissed rather quickly. To urge those involved in the implementation process to exercise discretion in any matter they see fit, other things being equal, compromises the integrity of a policy process at work within a democratic political framework. Elevating personal beliefs to the level of bureaucratic practice compromises the logic and purposes of democracy. Principles basic to democratic government, such as consent, majority rule, and minority rights, could be violated if a policy implementor's personal beliefs are transported, without proper justification, into a political context where public policy is directly affected. At the extreme, it could lead to a substantive redefinition of the ends and purposes of public policy based on the implementor's own preferences and predilections, not those of broader institutions and processes or affected client groups.

Similar difficulties also arise when the implementor's personal moral views call for the exercise of discretion. Many moral and political philosophers would justify a morally grounded exercise of discretion based on the presumed merit of the moral principles in question. Certainly such a view has the advantage of encouraging a process of questioning and reasoning about one's conduct. But save for moral dilemmas that crop up at the extreme—the kinds of problems raised in the Nuremberg principles, for example—a purely personal moral view seems unwise as a way of ascertaining the responsibilities of policy implementors. Again, the reasons are complex and require further discussion (see Burke, 1986, pp. 100–141, 161–178). Put simply, the problem is that giving personal moral or ethical beliefs such a privileged position in considering how officials ought to regard their conduct runs the risk of arbitrariness; that is, it may impose one's own preferences, albeit regarded as "moral," as binding in a more general political context.[5] Consider, for example, different moral views we have about matters of personal liberty such as rights to abortion, privacy, sexual practices, and other matters of personal conduct. Or consider different moral positions we hold in the area of social justice, for example, differing conceptions of entitlement, need, and fair distribution.

This is not to suggest that moral reasoning is wholly arbitrary. There may be moral views that are more commonly held—such as the Nuremberg principles—that officials may legitimately employ in situations where there are no other available guidelines. One task for further research is whether common moral principles exist that can be applied in public policy context in a nonarbitrary way.

In contrast to discretion that has its source in personal and moral beliefs, discretionary action might be permitted if additional arguments could be made on its behalf. That is, it is not only the implementor's personal beliefs or moral views that justify the act of discretion but other reasons can be marshalled as well. What precisely those other reasons are must remain for future discussion. Several interesting points are, however, worth mentioning. First, the ability of the implementor to give an account of his/her acts of discretion seems especially important. If officials cannot muster reasons for their actions, then they probably fail to meet the basic test of having an adequate sense of what their responsibilities are and being accountable, either to themselves or others, for their actions.

Second, the particular reasons they give for exercising discretion ought to have some linkage to serving the interests and purposes of the wider audience affected by the official's actions. Lipsky's (1980) discussion of street-level bureaucrats is especially interesting in this regard, since it suggests that "coping behavior," a form of discretionary action common among street-level bureaucrats, is often motivated by the need to serve client groups more effectively. Furthermore, differences in the expectations of client groups (or whatever groups or audiences are affected by policy decisions) could define the bounds of permissible discretion that officials might employ. Discretionary actions, for example, that might be embraced by one client group or community might be unacceptable to another (for example, nonenforcement of laws against prostitution in a large urban setting versus nonenforcement in a small town).

Lipsky's analysis of street-level bureaucrats suggests a third point that is useful in differentiating discretionary actions. Street-level bureaucrats also frequently exercise discretion, in Lipsky's view, in order to cope with the demands of the job and the limited resources at their disposal. Lipsky's depiction of the plight of street-level bureaucrats is compelling in light of the circumstances in which they are forced to operate. But their discretion seems particularly justified given their own personal skills, knowledge, and expertise in delivering goods and services to their clients. In a way, then, while their discretion is personal in its source—hence in Cell IV—it has characteristics that resemble those of professional expertise (Cell II). It is discretion that is job related and based on knowledge and expertise about what is necessary for the effective delivery of goods and services.

James Q. Wilson's analysis of policy behavior provides another suggestive line of argument concerning discretion exercises under conditions of Cell IV. In his study of police departments that were characterized by a "service" style, Wilson found significant amounts of discretion among police on the beat. According to Wilson, service-style police departments "take seriously all requests for either law enforcement or order maintenance . . . but are less likely to respond by making an arrest or otherwise imposing formal sanctions . . . .The police intervene frequently but not formally" (Wilson, 1968, p. 200).

Service-style exercises of police discretion by and large work well when there is a shared consensus in the community that supports police activities. Service-style police exercise discretion, but they do so as if they possessed some mandate from "higher authority" that is characteristic of Cell I (although note that instead of a formal mandate it is a community-based consensus on the need to exercise discretion).

Thus, in both Lipsky's and Wilson's analyses of bureaucratic discretion, we find officials exercising discretion on their own (hence, Cell IV), but for reasons that resemble the conditions of Cell I (Wilson's service-style police operating with the perception of a strong public mandate) or Cell II (Lipsky's street-level bureaucrats acting as quasi-professionals). This is instructive, since it suggests more general rules in resolving questions about the proper course of action in Cell IV–type situations.

Lipsky and Wilson are also instructive about the limits to the exercise of discretion in the cases they explore. Lipsky admits that discretion becomes problematic when it puts the street-level bureaucrat "in the position of manipulating citizens on behalf of the agencies from which citizens seek help" (1980, p. xiii). Here, manipulation and bureaucratic goals have replaced expertise and experienced-based delivery of goods and services, and the exercise of discretion leads to less positive policy consequences.

Wilson's service style, in turn, is likely to become problematic when the community's support of the police and the community's consensus about proper police activity break down. As Wilson notes, a service style is most likely to be found in "homogeneous, middle class communities . . . [where] the police see their chief responsibility as protecting a common definition of public order against the minor and occasional threats posed by unruly teenagers and 'outsiders'" (1968, p. 200). Where class and racial differences divide the community, other patterns of police behavior are called for. Departments can become "legalistic" in the enforcement of the law, and officers exercise very little discretion. Or they can become "watchmen," exercising significant amounts of discretion in preserving public order, but often at the expense of fairness in their treatment of minority groups. In both cases accountability weakens, responsibility suffers, and discretion is ill-advised.

CONCLUSION

It is important to note that, in evaluating discretion on the basis of the typology offered above, actual cases do not always fall neatly into each cell. Particular instances of policy implementation may share more or less in the characteristics of each of the four types, and some may in fact involve combinations of each. This problem is common to all classificatory schemas and typologies: the "real" does not neatly square with the ideal.

The purpose of the typology, however, is not to provide a schema in which cases of policy implementation can be neatly plugged in and analyzed. Rather, the purpose is to enhance our general theoretical understanding, so that the particular may be better evaluated. Thus, while something may be lost by simplification, something also may be gained in theoretical clarity.

Greater theoretical clarity, especially of a prescriptive sort, seems especially needed at this point in research on policy implementation. In their review of the implementation literature Nakamura and Smallwood present and then reject what they term the theory of "classical implementation":

An agent to carry out the policy is chosen by the policy maker according to technical criteria. The policy is communicated to the agent as a series of specific instructions. The agent implements (carries out) the specific instructions according to the policy guidelines specified in the communication from the policy maker. (Nakamura & Smallwood, 1980, p. 9)

Nakamura and Smallwood are right to reject such a neat solution to the problem of discretion. Officials involved in policy implementation are more active in the process and the relationship of policymaking to policy implementation is more "circular" and adaptive. The discretionary actions of those involved in implementation can contribute to the successful definition and implementation of policy.

But in considering when discretion should be exercised and by whom, it is also important to remember the place of the administrative process within a broader system of democratic government. Empirical observation alone cannot wholly determine when implementation can be regarded as legitimate; prescriptive evaluation must inform our judgments about proper policy goals and the role of bureaucratic discretion in their attainment. Thus, neither the empirical observations of more recent studies nor the concern for democratic theory in the earlier, "classical" approach alone will suffice. As understanding of the policy process develops, an important aim of contemporary observers of policy implementation must be to reunite both empirical and normative perspectives. Only on that joint basis can we properly answer the critical question: When should bureaucrats exercise discretion?

NOTES

1. It is interesting to note that a recognition of the place of discretion in the policy process can be found at earlier points in the history of public administration. Luther Gulick's 1933 essay entitled "Politics, Administration, and the New Deal" serves as an insightful reminder that much of what we think is new in scholarly investigation has been anticipated by our academic forbears. According to Gulick, "Discretion, the use of judgment, is the essential element in the determination of policy. . . . It is impossible to analyze the work of any public employee from the time he steps into his office in the morning until he leaves it at night without discovering that his every act is a seamless web of discretion and action. It is impossible to discover any position in government service, or in any other service for that matter, in which the element of discretion is absent. . . . What we have in administration is a continual process of decision-action-decision-action, like a man running after a high batted ball" (1933, p. 61). In his 1943 article in *Public Administration Review* on administrative discretion W. A. R. Leys offers a useful classification of types of administrative discretion: actions involving (1) evaluation of technical matters, (2) clarification of vague criteria, and (3) resolution of political disputes. Unfortunately Leys does not address the difficult issue of determining when and what kind of bureaucratic latitude is justified in each case, nor is the classification grounded in concrete cases or examples of bureaucratic discretion.

2. This ease of this "solution" to the problem of discretion is not unlike that offered by the formal-legal approach, although with obviously different conclusions. Thus, as the strong emphasis on democratic control and formal authority "drove" the formal-legal understanding of the empirical relation between politics and administration, the strong empirical emphasis in much of the literature on policy implementation may drive its normative and prescriptive conclusions.

3. Confusion results because in some instances, responsibility and accountability do seem to mean the same thing. For example, if one takes responsibility only to imply the rather limited sense of "responsibility to" then one is really implying the same as accountability. Similar confusion often results under formal-legal theories of bureaucracy; here one's sense of what one is responsible for is defined by those to whom one is accountable, thus responsibility tends to reduce to accountability. However, if one wishes to distinguish what actions one should or should not take (responsibility) from being held to account to others for those actions (accountability), then it seems useful to distinguish these two concepts.

4. That accountability may take various forms is important because it captures both

the concerns of an earlier period in the history of public administration that the bureaucracy should be answerable to higher political authorities (accountability to higher authorities) and the recognition of more recent observers that those involved in the implementation of policy are often better informed or situated to make substantive policy decisions about how policy should be carried out (accountability to self, peers or clients).

5. On this point about the limits of philosophy's role in a democratic political context see Walzer's (1981) more extended discussion.

10

Acquisition: The Missing Link in the Implementation of Technology

Carl P. Carlucci _____

In their first edition on implementation, Pressman and Wildavsky (1973) define implementation as "the ability to forge subsequent links in the causal chain so as to obtain the desired results" (p. xxi) and carefully point out that implementation begins after the adoption of a new policy, the agreement on a program, and the provision of funding. This definition fits a simple model of policy formulation, adoption, and implementation, but Pressman and Wildavsky added that unanticipated "technical details" of implementation plagued and delayed the implementation process. Similarly, Bardach (1977) and Yin (1982) also define implementation as a multistage process, including a preimplementation phase of technical testing and organizational acceptance.

Nakamura and Smallwood (1980) summarize the "classical" model of implementation as beginning after the invention and adoption of an innovation, and consisting of the choice of an agent to carry out implementation, communication of the innovation, and finally the implementation process itself. This model assumes that the process of invention or formulation and adoption is separate from the implementation process, just as policymakers are separate from policy implementors, and that after adoption, implementation is a relatively simple technical process.

The research done in "ironing out" the technical details of the classical implementation model challenges most of the model's assumptions. Nakamura and Smallwood (1980) suggest that simple linear models miss the complex and iterative nature of policy formation. Recent works conclude that implementation was rarely considered in the design of policy (Palumbo, 1987) and that implementors often participate in policymaking and adapt policies as they interpret policy goals in the process of implementation (Palumbo & Harder, 1981). Policies are likely to "evolve" as part of the implementation process (Cingranelli et al., 1981).

These works caution us on the importance of using the proper theoretical framework for analyzing implementation problems, for explaining the individual stages that occur during implementation, and for dealing with multiple levels of analysis (Elmore, 1982; Palumbo & Harder, 1981; Tornatzky et al., 1983; Yanow, 1987). The problem is that as the scope of implementation studies widens, we must regularly return to a consideration of basic notions and theories, using empirical findings to revise theoretical models.

A number of basic assumptions must be stated with the choice of an implementation process model. In studying the workings of government, Pressman and Wildavsky initially stated that the innovation must be fully adopted before implementation could begin. This means that the mandate, which in government would be legislation and in large private organizations would be a decision by management, must be in place; the funding must be provided and the agreements reached; or the technology acquired. We know from many studies that this is not always the case, that the explanation of implementation success and failure is not limited to postadoption factors (Yanow, 1987). In a practical sense implementation often begins before the adoption process is fully complete.

The extent to which adopters and implementors are the same people is also critical to designing an implementation model (Hargrove, 1975; Lambright, 1979; Nakamura & Pinderhaughes, 1981). Burke (1987) identifies four cases that distinguish implementation guided by external adopters from implementation that is directed by forces and persons internal to the implementing organization. In government, politicians and policymaking bodies often adopt innovations, whether policies, programs, or technologies, and assign agencies to implement them (Elmore, 1982).

Adoption and implementation can be physically separate processes carried out by different organizations, but we know that there must be a link between the two. What that link is and how it is formed must be considered. Where adoption ends and implementation begins is a critical factor in predicting the success of an implementation. In the model and analysis that follows this link is identified as acquisition, the stage between adoption and implementation of an innovation. Innovations are ideas, objects, policies, practices, or technologies new to a given organization or perceived as new by the adopting unit (Rogers, 1983; Tornatzky et al., 1983). Acquisition is defined in terms of the innovation, as a transfer of knowledge, authority, or responsibility in the case of policies and programs, and in this study of technological innovation, as the funding of a practice or purchase of an artifact. This is a simple stage model, in linear form, but it is appropriate because it is used to organize a body of empirical information about a sequence of decisions rather than as a means of defining a process (Tornatzky et al., 1983).

This chapter examines the stages in the implementation process and tests the proposed process model by studying the extent of use of the innovation by potential adopters. This work draws heavily on research done on the diffusion of innovations, which offers insights on both the development of stage models and research on specific components (Musheno, 1981). The result is an improved process model for use in works dealing with policy innovations related to new technologies.[1]

PROPOSED MODEL

The model used in this work includes three stages: adoption, acquisition, and implementation.[2] Adoption represents the culmination of a decision-making process in a single event, a decision, the intent of the leadership of an organization to do something, and in this case to do it a certain way (Rogers, 1983; Tornatzky et al., 1983). Implementation transforms the decision into reality. In a large government or hierarchical organization the link between adoption and implementation is the order that is issued by leadership or top management to those who actually manage the means of production. The message from top management can be an order, funding, or direct injection of an innovation into an organization's structure or operation. In the case of innovations employing technology, this link is quite clearly acquisition, the order to acquire, the funding to acquire, or the provision of an acquired innovation.

The more detailed the adoption decision, the more complete the acquisition phase prior to implementation. Alternatively, if the adoption decision is a simple approval to proceed, implementation will have to include the request for funds, the search for appropriate technology, and installation. In this case, where there is no clear acquisition step, the process proceeds along an "ambiguous" path.

There are obviously two different models of implementation in use by researchers, one considering acquisition as part of adoption and one considering acquisition as part of implementation. The appropriateness of either model depends on the organization and the case under consideration, but an explicit statement must be made to identify which of these models is in use.

Acquisition included in adoption is the case required by the implementation model constructed by Pressman and Wildavsky; yet it is clear that the separation of policy design and implementation causes problems that can be fatal. If acquisition is part of implementation, the process begins according to Bardach's model. Thus, there must be an assembling of money and information, and there may be various interorganizational "implementation games" between the unit assigned operating responsibility and top management or other groups in the environment.

In the proposed model, the acquisition link is analyzed separately. In large organizations we expect that the path of "well-defined policy," with acquisition associated with adoption, to increase the possibility of implementation. With the successful acquisition of a technology, or the provision of authority or resources, the likelihood of implementation occurring increases (O'Toole & Montjoy, 1984). Acquisition is an irreversible act, where adopters cannot later unadopt (Tornatzky et al., 1983).

With any technological innovation, a formal decision to adopt either is or is not made. Acquisition then confirms that adoption has taken place and paves the way for implementation. When it is determined that the innovation, or the funding, is in place, acquisition is complete and implementation begins. Acquisition is expected to have an impact on implementation to the extent that once it has been determined that the innovation is installed or contracted for, there can be no question as to the outcome of the adoption decision. There may be "implementation games," and the extent of the commitment made by the institution is still open to question, but the intent to adopt the innovation, even if only to let it fail, is clear.

TESTING THE MODEL

The primary purpose of this study is to examine the process of implementation. In the proposed model stages are causally related. There is also a causal relationship between the variables that relate to the process stages, but measuring the impact of these variables, or the extent of implementation, is secondary to the corroboration of the proposed model.

Case Study

The proposed model was tested using a specific innovation case, the use of computer technology by state legislatures in the 1980 reapportionment and redistricting process.

The case is significant. The reapportionment process consumes millions of public dollars and requires the efforts of thousands of elected officials and public employees. Reapportionment has been examined intensively to determine its impact on the public, but the process is little understood and ill defined. The reapportionment process may be carried out in essentially the same manner now as it was in 1789; yet technology to assist in the process is commonly available.

Studies of legislative decision making usually focus on legislative output: policy decisions (Shaffer & Weber, 1974; Matthews & Stimson, 1975; Weber & Uslander, 1977). These studies examine the adoption, by vote of the legislature, of policy mandates in various service areas. The focus of these studies is on the production of legislation and many times reflect a bottom-up process.

Studies dealing with the decisions of legislative leadership to make internal or organization changes are more top-down in nature and also consider implementation of the innovation. Such studies deal with the decisions of elected legislative leadership in restructuring the committee system in a legislature or the reform of the legislative process and staffing. In these studies decisions made by members of the legislature elected to leadership positions are carried out by members appointed to committee posts or by paid staff. These works identify organizational factors that influence implementation, such as type of organization, degree of decentralization in the legislature's operations, resource availability, and type of leadership.

State legislatures and the process of reapportionment are suitable as a test of an implementation model for a number of reasons. Since reapportionment takes place only once every decade, and legislatures have not maintained their capacities to reapportion during the intervening period, practices must be completely replaced.

All fifty states must redistrict themselves in a manner dictated by both law and custom and at approximately the same time. Congress is legally required to reapportion itself every ten years. The resulting redistricting by the states is primarily the responsibility of state legislatures. In forty-two states, the redistricting of congressional seats is under the control of the legislature. Of the remaining eight states, six have only one congressional seat and two are reapportioned by a special commission. At the same time, the reapportionment and redistricting of state legislatures is also required. It is, therefore, possible to observe all state legislatures as they perform the same task at the same time.

The elected leadership in each legislature has great latitude in the conduct of internal matters, and reapportionment and redistricting usually fall under the direct control of the leadership or a committee appointed by the leadership. While recently developed technology—computer hardware, software, and knowledge—to support the process is available to all states and the basic materials for reapportionment supplied by the U.S. Census Bureau are delivered on computer tape in a standardized format, the political requirements, history, resources, and abilities of the state legislative bodies vary greatly, and so the use of the new technology is an open question.

Implementation is examined by focusing on organizational factors as most significant in the implementation process. Three factors are identified and their impact analyzed: the legislature's "need" to use a new technology, its environment, and its history. A legislature's need is defined as the factors that cause its leadership to consider and adopt the use of a technological innovation: legal imperatives, perception of a performance gap, and political self-interest (Downs 1976; Rein & Rabinovitz, 1978). Environment reflects the social and economic characteristics that are postulated to facilitate generally or impede a legislature's ability to adopt or implement a new policy (Yin, 1977; Rogers, 1983). Organizational history indicates the degree to which a legislature has used other innovations (Walker, 1969; Feller et al., 1974) and will be likely to adopt and successfully implement a new technology (Danziger et al., 1982).

These factors are typically used to examine adoption as a part of implementation. In this study we expect the impact of these variables to behave differently in models with and without the acquisition step.

Methodology

The validation of the proposed model is based on a population census, a regression analysis, and the examination of selected cases.[3] The independent

Table 10.1
Variables by Stage

Stage Factor	Variable Name	Definition
Adoption	ADOPTION	Formal Decision
Need Legal	VRA	VRA Coverage
Need Technical	POP	State Population
Need Technical	DISTRICT	Number of Districts
Need Political	CONTROL	Degree of One-party Control
Environment Socioeco	WEALTH	Mean Income
Environment Socioeco	EDUCATION	Percentage of College Graduates
Environment History	FELLER	Feller's Technology Score
Environment History	WALKER	Walker's Innovativeness Score
Organization History	EV	Use of Electronic Voting
Organization History	1970	Use of Computers in 1970
Acquisition	ACQUIRE	Funding, Purchase or Delivery

variables representing the factors identified by the model are hypothesized to relate to the dependent variables representing adoption and acquisition and the specifics of this case (Table 10.1). Most of the independent variables have shown significant correlations with the dependent variables in other empirical studies. A logistic regression analysis designed to estimate the effects of independent variables on the dichotomous dependent variable showed no significant differences from the regression analysis results reported here.

Based on the proposed model, the fifty states are evaluated. Each state has three opportunities to use technology, for the two houses of the legislature and the congressional delegation, except Nebraska, which has a unicameral legislature. The result is 149 cases in the analysis.[4] Using regression analysis, the independent variables are examined to determine the effect of the factors they represent on adoption and acquisition. The model specifies a series of time-ordered linkages and relationships among the independent and dependent variables, making it possible to understand the link between adoption and implementation over time and to approximate the conditions of a controlled experiment.

There are ten independent variables expected to explain adoption, and they represent three factors: need, environment, and organizational characteristics. Need includes the legal imperative, as represented by Voting Rights Act (VRA) coverage, technical need as represented by population (POP), and technical complexity, represented by the number of seats to be redistricted (DISTRICT). Political need is represented by the calculated index of party dominance of the chamber (CONTROL). The nature of the environment is represented by the socioeconomic variables representing mean income (WEALTH) and proportion of college graduates (EDUCATION), and the historical measures of state program innovativeness (WALKER) and state technology usage (FELLER) (Walker, 1969; Feller et al., 1974). Organizational experience is represented by the use of electronic voting in the legislative chambers (EV) and the prior use of computers in redistricting (1970).

FINDINGS

According to the proposed model the relationship between adoption and acquisition should be strong, and the results of the analysis confirm this. According to the survey, thirty-four states reported having acquired a technical innovation, and of these twenty-nine (85 percent) had made a positive adoption decision. The legislatures in five states had made a positive decision to adopt new technology and had not acquired one (Alaska, Arkansas, Illinois, Ohio, and South Carolina), and five states had not indicated any intent to use a new technology, but had acquired it (Hawaii, Kansas, Mississippi, Montana, and Wisconsin).

The ten variables expected to explain adoption account for a statistically significant 31 percent of the variation in the dependent variable (Table 10.2). Individually, of the variables directly linked to adoption, population (POP), reflecting need, and use of technology in 1970 (1970), reflecting experience, have the largest BETA values and are statistically significant ($p < .01$). Two other variables have large BETA values and are significant at the $p < .05$ level, one-party control (CONTROL) and electronic voting (EV).

In terms of individual cases, 98 of the 149 actually acquired some new technology. Treating acquisition as a separate stage and analyzing these cases using a bivariate regression, adoption alone explains a significant 32 percent of the variation in acquisition ($RSQ = .324$, $df = 1/147$, $F = 70.67$, $p < .000$). Alternatively, acquisition is treated as the final stage of the adoption process in Table 10.3. Examining the variables that the model directly relates to adoption as if they were directly related to acquisition explains more than a third of the variance in acquisition (38 percent).

In this configuration adoption still has an impact on acquisition (BETA =

Table 10.2
Dependent Variable Adoption

N = 149

Regression Results

Variable	b	SE b	BETA	T	SIG T
1970	.240	.076	.245	3.144	.002
DISTRICT	-.0006	.0007	-.077	-.877	.382
CONTROL	.339	.151	.170	2.235	.027
VRA	-.152	.082	-.158	-1.861	.064
WEALTH	.00007	.00005	.139	1.332	.185
POP	.00003	.00001	.352	3.432	.000
FELLER	-.017	.028	-.056	-.606	.545
EV	.094	.042	.194	2.210	.028
WALKER	-.0004	.0005	-.078	-.781	.436
EDUCATION	.001	.019	-.007	.063	.950
Constant	.032	.332		.100	.920

Note: RSQ = .315, df = 10/138, F = 6.34, p .0000

.529), but the two major forces that contribute to adoption, population (POP) and 1970 experience (1970), become insignificant ($p > .05$), as do the other variables representing need and history. One of the environmental variables (EDUCATION) is significant, but this is the only support for variables in the environmental group. It may be that variables from the environmental group support the acquisition process, indicating the possibility that acquisition is still affected by the environment even after the decision to adopt is made. It is also possible that education may simply be correlated with acquisition through the interaction of other variables, such as WEALTH, with which it is highly correlated (.623).

Eliminating the adoption decision from the analysis restores the importance of the variables POP and 1970, and enhances the significance of the variables VRA and EDUCATION, but reduces the overall explanatory power of the regression greatly (RSQ = .192, df = 10/138, F = 3.28, $p < .0008$). It is apparent

Table 10.3
Dependent Variable Acquisition

N = 149

Regression Results

Variable	b	SE b	BETA	T	SIG T
ADOPTION	.526	.080	.529	6.530	.000
EDUCATION	.041	.018	.257	2.303	.022
DISTRICT	-.0003	.0007	-.043	-.518	.605
VRA	-.091	.078	-.095	-1.161	.247
CONTROL	.206	.146	.104	1.412	.160
1970	.036	.074	.037	.484	.629
POP	.000003	.00001	.035	.345	.731
EV	.023	.041	.049	.581	.562
FELLER	.039	.026	.128	1.463	.145
WALKER	-.0006	.0005	-.112	-1.165	.245
WEALTH	-.00006	.00005	-.123	-1.239	.217
Constant	-.027	.035		-.092	.927

Note: RSQ = .383, df = 11/137, F = 7.76, p 0.0

that treating the adoption decision itself as a separate stage adds to the predictive power of the model, as well as reflects the impact of variables representing need and experience in the acquisition of a new technology.

In the analysis of acquisition all cases were considered because the acquisition stage could be part of the adoption process, but in the case of implementation the proposed model requires that acquisition take place in order for implementation to begin, and in fact those states that did not acquire an innovation would have no data on innovation characteristics or performance data related to the implementation process. The result is that in a regression analysis with implementation as the dependent variable, acquisition would be eliminated because it is now a constant and those cases that did not successfully acquire new technology would be eliminated from the analysis. Given this finding, we know that any further implementation analysis should examine only the thirty-four states and ninety-eight separate chambers that actually acquired new technology.[5]

This makes it clear that acquisition is the stage that separates adoption from implementation, and should be analyzed as part of the adoption process. Acquisition is clearly dichotomous, and implementation cannot proceed without successful acquisition.

CONCLUSIONS

The growth of interest in implementation has produced works dealing with an ever-increasing range of topics. Implementation is the stated theoretical component of works in many different areas dealing with a variety of organizations, programs, and policies; yet some scholars have suggested that many of these works add little to our broader understanding of implementation beyond Hargrove's observation that implementation is often the "missing link" in the policymaking process (1975).

In this work a new implementation process model is created by the addition of the acquisition stage. Acquisition is the point at which a new technology is selected, funded, or purchased; and it is identified as the link between adoption and implementation. The result is an implementation process model appropriate for examining policies and programs relying on the introduction of a new technology. By examining this model we can draw conclusions both about modeling the implementation of technology and about the development of new implementation models.

Regarding the implementation of technology, it is clear that how adoption is defined, in regard to the inclusion or exclusion of acquisition, as a formal decision or as acquisition itself, will have a profound effect on the results of any analysis. Separating acquisition from implementation allows the separation of adoption and the processes that have been identified as part of adoption, such as agenda setting, the identification of solutions, and matching (the selection of an appropriate technology) from the implementation process. This is the condition that Pressman and Wildavsky require in order to separate the policymaking process, the identification and adoption of solutions, from the mechanics of implementation of the solution.

In regard to acquisition itself it is clear that acquisition seldom occurs without formal adoption and that successful implementation *never* takes place without successful acquisition. In this model, and clearly in the case of technology, the relationship between the three stages is sequential and unidirectional. Only when acquisition is complete are we sure that adoption is over, and only when acquisition is complete can we be sure that implementation has begun. Acquisition is empirically distinct from implementation and when included as a separate stage, forces elimination of nonimplementors from the analysis. Some studies that have included acquisition with implementation have produced distortions in the analysis of implementation. Such models, which ignore acquisition or that include acquisition in implementation, result in adoption factors being included in the analysis of implementation.

In the design of implementation studies dealing with technology we must account for the fact that all implementors are acquirers and all acquirers are implementors, but that all implementors are not adopters and all adopters are not implementors. This applies in all cases involving technology regardless of the setting. The implementation of a computer system in welfare case management or banking is equally dependent on the acquisition of the technology. Acquisition cannot guarantee successful implementation, but failure to acquire a technology guarantees that the innovation will not be implemented.

The broader implication of this work is the need for implementation models tailored to deal with specific policy innovations and organizations. In the case presented here there is strong control over implementation by the adopter of a policy, as identified in formal-legal and professional situations (Burke, 1987). This is more likely to occur in the physical services sectors of government than in the social services sectors. Policy innovations in the areas of environmental control, transportation, and communications are more likely to include analytical methods and practices and to be implemented as a result of formal direction by an external agent exercising legal control. In the areas of education and welfare services, policies are less likely to involve artifacts, and implementation is often guided by the discretion of street-level bureaucrats. Such differences require that the design of studies of policy innovations in social services organizations be based on process models appropriate to these innovations and organizations. The broader use of the acquisition model for implementation studies depends on the degree to which these organizations employ a top-down framework similar to that in the reapportionment case and the extent to which acquisition can be applied to nontechnological innovations.

NOTES

1. Policy innovations related to technologies are decisions to use a technical innovation to carry out a policy. There are three basic types of innovations: technical, policy, and program (Eveland et al., 1977). Technical innovations are identified as including: artifacts, materials, computer systems, or analytical methods and practices (Yin et al., 1977), or any tool or technique, equipment or method, by which an organization's work is done (Tornatzky et al., 1983). Purely policy innovations do not affect tools or procedures to do work (Tornatzky et al., 1983).

2. There are five stages in the process, but the invention and innovation stages have been eliminated, since state governments are not commonly the originators of new technologies.

3. Data describing the variables in the model represent three points in time. Organization and environmental data are prereapportionment. Adoption information was collected from a 1981 survey, and acquisition and implementation data were collected by a postredistricting survey.

4. While the six states with only one congressional seat are not required to redistrict, they have been left in the analysis to represent cases with no need to adopt the use of technology.

5. The states of Nebraska, Delaware, North Dakota, and Vermont produce only two cases each because Nebraska has a unicameral legislature and the other states have only one congressional seat.

_____ PART III

Epistemology, Methodology, and Implementation

11

Studying Micro-Implementation Empirically: Lessons and Dilemmas

Mary Ann Scheirer and James Griffith

Implementation as a topic for social science research has expanded in many directions over the past two decades. As the papers in this volume testify, the research threads concerning implementation have become interwoven into a complex tapestry of issues, designs, methodologies, and recommendations to program and policy managers.

One major distinction that helps clarify the issues facing implementation researchers is the difference between macro- and micro-implementation. As elucidated by Berman (1978), macro-implementation refers to the processes by which the federal government (or another large, umbrella organization) executes policy in order to influence local delivery organizations in desired ways. Studies of these processes usually focus on the linkages and interchanges among layers of organizations in loosely coupled systems. In contrast, micro-implementation refers to the change processes within local organizations after they adopt a program or innovation. Micro-implementation studies typically examine the changes in individual behaviors or organizational processes that are necessary to put a program into operation. Studies using these two approaches have proceeded almost independently of each other in developing research paradigms for implementation analysis.

One way to bridge the theoretical gap between macro- and micro-implementation is to view the study of micro-implementation processes as the "building blocks" for a better understanding of macro-implementation. This

This paper draws upon data collected under grant #DE–06895 from the National Institute of Dental Research. This article was written by Mary Ann Scheirer in her private capacity, before her employment by the National Institutes of Health. No official support or endorsement by the National Institutes of Health is intended or should be inferred.

implies that measurements must be taken at the micro level of specific user organizations, in order for the success of macro-implementation processes to be understood. It also means that studies at the micro level should be informed by the issues identified at the macro level, particularly the interlinked nature of organizations, and the strong influences of larger-scale political and regulatory processes on the actions of individuals within organizations. There is a need for greater interchange between the two perspectives, which raises issues of the congruence of their methodological assumptions.

This chapter identifies and discusses some conceptual and methodological problems incurred in attempting to do such research. We use material from an extensive study of the dissemination and implementation processes for one health promotion program, the fluoride mouth-rinse program in public elementary school classrooms, to illustrate the dilemmas involved. This study used data collected by survey methods to examine both adoption and implementation processes for a simple innovation with known effectiveness in decreasing the incidence of dental cavities among school-age children. A discussion of some methodological problems encountered in this research can usefully illuminate several issues that prevented us from drawing firm conclusions. These issues appear to require solutions before the field of implementation research will advance further toward accumulating an empirical base for reliable policy recommendations.

A central issue underlying our work is whether it is possible to develop and test generalizable, empirical models of implementation success. Further, can such models facilitate stronger interchange between the macro and micro perspectives? Is implementation assessment a topic that is amenable to fulfilling the standards for social science research, particularly the generation of potentially falsifiable propositions that accumulate into a body of knowledge about the phenomenon? Or is it destined to remain a managerial art, with descriptive studies to provide examples of good or poor practice under past circumstances, but no generalizable principles to provide reliable guidance for future action? In short, is program implementation a researchable social *science* problem?

EMPIRICAL STUDY OF THE FLUORIDE MOUTH-RINSE PROGRAM

The research project that provides the background for this paper was undertaken to examine the dissemination into public schools of the fluoride mouth-rinse program (FMRP). The term "dissemination" refers to the following processes that underlie the actual classroom use of the FMRP:

- The initial diffusion of information about the program among potential users (school districts);
- The processes leading to an adoption decision;

- The extent to which the program is fully and accurately implemented after it is adopted, and the individual and organizational processes relating to better versus poorer implementation; and

- The processes resulting in discontinuation among some user districts.

The FMRP study thus encompassed both macro- and micro-implementation perspectives, since it examined the means by which the fluoride mouth-rinse program entered the schools, as well as the operational aspects of classroom delivery.

The FMRP

The program that was studied, the fluoride mouth-rinse program in public elementary schools, is procedurally a simple innovation. As a dental caries preventive regimen, it requires school children to rinse with a 0.2% solution of sodium fluoride, within their classrooms, once a week throughout the school year. By distributing premeasured individual doses of the fluoride solution in paper cups to the children, the school staff can accomplish the program in less than fifteen minutes per week.

This program resulted from activities of the federal government's National Institute of Dental Research (NIDR) to develop and disseminate innovations that reduce the incidence of cavities. The safety and efficacy of the fluoride mouth-rinse procedures were established by well-controlled studies prior to 1973 (Horowitz, 1973; Silversin, Coombs, & Drolette, 1980a). If properly implemented, the FMRP significantly reduces the incidence of cavities, even in communities with fluoridated water. Its use has been widely endorsed by dental authorities, including the National Institute for Dental Research, the American Dental Association, and the Food and Drug Administration (see American Dental Association, 1975).

Since the efficacy of the FMRP was well established, the research reported here did not attempt to measure the extent of cavity prevention by the FMRP. Instead, its focus was on implementation processes, which must be widespread and positive in order for the FMRP to have significant impact as a public health measure. This program was particularly suitable for study of the processes surrounding implementation, since its effectiveness, if used, was well established and it is a very simple program, both to execute and to measure. Neither complicated program requirements nor unknown ultimate effects would interfere with the research focus on the processes of dissemination and implementation.

Methods

Data were collected by telephone interviews with several samples of informants across the continental United States. The sample construction and parts of the instrument design for the major survey were derived from a 1979 study by Silversin and Coombs (Silversin, Coombs, & Drolette, 1980b). The more extensive survey for this project was done in 1985 by telephone interviews with key informants from 784 public districts across the country, who were chosen to represent both "adopters" and "nonadopters" of the FMRP, and whose distribution is similar to a cross section of the nation's school districts. The interview developed considerable depth concerning the districts' involvement with the FMRP, particularly about processes concerning adoption and continued use or abandonment. In 343 districts offering the FMRP in 1985, a further telephone interview was conducted with an informant, usually the school principal, from one participating elementary school in the district, to collect data about the extent of use and processes surrounding micro-level implementation of the FMRP. This chapter primarily discusses data from this local-level principal's interview.

A second set of telephone interviews was conducted in 1986 with state governments' dental health offices in forty six states. This interview data with the state dental director and/or others on this staff was combined with other data about each state from archival sources. Its analysis provided extensive information about the roles of these state offices as dissemination linking agents between the federal government and the local school districts.

The telephone interviews were performed by the professional interviewing staff of Westat, Inc.'s Telephone Research Center. The interviewers were trained extensively to understand the meaning of each question, in order to probe respondents' answers appropriately. Since the respondents were serving as informants for organizational activities which occurred over a substantial period of time, they were also encouraged to consult with others in their settings to determine the best answers to key items. A further discussion of dilemmas arising from this data collection methodology is presented below.

Data analysis in this nonexperimental situation relied primarily on multivariate statistics to build causal models of the implementation processes occurring. Extensive descriptive analyses examined the nature of the activities surrounding the implementation of this school-based program, including inspection of univariate distributions and bivariate relationships. In addition, a number of data reduction activities were undertaken, including factor analyses and scale construction. Using multiple regression, we then examined a large number of relationships among variables suggested by the prior literature on the diffusion of innovations (cf. Rogers, 1983), and on the organizational processes surrounding micro-implementation (cf. Scheirer, 1981), to determine the predictive utility of each type of variable.

SOME LESSONS LEARNED

In this section, we describe data collected concerning the implementation of the FMRP. We focus particularly on several implementation issues for which substantive findings were possible. We also describe attempted analyses that were not so successful. The following sections then discuss methodological problems that remained unsolved.

Measuring the Variability in Micro-Implementation

The problem of defining and measuring "successful" implementation is a key element in this research area, which was raised by several of the authors in the *Policy Studies Review* (PSR) symposium. For example, Palumbo (1987) discussed the frequent lack of analytic distinction between implementation problems and program design failure as one major critique of implementation research. Linder and Peters (1987b) repeat this theme in noting that variations in the researcher's definition of "success" may change the meaning and feasibility of implementation. In short, program implementation success should be distinguished from program or policy effectiveness, and from organizational "effectiveness" in a global sense.

Measurement difficulty in macro-implementation research occurs frequently when the policies being studied have not been developed specifically enough to define their content. If one or more specific programs to operationalize the policy intentions have not been developed, then study of implementation is likely to be premature and unfruitful. Instead of implementation analysis, the situation may be better suited to program development activity, with accompanying formative evaluation.

Our approach to the measurement problem was to operationalize measures for the degree of implementation as a set of program elements or components. This approach was derived from Hall and Loucks's (1978) work on the configuration of innovations, which has also been used successfully in other dissemination studies (Blakely et al., 1984). The program being disseminated, the FMRP, had been carefully developed and tested prior to its attempted full implementation. Therefore, information was available to define what should be done for effective results in the field.

The National Institute of Dental Research, which had sponsored most development and testing for the program, promulgated four essential components for accurate implementation of the FMRP. These components are the following: (1) a weekly rinsing of children's teeth with a 0.2 percent solution of sodium fluoride (NaF); (2) the rinsing should extend throughout the school year; (3) retaining the fluoride solution in the mouth for sixty seconds; and (4) refraining from drinking and eating for at least thirty minutes after the mouth rinsing (Horowitz, 1981).

To measure the accuracy of implementing these program components, the school-based respondents were asked four open-ended questions: (1) Can you tell me how many weeks the children are rinsing this school year? (2) Do you know how often the children rinse? (3) Can you tell me approximately how many seconds the children rinse each time? and (4) Does your school have a

Table 11.1
Descriptive Statistics on Execution of the Four FMRP Program Components

| Program Component | Number Schools Executed: | | | | | | M | Mdn | SD | Range |
| | Properly | | Improperly | | Missing | | | | | |
	N	%	N	%	N	%				
1. Can you tell me how many weeks the children are rinsing this year? (At least 28 weeks in a year)	286	83.4	38	11.1	19	5.5	31.83	34.00	6.66	1-52
2. Do you know how often the children rinse? (At least once a week)	322	93.9	10	2.9	11	3.2	N/A	N/A	N/A	N/A
3. Can you tell me approximately how many seconds the children rinse each time? (At least 60 seconds)	259	75.5	51	14.9	33	9.6	54.16	60.00	15.81	2-120
4. Does your school have a guideline on how long after doing the mouthrinse the children may get a drink or eat something? (At least 30 minutes)	206	60.0	107	31.2	30	8.7	N/A	N/A	"Immediately" to "more than two hours"	

TOTAL N = 343

guideline on how long after doing the mouth rinse the children may get a drink or eat something? If yes, what is that guideline?

A summative scale was developed to assess the school's accuracy of implementation of the FMRP. To accomplish this, responses to open-ended questions were coded as dichotomous variables, indicating whether the school had met or exceeded the NIDR FMRP implementation standard (values of "1") or did not (values of "O"). "Don't Knows" and missing variables values on each of the four questions were treated as "O's," incorrect implementation, in order to avoid having many cases with missing data. Table 11.1 reports descriptive statistics for the four implementation components, to illustrate the properties of this type of data.

Even among these schools whose principals stated they were using the program, the percentage of schools that reported correct implementation varied. Having children rinse at least once a week during the school year was the most frequently reported component, in 94 percent of the user schools. The next most prevalent program standard was having children rinse at least twenty eight weeks out of the school year (83 percent), then having children rinse the full sixty seconds followed close behind, at seventy six. The least likely of the four implementation components to be properly executed was having specific guidance

Table 11.2
Descriptive Statistics on the Summative Scale Indicating the Number of the
FMRP Program Components Properly Executed

	M	Mdn	SD	Range
Summative Program Implementation Scale	3.13	3.00	1.02	0-4

	Number/Percent of Schools	
Number of FMRP Program Criteria Properly Executed	**No.**	**%**
None	8	2.3
One	17	5.0
Two	58	16.9
Three	100	29.0
Four	160	46.6

for children about eating or drinking after the fluoride rinse; about sixty percent of these schools reported the proper guidance.

To assess the overall accuracy of implementation, the number of components done correctly was summed across these four implementation variables. Table 11.2 reports descriptive statistics for the summative accuracy of implementation scale. Almost one-half of all schools reported executing all four implementation standards, and three-fourths fulfilled three of the four program steps. Yet, eight schools failed to execute *any* of the four program components, even though they were reported to be "using" the FMRP. Thus, accuracy of implementation varied considerably among these "adopter" schools: 24 percent of them reported proper implementation on only two or fewer of the four components.

A second scale was constructed to assess the extent of the target population reached. It is possible for a program to be carried out with great accuracy for a few participants, but not reach a large proportion of the intended target population. An example is a school that carefully executes the components of the FMRP in only one of its many classrooms, or in many classrooms but with only a few children participating in each class. A measure was then needed to assess the extent to which children actually participate in the FMRP. Responses to two variables were used. One question asked principals to report the percent of children who participated in the program in those classrooms offering the FMRP. Since parental permission slips had to be obtained before children could partic-

Table 11.3

Descriptive Statistics on the Percent of the Target Population Reached, and on the Component Parts of the Reached Measure

Component Parts	M	Mdn	SD	Range
Estimated Percent of Children Who Participate in Those Classrooms Offering the FMRP	88.5	95.0	13.7	1.0-100.0
Percent of Classrooms Rinsing in Adopting Schools	91.5	100.0	20.3	7.1-100.0
Percent of Target Population Reached	80.8	90.0	21.5	3.6-100.0

ipate, this figure should have been known to the respondents. Descriptive statistics to illustrate the method are presented in Table 11.3.

The second variable was the percent of classrooms in the school offering the FMRP, among the primary target population, namely kindergarten through sixth grade. Of the 343 adopter schools 254 (74.1 percent) indicated that all classrooms were participating in the FMRP. The range of the percentage of participating classes indicated that a small number of schools, however, had very few classrooms rinsing.

To estimate the total percentage of children reached, the percentage of children participating was multiplied by the percentage of participating classrooms. The results presented at the bottom of Table 11.3 showed that the bulk of the schools that had adopted the FMRP were quite successful in having most students participate in the program. Schools that had adopted the FMRP and yet had very few students participating were relatively infrequent. Only 38 (11.1 percent) of the 343 schools reported 50 percent or less of the target population reached. But again, there is substantial variability in the percentage of children reached *within* these adopting schools, indicating that the extent or scope of implementation is another key aspect in measuring the variability in degrees of implementation.

These two concepts, then, the accuracy of implementation and the extent of implementation, are both needed to measure the success of implementation at the local level, that is, to assess the amount of micro-implementation occurring. The data presented above illustrate that such measurement is possible, and that the results are likely to reveal substantial variability in measures of implementation success. For specific measures to be constructed, the researcher must be able to define the intended components and targeted participants a priori.

Further, these two criterion measures were not substantially related to each other: the correlation of the two overall scales was only .07. Three one-way analyses of variance also confirmed the absence of nonlinear relationships between the groups of schools according to their accuracy of implementation and the three variables measuring extent of the target population reached: the percent of children participating within classrooms, the percent of classrooms offering the program, and the overall total percent of children reached. These findings support the conclusion that how well a program is executed and the extent to which the target population is reached are separate aspects of the degree of micro-implementation.

Implementation Process Analysis

A major purpose of this research was to relate the variability in these measures of FMRP micro-implementation to variables drawn from the conceptual theories about micro-implementation, such as the structural characteristics of the schools, bureaucratic differences in the ways they administered or funded the program, and differences in the "political" processes that preceded the initial adoption decision. Previous literature concerning the adoption and implementation of innovations (e.g., Rogers, 1983; Greer, 1977; Scheirer, 1981; Tornatzky et al., 1983) was used to suggest the range and types of variables that have been hypothesized to relate to stronger implementation results.

It was hoped that the empirical results from this large sample of schools would help to sort out the most influential processes from among this large pool of variables. Such results, along with replications from studies of other innovations, could begin to accumulate into a body of empirically based knowledge concerning micro-implementation, drawn from generalizable samples of relevant organizations. In time, such knowledge should provide a more reliable basis for guidance to program administrators concerning management actions needed to strengthen micro-level implementation. Further, it would provide empirically based building blocks for macro-implementation study and policy guidance by indicating what local-level processes should be stimulated by the higher-level policy levers.

A large number of concepts about factors expected to lead to better implementation were extracted from the previous literature and included as items in the telephone surveys. In order to indicate the range of these variables, they are summarized as follows:

- Type of school—size; urban, suburban, or rural location; and the percentage of low-income students. Larger schools, especially those in the suburbs, might have more "slack resources" or more prior experience in implementing innovations. Schools with more low-income students might perceive a greater need for the program, and therefore push to reach a larger proportion of their students.
- Principal's characteristics—length of administrative experience; graduate education (versus undergraduate only); education related to health programs; and attitudes favoring the use of the FMRP in a school setting. Since the principal is a key supervisor in the school, all these characteristics were expected to support higher levels of implementation: more "cosmopolitan" principals should foster better implementation.

- Initial training provided for the FMRP—the availability and extensiveness of initial training; training provided directly to classroom teachers; training provided by those most expert in the program content (i.e., school and public health officials); and training focused on topics related to classroom administration. More extensive training, with more "on target" topics and sources, should relate to better implementation.

- Inservice or continuing training for the FMRP—the frequency of "refresher" training, its extent, and its focus on topics relevant to classroom administration. All these aspects of inservice training ought to promote better implementation.

- Administrative arrangements for managing the program—the continuing involvement of outside experts (state and local health officials); active interest of the school principal (who is the major enforcer of school system priorities); the extent to which the delivery tasks are a part of routine job responsibilities; the extent to which any delivery problems are identified and solved; and FMRP administration as an expected part of the school's routine each year. These administrative indicators ought to indicate more organizational support and more incentives for accurate classroom delivery.

- Financial support for the program—funding sources viewed as stable (regular school budget or state funds) rather than "ad hoc" (private donations or federal "seed money") ought to convince teachers that their efforts toward full implementation are worthwhile.

- Teachers' peer-group involvement in the FMRP—the extent to which teachers commented about the program and whether these comments tended to be positive, neutral, or negative. These indicators of group norms about FMRP among the teachers in a school might be powerful incentives toward full versus weak implementation.

Overall, more than eighty variables, some with several variations, were examined for their relationships with the two measures of the degree of implementation—accuracy and extent of children reached. While this methodology had the potential disadvantage of taking advantage of chance relationships, it had the advantage of comparing within one study the predictive effectiveness of concepts derived from a number of theoretical perspectives.

Unfortunately, the results of the exploratory multiple regression analyses, undertaken with several variable grouping and data reduction methods, did not come together to yield coherent, interpretable results. The final regression equation for assessing variables relating to the accuracy of implementation included only six variables with a statistical significance less than .05, only one of which had a probability value of less than .01. Several of the variables that remained in this equation referred to administrative arrangements that were quite rare among this sample of districts; these apparent relationships may well stem from just a few "outlier" cases. Further, the overall R^2 for this equation was just .11, indicating a very low proportion of variability accounted for in accuracy of implementation by the many variables included in the various stages of analyses.

The multivariate analysis results for the extent of target population reached were no more definitive. Only four variables with a statistical significance of less than .10 remained in the final equation, only two of them with a probability value of less than .01. The only strong relationship shown in this analysis was for a variable indicating the respondent's perception of the strength of parental support for the program. While this was in the expected direction, it might be viewed as nearly a surrogate measure for one component of this dependent variable, the percentage of children participating, since parental permission was necessary to allow participation. The R^2 for this equation, .14, is again unimpressive, especially given the extensive exploratory analyses conducted.

Thus, the multivariate analyses attempted did not prove fruitful in illuminating implementation processes empirically or in helping to select among the many competing concepts and variables being promulgated as explanations for differential degrees of implementation success, However, the disappointing results have prompted us to pursue some further thoughts concerning the nature of implementation research. Particularly puzzling is the issue of whether better procedures would somehow solve the problems we encountered, versus the possibility that these problems are endemic to empirical research on this topic.

IMPLICATIONS FOR FUTURE METHODOLOGY

The scarcity of confirmed relationships concerning implementation processes in the research just described raises a number of issues about the underlying methodology. Much of the influential writing on implementation topics has been based on case studies or descriptive analyses of the implementation of a particular policy change. On the other hand, perhaps studies that have attempted larger-scale empirical analyses have had difficulties similar to ours and therefore have not been publishable. A discussion of the methodological problems encountered should assist in creating a dialog about these concerns. This section addresses three types of issues raised by our research: problems with the conceptual framework, measurement issues, and dilemmas concerning statistical analysis techniques.

Conceptual Frameworks for Implementation Research

In this research, a social systems framework was employed to trace the effects of some initial environmental conditions, the processes used to implement the fluoride mouth-rinse program (particularly the potential influence of several aspects of training), and the ongoing administrative processes affecting its delivery. This approach was sufficiently broad to include a wide variety of variables that we believed ought to predict better implementation. For example, simply on the basis of logic, schools that had received initial training and continued inservice training should implement the program more accurately than schools that provided no training at all. While we would not expect that training alone would be sufficient to secure full implementation, we did expect it to show positive effects. The broad inclusion of variables also enabled us to examine the empirical influence of factors suggested by a number of theoretical approaches.

If we erred conceptually, it would seem to be on the side of attempting to include too many potential predictor variables in the overall research design, rather than too few. During analysis, however, we examined these concepts within manageable groups to be alert for their potential interrelations that might cancel out overall effects. Further, extensive bivariate analyses were conducted between the predictor variables and the two outcome indicators, to inspect the data for individual and nonlinear relationships. Therefore, it does not seem likely that the failure to uncover stronger empirical relationships with implementation outcomes was due to an inadequate scope of theory per se. None of the theoretical strands was empirically supported.

The multiplicity of mini-theories as partial explanations for implementation success has resulted in considerable conceptual confusion in this field. We had hoped that the results from this research would help to develop more parsimonious models of the major processes affecting micro-implementation outcomes. Certainly some means are badly needed to help researchers choose among the many ideas now blooming in the field of implementation research. Yet if large-scale empirical studies do not help in this endeavor, what alternative means are available for this theory winnowing task?

Measurement Issues

A number of measurement problems are endemic to large-scale organizational research, which may help to explain the lack of strong results. One such problem is that organizational informants undoubtedly want to show their organizations in the "best light." This social desirability effect suggests that the respondents might not necessarily report the actual state of affairs, but rather give the most socially acceptable response. In this study, this tendency probably applied more to the implementation outcome measures, namely the accuracy and extent of FMRP implementation, because these questions are clearly more "evaluative," than to the more objective aspects of the training, demographic characteristics of the school, and the initial setup of the FMRP. Open-ended items were deliberately used to discourage "guessing" the correct answer from prestructured alternatives. Nevertheless, the data for the program components may reflect the respondents' ideas about what was *supposed* to happen, rather than what *actually* happened concerning the FMRP in their school.

Further, retrospective reporting of events and processes that occur over a number of years is likely to result in lowered reliability in the data, with a consequent lower likelihood of detecting associations that do exist among variables. However, implementation processes typically take place over several years, which would require quite lengthy and expensive research for data collection to be carried out concurrently with the relevant events. Multiple informants per organization may be needed to obtain accurate data about the complexities of organizational processes occurring simultaneously, but multiple informants may also have conflicting perceptions of key processes, as well as adding considerably to the expense of data collection.

In sum, a number of measurement problems for this complex topic area may prevent uncovering real patterns of relationships that do exist between measures of implementation accuracy and extent, and the social systems within the target organizations. The problems of obtaining accurate and reliable data seem particularly intractable when studying implementation issues. In order to draw statistically significant, generalizable conclusions concerning the processes leading to full implementation, a large sample of implementing organizations is needed. However, if those organizations have adopted and implemented a program using naturally occurring processes (rather than under the artificial stimulus of a research project), the implementation processes are likely to occur over a wide span of time, both within and across organizations. Therefore, it is difficult for an outside investigator to obtain accurate data concerning what occurred, from a large enough sample of organizations without encountering recall and informant biases of various kinds. Further, who should be chosen as organizational informants and how many participant views are needed from each organization to obtain concurrence about organizational events is another thorny issue. The alternative of frequent, on-site data collection while implementation goes on is attractive but extremely expensive and likely to incur problems caused by the investigators' presence.

Statistical Analysis Dilemmas

This project intended to construct one or more empirically supported causal model of implementation processes, using statistical tools to aid in distinguishing among the many predictor variables that had been suggested by the previous literature. Multiple regression techniques were used to test the independent contribution of each type of predictor variable, while controlling for the effects of other parts of the social system that were also expected to affect the outcome criteria in this nonexperimental situation. Other data reduction methods, such as factor analysis, were also employed. Cluster analysis was also used to search for identifiable clusters of schools that had different implementation patterns. None of these statistical tools yielded interpretable patterns in the empirical data.

However, the use of multiple regression as the major statistical tool might not be appropriate for addressing implementation issues. The use of this technique carries with it the assumption that the processes affecting implementation are generally the same in most implementing organizations. If different organizations use different processes to achieve the same end—successful implementation— then the coefficients for estimating the effects of these processes would not be expected to be strong. For example, suppose some schools placed heavy emphasis on the structural arrangements for delivering the FMRP (e.g., assigned each part of the program as the responsibility of a specific staff member), while other schools emphasized training all staff members as the means to obtain their participation, while still others provided minimal formal training but included frequent monitoring by the principal or a public health staff person. The strength of the regression coefficients for each of these implementation processes would be greatly diluted by the fact that other schools did not use that particular process but still achieved high implementation.

In short, for implementing programs or policies at the local level, there may be many paths to success as well as many ways to fail. The linear, additive model assumed by the use of multiple regression is likely to be a poor statistical fit if this is the case.

A second problem with this type of statistical analysis is its fit with the longitudinal nature of implementation processes. The "snapshot" view of complex organizational processes obtained from data collected at a single point in time is likely to be inadequate for assessing which processes contribute most to different phases of implementation. Mohr (1978) discusses this dilemma as a contrast between "variance theory" and "process theory," and implies that processes cannot or should not be analyzed with statistical methods. Conceivably, the problem might be solved by frequent data collection from a reasonably large sample of organizations, followed by analysis using statistical techniques for panel data. This approach could capture the variance occurring in the processes of the organization, for analysis in relation to implementation achieved at a particular point in time, but would be quite expensive to carry out.

An alternative possibility is that quantitative models of implementation processes are not feasible, even hypothetically, because each organization may be unique in the manner in which its ongoing processes and characteristics fit the nature of the innovation and the implementation processes attempted for a particular innovation. An analogy that illustrates this situation is that of a lock and key, in which each part should match the configuration of the other in order for the lock and key to work together. In the case of implementation, a checklist of potential implementation variables can be developed (see Roberts-Gray & Scheirer, 1988), but it would not be possible to winnow down the list by conventional data analysis. The nature of the "fit" will differ between organizations, among the characteristics of the target program or policy, the organizational structures during the period of implementation, and the implementation strategies used in each organization.

In summary, then, there are several ways in which the linear, additive assumptions underlying the use of multiple regression may preclude its applicability: (1) The effects of the multiple variables suggested by existing theories may not be additive in their influences. Instead, they could be multiplicative, in which case a low value on any key variable would cancel out the positive effects of other variables in contributing to successful implementation. Or, the numerous potential influences on implementation may have very complex interaction patterns that are not yet predicted by current theory. Adding interaction terms or nonlinear effect estimation is certainly possible, but again adds considerable complexity unless appropriate interactions can be predicted in advance. (2) The fact that different variables affect the various stages of implementation processes differently may require the use of longitudinal data. (3) The notion of a unique configuration of fit between the organization, the innovation, and the imple-

menting processes used may preclude the development of generalized implementation models.

The foregoing discussion has suggested a number of methodological problems
that remain to be solved in implementation research. Our experience has suggested that undertaking research on this topic that is generalizable to new situations is a formidable task. It is particularly likely to require larger-scale research
projects funded over longer periods of time than has typically been available for
this line of study. Alternately, it would require close coordination among individual researchers studying implementation in diverse policy and program areas
in order to apply the same theoretical, measurement, and analysis concepts, thus
permitting comparison of results across projects. Yet it is unlikely that the field
will move beyond the stage of case study explorations and theory generation
without greater emphasis on empirical data to validate conclusions across the
numerous specific policy areas in which implementation occurs.

RELATIONSHIPS BETWEEN MICRO-IMPLEMENTATION
AND MACRO-IMPLEMENTATION

In spite of the methodological problems encountered, this research suggested
useful implications concerning the relationships between local delivery processes
and larger-scale policy and innovation dissemination. In other parts of the project,
we examined variables related to the decision to adopt the program by local
school districts (Scheirer, 1988) and the processes used by state government
dental health offices to promote the fluoride mouth-rinse program (Monahan &
Scheirer, 1988). Both analyses of dissemination (a macro-level implementation
process) provided fairly strong support for the importance of in-person contacts
for obtaining local-level adoption decisions. Even with strong empirical evidence
supporting the effectiveness of this program, written materials and scientific
evidence alone seemed insufficient to mobilize the local decision processes.

The decision processes for this program did respond to a ''top-down'' dissemination path, but the interpersonal linking agents supplied by state-level personnel
were a key to the dissemination process. The path of macro- to micro-implementation for this program involved at least the following links: federal government-
supported research and program validation; materials and information development by the federal staff for stimulating state-level activity; state and local health
officials promoting local-level adoption; a major involvement of school nurses as
the primary program champions inside the districts; and school nurses as trainers
and managers for local level delivery by classroom teachers at the elementary
level. The micro-level processes of adoption and implementation at the school
district level occurred only rarely in states where state government was not promoting the program (Monahan & Scheirer, 1988).

The role of evidence for program effectiveness as a reinforcer for implementation efforts becomes problematic in programs such as the FMRP that are
intended to prevent a long-term health problem. It is not feasible for each local

implementing agency to collect data documenting the effectiveness of the program, nor for the deliverers to see for themselves that the program makes a difference in the lives of the children who are its beneficiaries, for the cavities prevented would normally occur some years later. The local schools apparently recognized this, for few schools emphasized training for recordkeeping or other long-term means to document its effectiveness for themselves. Perhaps this was why the interpersonal role of the state and local health officials was so important: when the effects of the treatment was not immediately visible to the program implementors, they needed the credibility of knowledgeable health staff to support and reinforce their activities.

The potential usefulness of better knowledge about implementation processes is well supported by our research. Many different people at different levels of government, and with different formal job roles, were involved with a relatively simple program such as the FMRP. These findings reinforce the great need for clearer articulation of who should do what in this long-term process. Even if one were able to specify more clearly the types of factors leading to more accurate and more extensive implementation, these findings would still need to be translated into specifications for job roles of various kinds, in order for the research findings to influence practice.

CONCLUSIONS

In spite of the greatly increased volume of policy implementation research over the past two decades, its methodology still lacks a central paradigm that addresses the major problems. Investigators have separated the study of macro-implementation from micro-implementation, to the detriment of both parts of the overall process. Authors typically note the existence of an implementation "gap" between the formal objectives of a policy and its eventual outcomes in the field. Some analysts call for a more rational approach to planning for implementation, while others propose the applicability of a "garbage can" decision model. A third approach would be to trace the chain of activities that are set in motion by a policy promulgation or program availability, without necessarily comparing these activities against an a priori standard provided by a set of objectives. With this approach, measuring the detailed program components within micro-implementation provides the building blocks for further analysis.

This paper details an example showing how the accuracy and extent of implementation can readily be measured, if the components of the policy or program are specified and tested prior to widespread implementation. If the components have not been clearly articulated and tested for efficacy, at least on a small scale, perhaps it is premature for large-scale implementation to be attempted. Measures of the accuracy and extent of program implementation then become the outcome (or dependent) variables for analyses of implementation processes. Use of this paradigm will permit testing of the competing concepts of implementation, such as those suggested by Yanow (1987) or the procedural instruments suggested by Elmore (1987a).

Nevertheless, our work has raised a number of methodological issues requiring solution before further progress is likely. These involve specifying and operationalizing conceptual frameworks into researchable terms; collecting data from multiple organizational informants about the change processes as they occur, rather than retrospectively; and statistical analysis methods which do not assume linear, additive models, nor the same implementation process in all organizations. The question remains whether implementation research will become generalizable to new organizations, in order to predict with some accuracy what strategies will facilitate accurate implementation in each organization.

Researching the problem of implementation remains an unfulfilled promise. Certainly, better measurement tools are greatly needed to foster both clearer thinking and more accurate estimation of existing relationships. This chapter has suggested some guidance in this direction. Yet, in the absence of a methodological breakthrough or sudden conceptual synthesis, the field is likely to continue as more promise than empirically based prescription.

12

Studying the Dynamics of Public Policy Implementation: A Third-Generation Approach

Malcolm L. Goggin, Ann O' M. Bowman, James P. Lester, and Laurence J. O'Toole, Jr.

Nearly every academic treatment of public policy emphasizes the dynamic nature of the processes by which governmental issues are placed on the policy agenda, mandates are formulated and issued, policies are interpreted and made operative through an implementation structure, and policies are redesigned to fit more comfortably with their environments (Goggin, 1988). The centrality of dynamism in public policy is a well-developed organizing theme in the research literature of this field (e.g., Bardach, 1977; Kirst & Jung, 1982; May & Wildavsky, 1978; Pressman & Wildavsky, 1984; Ripley & Franklin, 1986; Goggin, 1987). Indeed, theoretical and empirical approaches to implementation—upon which this chapter focuses—invariably conceptualize the model's dependent variables as dynamic or evolutionary, that is, as changing over time and across space (Lester et al., 1987).

In some types of policy processes, notably those that encourage or require actions at multiple levels of government and/or incorporate substantial interlocal dynamics, the importance of dynamism—and the complexity it often generates— is magnified. Analysts are increasingly recognizing how frequently such cases actually occur. Both the interpretive or "adaptive" framework, which several investigators have used to analyze interorganizational behavior during implementation (Fox, 1987), and the "bottom-up" approach to studying implementation (Hjern & Hull, 1982; Hjern, 1982; Sabatier, 1986) document the importance of dynamism and diversity in such settings. Both approaches have contributed significantly to our understanding of the dynamics of implementation; but, as is discussed in some detail in the following section, as an analytical framework both have limitations, especially when it comes to either explaining or predicting implementation behavior.

Systematically studying the dynamics of implementation is a particularly difficult task. Until recently, most implementation research relied heavily on the
case study method to capture the dynamics of implementation. The first several
years of implementation research were marked by intensive analyses of small
numbers of such cases (see below). Although substantial progress was thus made
in identifying key variables and certain important facets of the implementation
process, implementation research in general must extend beyond designs restricted predominantly or exclusively to such intensive analyses of small numbers
of cases; otherwise, the field will be hindered in its scientific development.
Whereas such case study approaches aid description, and thus understanding,
relying exclusively on them makes it difficult to validate models of the implementation process.

This "too few cases/too many variables" problem (Goggin, 1986) is com-
pounded when the issue of dynamism in the implementation process is faced
squarely. The study of dynamic policy processes necessitates the refinement of
appropriately designed methods. Ideally, examining systematically the dynamics
of implementation, especially in settings of multilevel intergovernmental action,
means that researchers must make observations at several locations over many
time points regarding a number of cases. Only recently has a new, "third generation" of studies begun to emerge, empirical and theoretical research that
concentrates on comparative, diachronic methods of policy analysis (Goggin,
1986; 1987; Bowman et al., 1987; Lester et al., 1987).[1] Careful investigation
of the implications of this line of scholarly development reveals that the research
issues and trade-offs raised by such efforts are often difficult to sort out and
address satisfactorily (see Bowman et al., 1987).

The next section of this chapter outlines the contours of this "third-generation"
approach to implementation research. In the subsequent section we summarize
some of the systematic methods of analysis that third-generation researchers
might productively apply to the study of the dynamics of public policy implementation; this summary is developed through descriptions of some large-scale
empirical projects in which various methods of collecting and analyzing data are
being employed to capture aspects of the dynamics of policy processes. In the
final section, we illustrate the usefulness of combining research methods by
proposing a dynamic model of implementation and then outlining an appropriately variegated, polyphasic set of methods that one could use for examining
hypotheses derived from that model.

THE CONTOURS OF "THIRD-GENERATION" RESEARCH

Implementation is an exceedingly complex process—a series of administrative
and political decisions and actions that take place across time and space. Much
implementation also takes place in a bureaucratic setting and is intergovernmental, that is, it involves several administrative and political units in two or
more levels of government. While two distinct "generations" of scholarship

over the past twenty years have done much to advance our understanding of this complex, dynamic phenomenon, many scholars now believe that a new "third" generation of implementation studies is needed to overcome barriers to theoretical and scientific advance.

First-generation studies, starting with Pressman and Wildavsky's classic (1973; 1984), were single case studies that focused on the complexities of the implementation process. Second-generation studies recognized implementation's variability over time and across policies and units of government. Thus, second-generation research, to which each of us has made a contribution, has concerned itself with explaining implementation success or failure and has relied heavily on an explicit or implicit model of the policy implementation process.

As a framework of analysis, second-generation scholars employ either a hierarchical "command and control" model, with emphasis on federal mandates and local compliance with them, or an adaptive model which conceptualized implementation as a field for bargaining and accommodation about programmatic goals and strategies between implementors and those affected by implementation (Fox, 1987). The former is a deductive approach that predicts future behavior and then compares what actually happened with what was supposed to happen in order to draw conclusions about the degree of success or failure of program implementation. The second, mostly European brand of second-generation research is a good example of analytical induction, which starts with individual observations of interpersonal behaviors at the local level and aggregates these into a single observation of a more general policy network.

Both types of second-generation approach have been criticized. Researchers from the two schools cannot agree on a common definition of "implementation"; there are vast differences in the role of implementors in the two models, especially with respect to the degree to which they are autonomous actors; and neither approach has been able to explain why implementation occurs as it does or predict how implementors are likely to behave in the future. Indeed, some middle-range theorizing with substantial potential utility has emerged from this line of work.[2] However, a number of the propositions available in the research literature have proverbial rather than scientific characteristics. The need is apparent, then, for more careful, systematic inquiry.

The notion of a third generation of implementation research refers to efforts designed to address this need. More specifically, in this chapter the term is used to designate studies crafted to achieve an ambitious and difficult goal: theory building and validation based on more rigorously scientific, quantitative (both comparative and longitudinal), hypothesis testing.[3] These approaches have thus far been attempted only to a limited degree in this subfield of the discipline (for example, see Lester, 1985; Thompson & Scicchitano, 1985; 1987; Goggin, 1987; Lester & Bowman, 1989). In making a conscious effort to be more scientific in approach, third-generation scholars like those discussed in the following section are trying to overcome several conceptual and measurement problems that have plagued earlier studies. The peculiar difficulties that are likely to attend such

efforts in implementation research have to do with achieving rigor without sacrificing the richness and dynamism of the implementation process itself, and
without making unacceptable choices about important issues like validity and
reliability of measures.

METHODS FOR ANALYZING IMPLEMENTATION DYNAMICS

Thus far, we have argued that a new generation of research, one based on
diachronic, comparative methods of analysis, is needed to test and not simply
generate both explanatory and predictive theories. Now we will highlight several
promising methods that are currently being employed in some ongoing empirical
studies that bear on the directions for third-generation study of the dynamics of
implementation.

Time Series Analysis

A study by B. Dan Wood (1988) analyzes the sequence, magnitude, and
duration of changes in the implementation process across time. The method of
analysis that Wood used in this study is the time-series quasi-experiment (Campbell & Stanley, 1966); that is, the response through time of a particular bureaucracy to a particular set of policy initiatives. His focus is on EPA's clean air
policy and how this bureaucracy responded to the Reagan presidency's policy
initiatives from 1977 to 1985. His research thus employs a longitudinal design
with finely divided intervals (i.e., monthly) to capture an empirically rich and
dynamic implementation process.

The specific technique used in his analysis is time-series impact assessment
(Box & Tiao, 1975). This method requires the identification and estimation of
mathematical components that separately describe the stochastic and deterministic variations in the series (Wood, 1988). According to Wood, modeling the
series offers both an excellent way to control for the independent effects of series
noise, as well as an elegant description of the series response to events of interest.
The goal of Box-Tiao modeling is to produce a parsimonious yet theoretically
complete explanation for the variance in the time series process.

Dynamic Modeling

A recent approach by John Chubb (1985) integrates the general insights of
policy implementation research with the methods of public finance, using economic models of fiscal choice as a foundation. By using an econometric model,
the effects of national policies on state and local decision making are estimated.

He suggests that pure economic models are inadequate because they ignore
the "complicated hierarchy of political and administrative factors that implementation research has taught us are so critical" (Chubb, 1985, p. 995). His

resulting political economy framework is then tested econometrically with an analysis of the performance of two major federal grants programs in the fifty states during the years 1965–1979.

His approach has certain advantages. First and foremost, it provides a framework for analyzing empirically important noneconomic, as well as economic, elements of policy implementation. Second, the framework permits an analysis of the political environment as a determinant of policy implementation; typically, studies of policy implementation focus on the bargaining and interaction between the bureaucracy and its clientele. Finally, the approach permits the formal specification of hierarchical relationships across time and the rigorous derivation of positive and normative results (Chubb, 1985, pp. 998–999).

The major disadvantage of this technique, however, is that it requires a certain familiarity with the methods of public finance. Unfortunately, few political scientists who study policy implementation are familiar with these econometric approaches.

Network Analysis

This approach, developed largely by Benny Hjern and his colleagues—David Porter, Ken Hanf, and Cris Hull—starts by identifying the "network of actors" involved in service delivery in one or more local areas and asks them about their goals, strategies, resources, activities, and contacts.Essentially, the researcher sets out to reconstruct what actors are part of the implementation process, and their patterns of social interaction are described and analyzed (Hjern & Hull, 1983). This approach then uses the contacts as a vehicle for developing a network technique to identify the local, regional, and national actors involved in the planning, financing, and execution of relevant governmental and nongovernmental programs (Hjern & Porter, 1981).

As Sabatier (1986) notes, this approach has several strengths. (1) It represents an explicit, reliable methodology for identifying a policy network, that is, an "implementation structure"; (2) the approach allows one to assess the relative importance of a variety of governmental programs vis-à-vis private organizations and market forces in solving these problems; (3) it allows one to see all sorts of unintended consequences of governmental and private programs; (4) it is an approach that can deal with a policy/problem area that involves a multitude of public (and private) programs, none of which are preeminent; and (5) this approach is well equipped to deal with strategic interactions over time (Sabatier, 1986, pp. 33–34).

However, this approach has several limitations as well. First, it tends to overemphasize the ability of subnational implementors to frustrate the goals of national implementors. Second, it takes the participants in an "implementation structure" as given without examining the prior efforts of various individuals to affect participation rates. Finally, it fails to start from an explicit theory of implementation to guide the inquiry. That is, this approach needs to be related to an explicit body of theory (composed of social, economic, and legal factors) that structures the perceptions, resources, and participation of these actors (Sabatier, 1986, pp. 34–35).

Discriminant Function Analysis

A study by Lester and Bowman (1989) uses discriminant function analysis to determine the "critical" variables affecting the implementation of the Resource Conservation and Recovery Act of 1976 (RCRA) among the fifty American states. The purpose of their study was to identify systematically the factors promoting or inhibiting state implementation of RCRA using the conceptual framework developed by Sabatier and Mazmanian (1980). This particular technique provides a way of determining how selected independent variables work in combination with each other in explaining policy implementation. Also, by using a stepwise procedure, redundant variables may be eliminated from the analysis.

Discriminant function analysis can also be used to classify cases. In this instance, if one were to discover states about which there was no information as to implementation status, discriminant analysis could assign the states to groups based on their values on the most salient variables.

Content Analysis

Although content analysis as a technique is not new, it has recently been used by Paul Sabatier and his associates to explore the beliefs of relatively large numbers of policy elites over periods of a decade or more (Sabatier, Brasher, & Jenkins-Smith, 1987). They use content analysis of public hearings, other government documents, and interest-group publications to explore the determinants of policy change.

Such an approach has numerous advantages. (1) It permits a much more detailed analysis of beliefs than can be captured by partisan affiliation and interest-group scorecards; (2) the content analysis of policy documents is better suited than attitudinal surveys to the examination of changes in beliefs of elites over time. It does not automatically limit analysis to the replication of previous work nor does it require scholars to maintain an interest in a topic for an extended period of time. Public documents spanning an enormous range of topics and time periods are relatively easy to obtain, and coding several decades' worth of records can be done in a year or so; (3) the researcher is not limited to studying elites from legislatures or any other particular institution. In fact, most public hearings contain testimony from individuals representing a wide variety of interest groups, administrative agencies, legislative districts, research organizations, and so on (Sabatier, Brasher, & Jenkins-Smith, 1987, pp. 3–4).

Content analysis also, of course, has limitations. First, there is the difficulty of developing a coding frame that indicates the range of items that will be coded.

Second, there is the problem of validity. How does the researcher know if actors are expressing their "true" opinions? Finally, there is the problem of coder reliability. For example, if one uses a "thematic statement"—that is, a clause, sentence, or paragraph that expresses an opinion or belief—as the codable unit, one becomes acutely aware of how easy it is for different coders to interpret a piece of testimony in quite different ways (Sabatier, Brasher, & Jenkins-Smith 1987). Thus, there is no such thing as immaculate perception.

Nevertheless, preliminary findings from these scholars indicate that much can be learned about policy implementation and elite beliefs through the method of coding the content of policy changes (Jenkins-Smith, St. Clair, & Martin, 1987).

The Social Experiment

Studies by Richard Nathan and his associates (1983) use field network evaluation methods to assess the impact of the Reagan administration's domestic programs on state and local government. The research approach has five key elements: (1) In each jurisdiction, a field associate analyzes the effects of the federal policy or policies being studied. In preparing the analysis, an associate interviews officials of government and nonprofit agencies and examines both unpublished and published records and reports containing program and fiscal information and statistics; (2) a central research staff, in consultation with all of the field associates, develops a common analytical and reporting format for the associates to use in developing and writing up their findings; (3) information is gathered at several times over a period of years to analyze the effects of federal policy changes on a longitudinal basis; (4) the analysis focuses on the nature of the actual changes in federally aided programs in each local area, the effects of these changes, and ways in which the grantee government responds to them; and (5) a central staff coordinates the research and prepares reports that summarize the field analyses and present generalizations across the states and over time (Nathan et al., 1983, pp. 10–11).

The primary advantages of this approach are that it is diachronic in design, intensive in its analysis, and extensive in terms of its comprehensiveness. However, it is limited by the fact that substantial amounts of time and financial support are necessary to carry out the project.

Regression Techniques

A number of scholars have used multiple regression analysis to assess the unique effects of several variables hypothesized to affect policy implementation in the fifty states (see, for example, Lester et al., 1985a; Thompson & Scicchitano, 1985; 1987; Crotty, 1988).

The technique of multiple regression analysis is an important (and often used) tool for social scientists in the analysis of nonexperimental data. The technique has a number of assumptions: (1) an absence of specification error and interval-level data; (2) no measurement error; (3) for each observation, the expected value of the error term is zero; (4) the effects of the independent variables are additive; (5) linear relationships between X and Y; (6) uncorrelated and normally distributed error terms; and (7) no independent variable is perfectly linearly related to one or more of the other independent variables in the model (Lewis-Beck, 1980). When the assumptions of regression are met, the coefficient estimates derived for a random sample will have many desirable properties; however, when one or more of these assumptions are violated, the application of regression analysis may produce misleading or problematic coefficient estimates (Berry & Feldman, 1985).

A "MIXED-METHOD" APPROACH

Thus far, we have reviewed a number of methods that hold promise for the development of an empirical third-generation of implementation research, and we have cited examples of those cases in which scholars are currently at work along these lines. Each study emphasizes the importance of collecting data over time. Most of these projects examine processes retrospectively. One, the naturally occurring experiment, analyzes policy dynamics as they unfold. All the approaches offer some encouragement to those who desire scientific development in this field; yet the coverage above makes clear that each method brings weaknesses as well as strengths to implementation research. Accordingly, we argue that testing a dynamic model of implementation, particularly when multiple levels of government are involved, is especially advantaged by an approach that is variegated and polyphasic. This "mixed-method" approach to data collection and analysis means that several methods are combined and that they are pursued in multiple, carefully scheduled phases.[4] The remainder of this section is devoted to a description and discussion of an approach to the study of the dynamics of implementation that could lead to an explanation of variance in implementation decisions and actions. More specifically, the section outlines a "mixed-method" approach to testing two propositions derived from the model in Figure 12.1.

Figure 12.1 depicts a dynamic model of the implementation process. It presumes: (1) cooperation and conflict between national and subnational governments; (2) a degree of state-level discretion as to the interpretation and operationalization of either a federally initiated mandate or a locally generated problem that is in need of a solution; and (3) a variable pattern of implementation across time or jurisdictions. While the model cannot be explained in detail here, a brief discussion will serve to highlight its most salient features.

The model of intergovernmental implementation schematized in Figure 12.1 conceptualizes the implementation process at the state level, as well as its product (process, outputs, and outcomes), as resulting from choices made by the state. State choices are not made in a vacuum, however; those policy decisions are made in the context of an implementation subsystem.

Figure 12.1
A Conceptual Model of Intergovernmental Policy Implementation

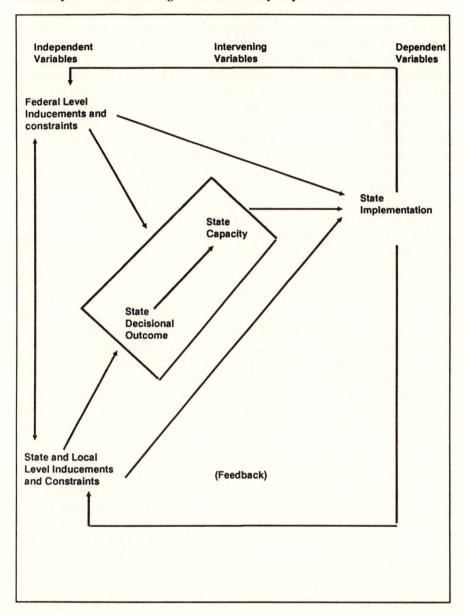

SOURCE: Goggin, Bowman, Lester, and O'Toole (1990). Reprinted by permission of Scott, Foresman and Company.

The Implementation Subsystem

The essential components of this subsystem—the "black box" of state and local politics—are: (1) one or more bureau chiefs in each state, who receive federal communications and act instrumentally to assure agency survival and to enhance their own welfare; (2) one or more bureaucratic organizations in each state whose organizational structure (and whose quantity and quality of financial and human resources) impinge upon individual agent behavior; (3) spokespersons for organized interests in each of the fifty states, whose main interest is in maximizing benefits for group members and who also communicate their preferences to state-level implementors; (4) two or more state legislative committee and subcommittee chairs and one governor in each state whose principal driving force is reelection; (5) a wide variety of local-level actors with significant levels of interlocal diversity in interest and motive who also communicate their desires to state-level implementors; (6) fifty states, each with its own level of capacity to act on its collective preferences; and (7) feedback loops that permit those affected by implementation decisions and actions and their distributional consequences to communicate their reactions to authorities at both national and subnational levels in the federal system.

The Interaction among Components

The most salient feature of the model is that it is dynamic: it takes into account important political and administrative behavioral changes over time, and across policies and states. Hence, the seven components of the subsystem sketched above are interactive, interdependent, and multidimensional. In essence, the implementation decisions made and actions taken at this level in the federal system are the joint product of individual judgments made by the managers in charge of program operations, the preferences of state elected officials, and the cross pressures brought to the bargaining table by consumer and provided advocates.

These individual judgments are reached, at least partly, as the result of bargaining among various interests, each interest having its own expectations, goals, resources, stakes, and power (Allison, 1971; Lowi, 1964). These joint decisions are also constrained by the political, cultural, and economic environment, and the capacity of "focal" organizations to act on the state's collective choices.

The interdependence of these actors—federal principals, local interest groups, the governor, state legislators, local elected and appointed officials, and appointed officials in the state's bureaucracy—and their respective institutions is assumed (Bendor & Moe, 1985; Chubb, 1985; Moe, 1985). Finally, individual actors in this model are constrained by the nature of the decision-making process itself (Braybrooke & Lindblom, 1963; Cyert & March, 1963; Simon, 1957). Each institution is assumed to deal with the problem of information costs of decision making by specializing and by dividing tasks. Because of specialization and division of labor, power is usually concentrated in the hands of committee and subcommittee chairs in the legislature, bureau chiefs in state administrative agencies, and the leadership of organizations for consumers and providers of services as well as direct beneficiaries and cost-bearers.

This theoretical argument plunges us headlong into what Richard Elmore (1987b, p. 278) has called "the disorder that is policy implementation." In attempting to make sense of important aspects of the political and administrative behavior associated with the intergovernmental implementation of public policy, the critical decisions and actions are, first, whether to go ahead with implementation at all; second, the timing of implementation action; and third, the nature and degree of change, if any, in policy intent. Implementation decisions of this sort are frequently sequential. However, whatever their order, decisions about the timing of implementation and the nature and extent of change in program content are usually jointly made and reflect the supports and demands of both federal sovereigns and local interests as well as the interests and motivations of the state bureau chief, the state governor, and policy influentials in the state legislature.

Testable Hypotheses

In fact, the dynamic model of implementation that is schematized above suggests a number of testable hypotheses. One of these is that cross-state differences in the timing of implementation and degree of change in policy content during implementation are systematically related to variations in communications patterns. At both national and subnational levels of government, there are significant variations in message form and content and in the senders' standing in the community across programs, across units of government, and over time. These differences account for differences in implementation decisions. A second proposition is that variability in implementation action across states, for example, whether or not a state actually transforms intended policy into effective policy or exercises administrative discretion in interpreting a federal mandate is systematically related to organizational capacity. All other things being equal, the more capable the state organization that is responsible for implementation is, the more likely that state will implement the program promptly and without major modifications.

Given this testable hypothesis, the critical methodological questions are, How should the investigator conceptualize, operationalize, and measure: (1) the timing of implementation; (2) the nature and extent of modification in program content; (3) communications patterns; and (4) organizational capacity? and What methods of data collection and analysis should the investigator use? To answer these questions, we now turn to a discussion of the three elements of this "multi-method" approach, namely, elite interviews, a mail questionnaire, and content analysis.

Elite Interviews

One use of interviews with elites in the implementation subsystem is to de-termine the timing of a state's implementation and the nature and degree of the state's use of discretion during implementation. What is proposed is historical reconstruction of the experiences of each of the fifty states relative to the im-plementation of a public policy. In reconstructing what happened in each state over an entire implementation period—including both take-off and capacity-building phases—two empirical questions need to be answered. First, has the state carried out the intent of the policy, and if it has, at what point in time did the state put that policy into effect? Second, has the state modified the policy in the course of implementation, and if it has, have the modifications helped or hurt the state's chances of achieving programmatic goals or the chances of satisfying clients' demands?

Armed with answers to these questions, any case of implementation can be classified as one of four implementation styles:

- defiance (delay with modifications that hurt the state's chances of achieving goals)
- delay (delay with no modifications)
- strategic delay (delay with modifications that help the state's chances of achieving goals)
- compliance (prompt with or without modifications that help the state's chances of achieving goals)

Elite interviews can be either face-to-face or conducted by phone. A tape recorder can be used to record answers to open-ended and fixed-response ques-tions, or notes can be taken and the responses transcribed immediately upon completion of the interview. Given the wide geographical distribution of elites and the high cost of face-to-face interviews, a telephone interview schedule is arguably the most appropriate instrument for collecting the facts about how a policy has been implemented in all fifty states. The interview schedule is also probably the most appropriate instrument for collecting data relative to state level inducements and constraints. Since the model in Figure 12.1 suggests that the state's response to a federal mandate to comply with the law is jointly arrived at through bargaining among decision makers in three interdependent institutions within the state, influentials in the state and regional bureaucracy, among state elected and appointed officials, and among the ranks of local interest groups who either oppose or support the policy's implementation should be the ones to be asked a set of questions about the nature and extent of their participation in state implementation decisions.

The interview schedule would make use of both open-ended and structured questions and would be divided into two parts. In the preliminaries to each interview, elites would be told that notes will be taken, that they might be quoted, but that if there is anything that they wish to say "off the record," their wishes would be respected. In the "focused" portion of the interview schedule, a set of common questions would be asked of each implementing actor, but follow-up and probing questions would vary, depending on individual responses (Merton, Fiske, & Kendall, 1956).

The first part of the interview would "focus" on the individual respondent's personal involvement in the implementation experience in his or her state. By asking a broad, open-ended question about a particular facet of the implementation process, and then by using a funneling technique to narrow the focus of the interview, patterns of the implementing actors' behavior could be identified that, upon reconstruction, will provide a basis for individual case studies and later a comparison of cases. Furthermore, questions would be worded in order to elicit details about the interpersonal and interorganizational behaviors that characterized the bargaining among interdependent institutions that may have led to any key joint decisions during the course of a program's implementation.

Recognizing that memory loss is a serious threat to validity when asking elites to recall their involvement in implementation five, ten, or fifteen years after the fact, one successful technique which we have used elsewhere would be to ask the respondent for internal documents that chronicle the history of the program's implementation in the state. Such documents are frequently found in the files of state program managers.

The second part of the interview could be more structured, and could include a number of fixed-response questions about: (1) the personal characteristics of the individual who is being interviewed; (2) his or her perceptions of the form and content of federal laws and regulations (the federal-level message); (3) his or her perception of the reputation of the focal agency that is in charge of making the particular program work (the federal-level sender); (4) subjective assessments of other political and bureaucratic elites and members of the attentive public for the particular policy subsystem within the state (the state level senders of messages); and (5) individual world views and psychological predispositions toward the ends of the program itself, as well as toward the various alternative means of achieving program objectives (the state-level messages).

Mail Questionnaire

Besides the elected and appointed officials and local interest group advocates interviewed by telephone, others who have been influential in the implementation of each program under study can be identified through a snowball sampling technique. Each "influential" interviewed by telephone would be asked five open-ended questions:

1. Who has been the most influential state-wide politician during the course of this program's implementation?
2. Who has been the most influential elected or appointed official in local government during the course of this program's implementation?

3. Who has been the most influential state-level bureaucrat during the course of this program's implementation?

4. Who has been the most influential opponent representing an interest group during the course of this program's implementation?

5. Who has been the most influential proponent representing an interest group during the course of this program's implementation?

In this manner, a list of names, titles, and, if possible, the addresses and telephone numbers of the persons each of the respondents deemed to have had the most influence on implementation in the state can be generated. Each person on this list would then be sent a mail questionnaire.

The interview data and responses to items on a mail questionnaire could be subjected to both intensive and extensive analysis. Responses to open-ended questions would be coded for content, and, when combined with data from state-generated reports to the federal agency, would provide the basis for brief case studies to be prepared for each implementation experience in each state. These case studies would focus on: (1) the nature of the implementation process (the time that it took to get the program off the ground in the state and the nature of any changes in program goals during the course of implementation); (2) the extent to which programmatic goals were achieved in the state; and (3) changes in program outcomes over time that were affected by the achievement of program objectives.

Strict categories would be used to code responses to questions in the second half of the interview schedule. From responses to these questions frequency distributions by program, by state, and by type of elite would be prepared. Another purpose of these questions would be to collect data that, when combined with data from other sources, permit the preparation of profiles of each organization— and the political bargaining among them–and each manager within those organizations who is responsible for making his/her program work. This data set would then be used to test hypotheses linking differences in communications patterns and organizational attributes to differences in implementation process, outputs, and outcomes.

Content Analysis

Besides the instruments discussed above, the third element of this "multi-method" approach is a coding sheet. To examine systematically differences in messages, senders, and organizations at all levels of government, one can use coding sheets in order to analyze for content: (1) top-down messages such as federal statutes and amendments, regulations, guidelines, major policy statements from the executive, legislative, and judicial branch of government, agency reports to Congress, and their routine directives to the states; and (2) bottom-up messages such as state enabling legislation, state regulations, ordinances, state-generated reports to regional and federal offices and to Congress, and major policy or position statements issued by the state legislature, the state bureaucracy, and spokespersons for various organized interests. Messages can be analyzed for content, and they can also be systematically compared in terms of their clarity, specificity, and consistency over time.

To help construct an index that captures levels of organizational capacity, content analysis could also be used to examine the internal documents of focal federal and state agencies, including mission statements, annual budgets earmarked for serving clients as well as for implementation and administration, personnel strength, social and political functions, organization charts, and dependency relations with other organizations. A rigorous analysis of these archival materials permits a reconstruction of each organization's "power setting" (Downs, 1967, Chap. 5), thus providing a basis for assigning values with respect to organizational resources, and the degree of fragmentation within each organizational set.

Careful construction and pretesting of a standard coding sheet (with conceptual categories that are derived directly from the model of intergovernmental implementation in Figure 12.1) is essential if intersubjectively reliable data are to be collected. Standard instructions for categorizing and recording data must accompany the coding sheet. To assure reliable measures of message form and content, and attributes of senders and organizations, for example, a number of coders—each of whom is trained and briefed by an experienced investigator—should be assigned. A critical element of content analysis is that coders make independent judgments. To assure uniformity, documents can be divided into paragraphs and read systematically, with the unit of analysis being the thematic statement. To be consistent with other methods of data collection used in this "mixed-method" approach, when coding and assigning values, coders use a standard scale with five intervals.

CONCLUSION

In less than two decades of research, the field of implementation has burgeoned. Its accomplishments, especially the generation of promising theoretical work, has been impressive. Its practical import, in today's world of complex programs, high expectations, and constrained budgets, is obviously high. Yet if the study of policy implementation is to achieve its full potential, the creative and sensitive development and application of methods for systematic empirical research must also be a top priority.

After passing through two stages, or "generations," the focus of implementation research is gradually changing from theory construction to theory testing. At center stage of this new "third-generation" scholarship is an emphasis on conceptual clarification, and the careful operationalization and measurement of variables; equally important is a set of policy analytical techniques that are both comparative and longitudinal. Some of the latest scholarship illustrates how these techniques have been used, and we have proposed a "multimethod" approach to studying the dynamics of implementation.

While by no means the only approach to advancing our understanding of public policy implementation, this promising research design is one that combines content analysis (if appropriately administered, a method strong on reliability) with elite interviews—telephone and/or face-to-face—and the careful administration of a mail questionnaire (procedures that, in combination, can tap aspects of implementation dynamics and assist in establishing validity). While each of these methods for collecting data has its limitations, the combination—when supplemented by the analysis of archival documents and the intensive, on-site investigation of selected cases[5]—for analyzing data retrospectively is appropriate and defensible. In particular, we have tried to show how these three types of instruments could be combined to yield intersubjectively reliable data that could be analyzed in order to shed new light on the causal complexities of implementation, especially with reference to the effects of organizational capabilities and "top-down" and "bottom-up" communications patterns on state-level implementation decisions and actions as well as their distributional consequences.

NOTES

1. For a more comprehensive explication of our dynamic model of implementation and a detailed description of a design for testing it, see Malcolm L. Goggin, Ann O' M. Bowman, James P. Lester, and Laurence J. O'Toole, Jr., *Implementation Theory and Practice: Toward a Third Generation* (Glenview, IL: Scott, Foresman/Little, Brown, 1989).

2. See, for instance, the summary of several important studies reported by Palumbo, 1987. He identifies as particularly noteworthy the efforts reported in Berman (1980), Elmore (1987b), O'Toole and Montjoy (1984), Salamon (1981), and Van Meter and Van Horn (1975). See also Ingram and Mann (1980), and Mazmanian and Sabatier, 1981; 1983). However, as O'Toole and Montjoy report, "there is, as yet, no general agreement on a predictive theory of implementation or even on what variables are most important to consider" (1984, p. 491).

3. A discussion of one alternative to the epistemology of logical positivism—naturalistic inquiry—can be found in Lincoln and Guba, 1986. We agree with Guba's point that a value-free analysis of policy is unlikely; nonetheless, there is still value in using analytical techniques—with explicit caveats clarifying their limitations—that are designed to test the validity of conditional, explanatory, and predictive hypotheses. For the positive case for the use of a more "scientific" third-generation design for examining implementation hypotheses, see Goggin et al., forthcoming.

4. For discussions of the advantages and disadvantages of a "mixed-method" approach, see Diesing (1982); Jick (1979); Yin (1982). For examples of how mixed methods have been used in the study of political phenomena, see Sieber (1973); and Whiteman (1985).

5. Because a comparative analysis of the ten- to fifteen-year implementation of three policies in all fifty states would yield at least 1,500 observations, a wide variety of quantitative methods, including pooled cross sections of time series, is quite possible.

But one legitimate concern is that the richness of the implementation process might be lost in the analysis. To remedy this, Goggin (1986) has suggested combining large- and small-*n* studies. There is little doubt that a more intensive examination of carefully selected cases could enhance the value of the quantitative work significantly.

13

Implementation Research: Why and How to Transcend Positivist Methodologies

Charles J. Fox

One of biology's most provocative insights is expressed as "Ontogeny recapitulates phylogeny." Each individual, from conception to birth, retraces the developmental stages of the species. Thus human fetuses try out and then reincorporate and transcend, gills, tails, and paws. Similarly, in a truncated time span, implementation literature has recapitulated the development of twentieth-century social science. Are we now then poised to give birth?

Central to the development of research methodologies in social science has been logical positivism-empiricism (hereafter LP/E) and the myriad of techniques it has informed and inspired. Established and now widely practiced, it was—in its youth—a revolutionary movement against excessive, complacent, and moribund idealism; it swept away the cobwebs of metaphysical speculation and got down to the facts of the matter. The incarnation of positivism in political science has been behavioralism-thought by its practitioners to be a tough-minded realism (Ricci, 1984; Seidelman, 1985).

Although specific tenants of LP/E can, and will here be, identified, it and its persuasiveness cannot be separated from the larger social context within which it occurs and of which it is such a significant part. Book-length treatments would fall short of tracing all the interconnections (but see Horkheimer & Adorno, 1972; Husserl, 1954; Marcuse, 1964.) Among its central conceptual trappings, it is sufficient to mention only industrialization, capitalism, technology, "mastery" of nature, means-ends, cause and effect, instrumental rationality, functional architecture, precision calibration, and the like. As in a holographic film, a laser beam passing through any of these microcosmically entails all the others from the standpoint of that aspect illuminated. It follows that the attempt to move beyond positivism in the sub-sub field of policy implementation marches in rank with similar efforts across the intellectual front to rethink the relationships between who we are as human beings and the mechanical things that are our creations. Thus implementation research has moved from positivistic systems-theory-dependent "top-down" approaches (e.g., Pressman & Wildavsky, 1986; Mazmanian & Sabatier, 1983) to phenomenologically influenced "bottom-up" perspectives (e.g., Elmore, 1982; Hull & Hjern, 1987) to attempts at synthesis (e.g., Elmore, 1985; Knoepfel & Weidner, 1982; Palumbo, 1987; Sabatier, 1986). Some implementation theorists, in step with latest developments in social theory, now emphasize such intriguing concepts as the salutary uses of metaphor (Yanow, 1987), the social construction of reality (Moore, 1987), historicity (Fox, 1987), and the human logic of politics (Stone, 1988).

This chapter argues that our understanding of policy in general and policy implementation in particular should transcend positivism while at the same time incorporating it. The next section articulates why this should be done; the final section suggests how it might be done.

HOW POSITIVISM LEADS IMPLEMENTATION
LITERATURE ASTRAY

This section discusses reasons for focusing on LP/E epistemology; LP/E weak-nesses as an epistemological paradigm, and specific affects of LP/E on imple-mentation research.

Why Epistemology

LP/E is essentially a philosophy of science in the realm epistemology. Epis-temology is that branch of philosophy that deals with questions of knowledge: what can be known and how we can know it. As a general rule epistemological theories entail ontological ones. Ontologies, in turn, are theories or assumptions about the nature of reality or being. What is, of course, codetermines what can be known while we need simultaneously to know how we know what is (Cook, 1985).

Epistemology may be seen as the philosophical foundation of methods. Every method implies an epistemology, and epistemologies imply methods. While practicing social scientists need not generally concern themselves with the phil-osophical underpinnings of their craft, in periods of paradigmatic turmoil a reexamination may be called for. We have been in such a period for a couple decades with different concatenations in different disciplines. It is suggested that this condition now also typifies implementation studies.

The debate is over how to conceptualize implementation and how it should be studied. By back-tracking to epistemological presuppositions, we can at least pinpoint our differences and either settle them or agree to disagree. The dispute between top-downers, bottom-uppers and synthesizers may well be a deeper dispute over the nature of knowledge and being. Having sketched the importance of epistemology, an explication of LP/E and its faults is appropriate. It will then be possible to see its continued influence on the implementation problematic.

LP/E and Its Weaknesses

At the outset it should be noted that there are few, if any, hard-core LP/E advocates among practicing philosophers of science. Its precepts are rehearsed here only because the news has not reached those who advocate methodological protocols for which only LP/E residues can be invoked as justification.

LP/E may be reduced to four major principles: (1) the objective-subjective dichotomy; (2) the fact-value dichotomy; (3) the nomothetic-deductive theory of explanation/prediction; and (4) the belief in cumulative knowledge.

The two dichotomies express LP/E's realist/objectivist ontology. Positivists are ontological dualists. They view being as bifurcated into two distinct realms: physical and mental. The mental side, subjectivity value, is inside human minds. The physical side, objectivity factual, lies outside and has an existence independent of human perception. The physical side is thought to be determined by regularities that can be discovered and gathered up as laws. This is the task of science. In this conception, the outside is fixed and determinative. Minds, subjects, theories and hypotheses must try to find and adjust to fundamental objective reality. How persuasive this view is, is suggested by ordinary language: "be objective!"; "don't be so subjective!"

Despite its surface plausibility, which itself may be but a testament to its historically contingent cultural hegemony, it runs afoul of both logic and perceptual theory (Merleau-Ponty, 1962; Fox, 1980). Objects, at least as we encounter them, cannot be known apart from our intentional projects to know and use them. Conversely, subjectivity is not as ephemeral as LP/E supposes. Subjectivity finds its density by its projects to transform and envelop objects. In short, there is a dialectical relationship between subjects and objects (if they can be seen as separable at all) which confounds the dichotomy relied upon by LP/E. Similarly, facts do not just lie about, discrete and invariant, waiting to be discovered to confirm or disconfirm hypotheses. From an infinite number of possible facts available to one's senses, only some are chosen. Those that are selected owe the honor to their *value* to our intentional projects.

The nomothetic-deductive model of explanation postulates analytical theory or hypothesis construction on the mental-subjective side and confirmation by way of observation of the physical-objective side. This view is difficult to sustain without the two dichotomies. Laws, theories, hypotheses, and predictions cannot be irrefutably confirmed or falsified by reference to objective reality when its *independent determinative* status is questionable. If the relationship between subjectivity and objectivity is dialectical; if objects do not perform the reality check to which LP/E science is committed, then self-fulfilling hypotheses are as likely to be sustained as any other kind. If this is an even more salient criticism in relation to the social sciences, where subjects resist becoming mere objects, so much the worse for LP/E inquiries about individual and aggregate human behavior.

The previous three concerns of LP/E lead to the most important issue facing implementation studies. From the perspective of the author of this chapter the issue is historicity or ahistoricity. To what extent is implementation itself and implementation research contingent? In day-to-day research, dissertations, and academic self-definitions it is more often than not assumed that knowledge is cumulative; we know more and more by gathering up the studies and theories of the past and incrementally adding to them in the present. Dissertations, research, and publications are judged and rewarded on the "addition to the body of knowledge" criteria. "Significant contribution" means, practically, adding a brick to the edifice of one's discipline. In other words social scientists naively assume that knowledge progresses from ignorance to approximations of perfect cognition.

The proximate intellectual heritage from which this faith is derived is LP/E's assumption that knowledge is ahistorically cumulative. At an epistemological level this belief is undermined by the incoherence of the previous three LP/E precepts. If knowledge cannot be purely objective or factual, and if values inevitably intrude in the process of inquiry, then the particular and contingent culture of the times must influence values and be entailed in subjectivity. Social science truths, both because the researcher is historically situated and influenced by his or her times, and because the social facts that are the object of study vary over time, cannot even in principle be immutable, essential, universal or, without remainder, cumulative. It cannot be the case that immutable laws of social action and interaction (unless trivial) can be incrementally built up over time to approach perfect knowledge. Contrary to LP/E both objective and subjective sides are malleable, often reciprocally so.

Having laid bare the premises of LP/E and their vulnerabilities we are properly prepared to trace their effects on implementation studies.

Effects of LP/E on Implementation Studies

Turning now to consideration of the adverse effects of LP/E on implementation theory it should be reemphasized that this chapter is not arguing that every human effort in any way connected to LP/E is or has been fruitless. The standpoint here is evolutionary not manichean.

Despite the withering away of LP/E as epistemology, it lives on and finds its way into implementation studies through the methodological protocols of "normal" or "good" science. Textbooks generically express the orthodox view. In Ripley's (1985, pp. 9–11), for instance, good science is defined as data, hypothesis testing, establishment of cause and effect, search for regularities, replication, and designing research based on the "belief that knowledge is cumulative" (see also Langbein, 1980; Nachmias, 1979, pp. 3–4).

While some of the methods mentioned by Ripley, Nachmias, and other texts are useful, they do not, by themselves, constitute "good science," or the scientific approach as these authors imply. Science, more generally, means disciplined study, and these tools are not the only ways to achieve discipline. Historians, ethnographers, philosophers, and literary or art critics are also disciplined in ways appropriate to their concerns. Many scholars since him have agreed with Aristotle's observation that no more precision can be called for than the subject admits.

Lester et al. (1987) state that implementation studies are poised at the brink of their third generation. We have but to overcome "three inadequacies: (1) theoretical pluralism, (2) restricted context, and (3) a lack of cumulation" (p. 200). Similarly Linder and Peters (1987b, p. 116) argue that if the two conventions they identify (selective relativism and limited contingency) could be abandoned, implementation studies could "make important prospective statements about policy." It is here suggested that these assertions are representative of how some implementation scholars negatively assess the work of others by way of squelches themselves dependent on unexamined and no longer credible dogmas of LP/E. Before discussing three such caveats it is necessary to situate their use in the ongoing debate between the two dominant schools of implementation studies.

In the 1980's implementation studies have divided into two schools: "top-down" and "bottom up" (see especially Sabatier, 1986; Linder & Peters, 1987a, 1987b; Palumbo, 1987). A more elegant rendering of the distinction may be: "top-downers" are unilateralists, "bottom-uppers" are multilateralists (see Fox, 1987, p. 129). Expressing the distinction this way highlights a difference of opinion between the two on the efficacy of representative democracy and the appropriate degree of bureaucratic discretion, usually obscured in strictly implementation studies. Unilateralists are more closely associated with the orthodox political science and public administration view of representative democratic accountability. They accept the common assumption that elected officials and their appointees are the legitimate policymakers because only they can be held accountable to the people through the ballot box. Linder and Peters (1987a, p. 466), for instance, argue against bottom-uppers who are charged with celebrating bureaucratic discretion. Their view, obversely, stems from:

positing good democratic values that those who are elected to occupy central positions in governments are elected to make policy. . . . If the implementing classes do not like that then perhaps they should stand for election at the next opportunity.

More than a few observers (see, for instance Bachrach, 1967; Bachrach & Baratz, 1970; Domhoff, 1979; Dye & Zeigler, 1987) question this faith. Without digressing into the shopworn debate between elitists and pluralists it is still possible to ask whether the electoral process produces policy mandates of sufficient clarity that they can be the concrete expectations against which the actions of the "implementing classes" can be found wanting. Policy accountability would seem to require more attentiveness than the American electorate has demonstrated, more precise policy statements from candidates than recent electoral history has recorded, and higher degrees of differentiation between candidates and parties than is usually the case. If such considerations carry any weight, multilateral policy formulation and adaption through implementation may not be as dangerous to the actual workings of democracy as unilateralists fear. It may be seen as quite democratic indeed (in a polyarchy sense; see Dahl, 1971) that mutual adjustment between individuals, agencies, interest groups, and levels of government occurs in both the legislative and implementation spheres.

The affinity between unilateralists and mainstream assumptions is, naturally enough, carried through to epistemology. Thus do they fall back on caveats derived from LP/E to meet the stiff challenge they face from multilateralists. Unavoidably, then, what follows has a polemical taint as multilateralists are defended against the recently mounted attacks of resurgent unilateralism. Two caveats will be discussed in this section: (1) a move from description to prescription is illegitimate; (2) we must construct a predictive theory using precise terms of "meaning invarience." The putative meanings of these caveats will be addressed and then subjected to closer scrutiny than their users have done.

A Move from Description to Prescription Illegitimate. This squelch stems from the fact-value dichotomy discussed above. Again, the fact-value bifurcation relies on the ontological distinction between "really real" physical objective reality and the more ephemeral mental reality. Since science is about discovering regularities "out there," contamination by subjective desires, dreams and fantasms must be avoided.

While the caveat against conflating empirical and normative statements is ever available to even sophomoric debate ("that's just your opinion," "that's subjective") it has recently been used as the cornerstone of Linder and Peters (1987a; 1987b) critique of what they call bottom-up and evolutionary approaches (i.e., multilateralism).

Linder and Peters believe that bottom-up approaches that begin by describing the mutual adaption and bargaining that actually occur in street-level implementation, end up implying if not actually stating, that such an arrangement has its virtues (a normative statement). From their "design perspective" (i.e., unilateralism) this is anathema; it deprives policymakers of any standard of success. "Implementation becomes a tautology: implementation was a success because what was implemented became the policy" (1987a, p. 466). Linder and Peters (1987a, p. 471) think the game is over with this ace: "Our most fundamental critique of the existing implementation literature has been its tendency, particularly manifest in the bottom-up approach, to conflate empirical and normative statements." Game, set, match to LP/E.

But what foul has actually been committed? Elmore (1982), the chief target of Linder and Peters (1987a, p. 46), simply notes in passing some of the insights developed in organization theory by the human relations school (see Mouzelis, 1969): that it is often better to "capitalize on discretion as a device for improving the reliability and effectiveness of policies at the street level'' (Elmore, 1982, p. 26). In other words, it is good management practice to permit that exercise of discretion which cannot, in any case, be avoided. Involved street-level bureaucrats and professionals will exhibit higher morale and deliver services more effectively. It seems manifest that such conclusions are not, as Linder and Peters aver, simply opinionated value judgments. Rather it is a conclusion derived from over half a century of research and thought.

Furthermore, if Elmore and the multilateralists should be censured for their error of conflating, Linder and Peters must be convicted of the same crime. They agree (1987a, p. 466) that mutual adjustment is an important fact. ''However, it is important only to the extent that it allows *policymakers* [emphasis added] to be successful in implementing policies.'' In other words (1987a, p. 465), ''those elected by the public to government should be able to place their policies into action.'' One may agree with this noble sentiment, but it is not a purely factual description.

Both unilateralists and multilateralists should be afforded their value choices and should back them up with reasons. Invoking the fact-value dichotomy as a squelch on such a debate diverts attention from the important issue of unilateral or multilateral democratic accountability.

We Must Construct a Predictive Theory. Lester et al. (1987, pp. 200–201) think implementation studies are backward. While many variables have been found:

the ''critical'' variables have not been specified; and the operationalization and measurement of key variables, as well as the careful testing of hypotheses, have only just begun. . . . Even the most sophisticated schemes have provided only a general map of the broad terrain of implementation behavior when what is needed is a topographical map that characterizes the terrain in precise terms, indicates quantitative measures, and specifies precise relationships among the various elements.

In other words, to move ahead, implementation studies need to follow the protocols of ''good'' science. From what has already been said, it must be obvious that this prescription has been found wanting. But Lester et al. represent only the extreme of many unilateralists (Sabatier, 1986; Linder & Peters, 1987a; 1987b) who decry the absence of some consistent framework.

Lester et al. is so chock full of ''good'' science precepts and LP/E presuppositions it is not possible in the space afforded here to sort them out and pick them off one by one. The two overlapping LP/E assumptions at stake here are the already discussed hypothetico-deductive model of explanation and prediction and, again, the faith in ahistorically cumulative knowledge. The methodological protocols that follow from them at a lower level of abstraction are (1) hypothesis testing, (2) replicability, and (3) precision, including quantification.

No one can deny the virtues of hypothesis testing. We all do it many times a day. It is a good way to think about things, and we learn a lot from it. Under positivism, however, hypothesis testing takes on a more grandiloquent meaning than this mundane sense. Confirmed hypotheses, those successfully tested against "outer" reality, are to "good" scientists little pieces of fixity. This is especially true if they have been observed by more than one subject. Then they possess intersubjective reliability (compare Sabatier, 1986, p. 32). If one could develop a standard set of hypotheses, indicate how they should be observed by others to see the same things, then one would have an intersubjectively reliable methodology producing little pieces of fixity which could be aggregated at the theoretical level allowing us to predict (a form of hypothesis). To do all of this requires that we agree on the precise meaning of what we are studying. We cannot be saying something different with the same words lest we sacrifice our intersubjective reliability. This is why quantification is greatly to be desired because numbers are less likely to be ambiguous; their meanings are invariant and incorrigible.

The most recent works of those identified with the unilateralist school (especially Sabatier, 1986) suggests that they are no longer strictly top-downers. They believe they have learned valuable lessons from bottom-uppers, and they wish to incorporate some of these. Still, most of the bottom-up studies cannot really be incorporated because they lack "an explicit and replicable methodology" (Sabatier, 1986, p. 33 discussing Hull & Hjern, 1987). Similarly, Lester et al. (1987) have developed a model of state implementation of federal programs that is "dependent upon both 'top-down' and 'bottom-up' types of variables" (p. 207), yet case studies must suffer "lack of cumulation" (p. 200), because of overdetermination "where two variables explain equally well variations of a particular phenomenon" (p. 201). Here we suggest that the standpoint of such efforts to coopt bottom-up multilateral studies is still very much unilateralist. Further, a synthesis of the two perspectives is impossible from the standpoint of top-downers because of their methodological predispositions. LP/E science is designed to predict and control (nature in the physical sciences, but what in the social sciences?). The kind of models they seek can be of use only for central authorities to get their way unilaterally. If the key variables are isolated in the way Lester et al. propose, the behavior of the "implementing classes" would be predictable and hence malleable to the wishes of those at the apex of an implementation hierarchy. Street-level implementors must cringe at the prospect of being rendered putty in the hands of their superiors by way of "scientifically" derived controls.

Fortunately, then, the positivistic project has little chance of success. As Cook (1985, pp. 24–25) puts it:

Most social phenomena are multiply determined; each unique cause may itself be complexly and multiply determined by other forces that are not themselves direct causes of what is being explained. To practicing social scientists, causal explanation is not likely— in the near term at least—to involve simple relationships that look like parsimonious laws.

While the utility of orthodox methods should not be denied, neither should following them become a fetish by which other methods of disciplined study are delegitimized. Case studies, for instance, should not be demeaned simply because they are not replicable and do not test hypotheses. Case studies often occur in particular times at particular places and are studied by scholars usually uniquely positioned to do so. This must continue to be the fate of implementation studies because only rarely are legislatures willing to use their offices to experiment on their constituencies with model or pilot programs. Studies such as the guaranteed income experiments (Pechman & Timpane, 1975) are extremely valuable, but they are likely to occupy only a small corner of the implementation universe and even they are not as conclusive individually as Lester et al. would like the entire field to be.

Defining our terms with the precision called for by orthodox social science seems also a chimerical goal. Stone (1988, pp. 4–6) is on target:

paradox is an essential feature of political life, politics and policy are beyond the reach of rational analytic methods. The very categories of thought underlying rational analysis are themselves paradoxes, defined in political struggle. They do not exist before or without politics. Instead, we must understand analysis in and of politics as *strategically crafted argument*, designed to create paradoxes and resolve them in a particular direction.

Political reasoning is reasoning by metaphor and analogy. It is trying to get others to see a situation *as* one thing rather than another.

Just as Frederick Winslow Taylor was mistaken that science would settle the issues between management and labor, so too is the belief that a well-structured scientific model can mediate between unilateralists and multilateralists, interest groups, agencies, and levels of government. With Cook (1985, p. 29) it is time for implementation scholars to recognize that positivism and the methods it has inspired must be, while not abandoned, transcended:

It is now not easy to assume one is trying to describe a social world that is lawfully fixed, deterministically ordered, and can be perfectly described with elegant and simple functional relationships; it is not now easy to assume that everything of importance can be measured, that value-free measurement is possible, and that our theories are perfectly specified.

Having specified why LP/E needs to be transcended, it is time to turn to the more difficult and hence tentative task of how.

WHAT WOULD GOOD IMPLEMENTATION RESEARCH LOOK LIKE?

In the spirit of what Cook (1985) calls "postpositivist critical multiplism," what follows is a conjecture (Popper, 1968). It would not do to call for the demise of one overly rigid paradigm only to offer another one. Lester et al. (1987, p. 208) disdain of theoretical pluralism is not here endorsed. Further, as is usually the case in such efforts, the suggestions for the future pale against the critique of the present and past. Remarks will be structured in three subsections dealing with scope, multiple standpoints, and expanded empiricism.

Scope

To expand the scope of implementation studies three recommendations are suggested.

Recommendation one: Focus on a policy area rather than specific legislation or decisions. Focusing on single central decisions may give a distorted picture of implementation successes and/or failures. While analysts may often be called upon to look at the effects of a particular law or judicial decree they should keep in mind the contours of an entire policy problematic and should be generally well informed about it. A specific initiative might by itself be either a success or a failure but at the same time be a part of a series of initiatives that are on the whole failing or succeeding. A macro example of this would be the school bussing initiative within an overall effort to reduce racial discrimination. As a single initiative bussing has been judged a failure. But when taken as a measure of the firm national resolve to reduce discrimination—as perhaps even a symbolic aspect of the entire effort—it may be judged as an aspect of overall success (Fox, 1987). It should at least be considered in evaluating this policy that something like this message was communicated to the collective conscience of the nation: "so serious is invidious discrimination that we are willing to spend billions on busses, drivers, energy, and aggravation."

A second example arises from the classroom experience of the author; it involves the efforts of graduate students to evaluate the implementation of a program in Texas to provide prenatal care for indigent women with "at-risk" pregnancies. Most measures pointed to relatively successful implementation. Only when considered in the larger context of Texas's indigent health care policy did its shortcomings become apparent. What the legislature had done was to set up a discrete program, with its own bureaucracy and exclusive state funding, ignoring a simple alternative solution of expanding Medicaid eligibility criteria, which would have brought federal matching funds and would have used existing administrative resources. Seen in the light of this design flaw, the program was too redundant and too confusing to both clients and providers.

Focusing on policy areas has an additional advantage of mitigating one of the problems in implementation studies pointed out by Linder and Peters (1987b). They complain that especially bottom-up approaches suffer from the same maladies as incrementalism. That is, little innovation can be expected in new policy initiatives when we are all convinced that the implementation processes cannot be sufficiently altered to allow anything radically (to the implementors) new. Policymaking strategies that advance along a broad front using several legislative or judicial vehicles may be able to overcome the inherent conservatism and incrementalism of particular implementing units taken alone. The reforms and increased professionalism generated in the wake of Supreme Court decisions protecting the rights of suspected criminals comes to mind. Thousands of implementing units incrementally wrought a very large change. They didn't like it, but they did it because everyone else was doing it and it became a mark of professional pride to do it well without unduly sacrificing arrest-to-conviction ratios.

These examples illustrate that implementation studies will lead us astray if we take them to be exercises in recipe book science. Analysis is part science but also part craft.

Recommendation two: cultivate an awareness of historicity. As indicated above, ''good'' science supports the arrogance that research findings can be ahistorically cumulative. Awareness of historicity would be the opposite of this. As stated elsewhere (Fox, 1987), implementation studies developed a deserved reputation for negativism because the policies they evaluated were begun during the optimistic ''we can do anything'' years of the ''American Century'' but assessed in the pessimistic years of stagflation, Watergate, and the failures in Vietnam. Mood shifts in national cultures are not really that difficult to sense; they need only to be taken into account and not sublimated by overly rigid methodological protocols that assume that human behavior is a constant regardless of the times.

There is a more transcendent point here that is difficult to express. Some policies seem destined to find a commodious environment because they ''go with the flow.'' Others will find a hostile environment for which they are ill fitted to survive. Some of the latter will nonetheless find a niche to occupy, while others will not. Analysts probably have these kinds of intuitions, but since they are unexpressible in the jargon of scientific social research, they often go unmentioned. An interesting policy problem is drunk driving. Groups like Mothers Against Drunk Driving (MADD), and Students Against Drunk Driving (SADD) have formed to resist the lethal coexistence of drinking and driving. From a narrow policy perspective they have successfully lobbied for stiffer penalties against those who practice it. Now a narrowly trained policy analyst might look at death rates, incidence rates, conviction rates, penalty increases, and various other outputs of the policies. Assume for the sake of argument that by all such indicators that the policies are successful. ''Billiard ball'' implementation analysis would take the laws as cue and the indicators as pocketing. But is mere fear of punishment really what caused the change or was it a subtle shift in the *Zeitgeist* (spirit of the times) of which the laws themselves are only a part? Consider the publicity surrounding the passing of the laws, the tearful stories in technicolor of parents with children sacrificed in the carnage, the TV movies generated by the protest, the aging of a population that is more health conscious now anyway. What affect did these shifts have on the probability of successful policy? The happy-go-lucky social drinkery of great party wit now is regarded as a potential perpetrator of homicide—the social legitimacy of his heretofore successful behavior pattern has been undermined. Reaching for the realities of historicity without fear of positivistic recriminations would at least allow us to consider such factors.

Recommendation three: try to incorporate longer time spans. As Sabatier

(1986, p. 21) has recently stated "the 4–6 year time-frame used by most implementation research misses many critical features of public policy making." He goes on to recommend ten- to twenty-year periods. He is right, although empathy should be extended to analysts who contract to do studies more quickly and academic researchers competing for a scoop. Those who are compelled by circumstances to do short studies should, however, adopt a tentative attitude and avoid at all costs the presumption of finality. Organizational learning is real, but it does not occur overnight.

Multiple Standpoints

It may be laid down as a general rule that almost everybody makes sense to themselves. When asked, virtually all people have a reason for what they are doing. Not all reasons are equally coherent, logical, or sufficiently general. Nor will implementation analysts be always themselves sufficiently general to judge. But, as long as the social world retains its extant degree of ambiguity, it would seem prudent to take into account as many standpoints as one can try to empathetically occupy. Thus: *Recommendation four: try to incorporate multiple standpoints to triangulate on a policy implementation problematic.* This is a multilateral approach that probably does not differ in practice from what bottom-up analysts have been trying to do. Although unilateralists accuse multilateralists of ignoring the desires of legitimate central decision makers it is hard to believe that multilateralists would ignore laws and the legal parameters of any particular implementation process. The intentions of central decision makers are microcosmically entailed in the minds of the implementors anyway; power is rarely invisible. It follows that top-down perspectives must be taken into account in any implementation research. Top-down versus bottom-up is a false dichotomy.

In practice this means that implementation researchers should try to interview representatives of all groups and strata involved in any particular implementation process. The perfect implementation study would incorporate the perspectives of those at the top, the bottom and, perhaps most important, all those managers and supervisors in the middle. Implementation studies supervised by the author have generally found middle-level management to be the best source of information about both design failures originating at the top and implementation problems inherent in the structures at the bottom.

Expanded Empiricism

If implementation studies can transcend the strictures of LP/E, they can claim empiricist legitimacy to which they are entitled. The narrow band of methods accepted by "good" science should not be allowed to claim the mantle of empiricism alone. Case studies, whether they confirm hypotheses, are replicable, or if they fit into someone's conception of a parsimonious testable model, are empirical. They explore, however dialectically, the realities of implementation.

Reality, in other words, is not only objective; it is infused with the values of the implementors and the analysts. Since this cannot be avoided, it must be embraced. The best way to do this is not to try to eliminate subjective impressions but to balance them one against the others.

Case studies find their real utility, their real aggregation to scholars and analysts in particular subfields. Health studies, for instance, are of interest to health policy specialists and are aggregated in their understanding of their field. Although they may not contribute to some overall paradigm of implementation they are nonetheless valuable. That value should not be underestimated on account of positivistic ideals.

This chapter opened with a biological metaphor: ontogeny recapitulates phylogeny. The question was asked: are we now then poised to give birth? The answer is that all aspects of the life cycle occur and reoccur simultaneously along a multitude of trajectories. We actually know, collectively, a great deal about implementation—we give birth repeatedly. Much of it is really wisdom, a seemingly archaic term too often demeaned by the blinders slapped on our heads by the unreasonable strictures of "good" science promoted by LP/E. It comes down to this: to the positive benefits of modern social science must be added respect for the disciplined employment of sound intuition itself born of experience not reducible to models, hypotheses, quantification, "hard" data, or little pieces of incorrigible fixity.

NOTES

1. Positions in this chapter are close in spirit to those of Stone (1988) and Yanow (1987). The main difference is in the identification of what needs to be overcome. Stone's target is what she calls the rationality project; Yanow's is the "ontological perspective." From the more epistemological lens adopted here, the way they label the problematic gives more ground to LP/E than seems warranted. It has always been one of positivism's most irritating ploys to capture the meanings of concepts by reduction. A term like science, for example, had originally the transitive meaning of disciplined study. Under positivism it becomes only positivism; other claims are simply defined out of existence as science (see Fox, 1980). Stone and Yanow err, from this perspective, because they begin their reconstructions by allowing reductionist meanings of rationality and ontology. By rationality LP/E means only instrumental rationality, a meaning that Stone unwittingly grants. By ontology Yanow means LP/E's realist or objectivist ontology; yet there are many ontologies in the history of philosophy.

2. The disarray (albeit creative) of implementation studies is apparent in the recent *Policy Studies Review* (1987), pp. 91–245, on implementation. This book, of course, is offered as a corrective.

3. Jennings (1983) expresses it well:

if positivism and empiricism are now on the wane as epistemologies, the research procedures and protocols that have grown out of them remain firmly institutionalized in legislative and administrative requirements, funding structures, graduate curricula and professional reward systems. Positivism is the basic methodological orientation of the social sciences and will surely remain so for some time, even though it has now lost the secure philosophical warrant it once enjoyed.

4. LP/E is a complex and often sophisticated philosophical tradition. See especially Ayer (1959). It deserves more respect than can be expressed here. This section of the chapter does not refute LP/E. Rather the existence of a refutation is simply reported. Accessible secondary literature includes Fox (1980) and Gunnell (1975).

5. For intentionality see, for instance, Fox (1989; 1980) and bibliographic sources listed therein.

6. The term "normal science" owes its current meaning to Thomas Kuhn's (1970) book and the disciplinary self-examinations it generated. Kuhn's thesis was that the history of science was marked not by the steady progress of incremented knowledge accumulation, but by radical paradigmatic revolutions. Pieces of knowledge owed their existence as knowledge to the historically contingent paradigm of the time. During any particular era normal science busied itself with cleaning up corners of the structure. But, in this process, anomolies would eventually appear that were inexplicable by way of the prevailing view. Explaining anomolies eventually requires a transcendent new paradigm that explains the new and rearranges what can be salvaged from the old. Kuhn's insights shook the self-confidence of the social sciences to their foundations, in other words, LP/E and its theory of cumulative knowledge. In political science it marked the end of the behavioralist era and the beginning of "post-behavioralism." This, by the way, also marked the renewed emphasis on policy studies as a way of recapturing lost "relevance."

The absorption of Kuhn is an interesting case study of cooptation. Rather than discarding behavioralist research protocols, they were redefined as the normal science of the contemporary era. They may not be immutably and universally true as we had supposed, but they are what we do until a paradigmatic revolution is fomented. Given the sociology of knowledge and the political economy of disciplinary structures, however, this tends to rule out "abnormal" science (Ricci, 1984, chaps. 5 & 6).

14

Tackling the Implementation Problem: Epistemological Issues in Implementation Research

Dvora Yanow

The role of organizational theories in policy analysis has a long history. Over twenty years ago, Herbert Kaufman (1964) pointed to similarities of analytic approach between organizational theory and political science. More recently, the importance of one for the other has been noted with specific reference to the analysis of public policy implementation (e.g., Elmore, 1978; Hasenfeld, 1980). The centrality of organizational theories to case studies in policy implementation has been largely implicit to date, although it has been treated more explicitly in some implementation theories (e.g., Burke, 1987; Scheirer, 1981) than in others.

It can be noted that conceptual attributes of the organizational studies field have had a hand in shaping our analytic capacities for understanding implementation, as well as in forming our definition of "the implementation problem." This hand may be seen in three areas in particular. First, the conceptual pluralism which characterizes the field of organizational studies (Berman, 1978; Elmore, 1978) may underlie the often-bemoaned lack of agreement among implementation theorists on what factors constitute the key variables worthy of study (see, e.g., Lester et al., 1987).

Second, this conceptual pluralism is not without pattern. A logic underlies the variety, which links a set of analytic concepts with the particular organizational level under study, in a system of four lenses of analysis (Yanow, 1987). The tendency of this system of analytic lenses to focus study on one level of an organization or another may have contributed to the noted dichotomy (Palumbo, 1987) between "top-down" and "bottom-up" approaches to the study of implementation.

Third, the ontological positivism of traditional organizational analysis may have contributed to the way that research agendas have been framed in implementation analysis and thereby our definition of the implementation problem.

To address the impact of this hidden conceptual hand, this chapter outlines the system of four lenses, suggesting how each lens embodies a definition of the problem of implementation and proposes a solution to it. The ontological logic shared by these four lenses is analyzed and an "interpretive" logic is presented that more accurately reflects another reality of implementation, where societal values expressed through public policies are seen to influence implementors' behaviors. The research implications of the interpretive approach are discussed, including their impact on the recasting of the implementation "problem."

FOUR LENSES OF ANALYSIS

Most implementation case studies have focused on organizations or on individuals acting within organizations, the analytic domain of organizational theory and behavior. Implementation studies cover the gamut of organizational levels, from individual actors within organizations to the agency's structure, from groups within the organization to the agency's interorganizational environment. Analyses of each level use a particular set of analytic concepts. These levels and their related concepts may be grouped into four "lenses," according to the level of organization that is the primary analytic focus of each lens and the corresponding set of theoretical concepts that are commonly used to examine behavior at that level. These lenses are:

1. The human relations lens, which looks at the behavior of individual actors within organizations and traits of interpersonal behavior;
2. The political lens, which examines dynamics within groups and relations between and among groups;
3. The structural lens, which focuses on the organization itself as a designed set of behavioral rules;
4. The systems lens, which targets organizations as they relate to one another in a particular environment.[1]

Each lens embodies an idea of what is of key importance in studying implementation, as well as a set of terms appropriate to that study. The *human relations* lens focuses on the behavior of the individual implementor and on interpersonal dynamics between implementors as those dynamics affect the behavior of the individuals. Its dominant metaphor is the organization as a traditional, supportive "family." Analysis focuses on a social psychology of roles, expectations, norms, needs, motivation. Ineffective behavior, poor interpersonal skills, and ignorance in motivating others are sources of problems. Edwards (1980), for example, lists individual implementors' "dispositions"—their desires, motivations, attitudes, incentives—as one of three keys to successful implementation. Mazmanian and Sabatier (1983) include the amount of behavioral change required of individuals by policy innovations as one of three factors affecting implementation success.

Analyses of street-level bureaucrats' implementation behaviors (Lipsky, 1980; Weatherley, 1979) depend on role definitions, expectations, and norms. Studies that focus on the use of sanctions, incentives, and other means of enforcing compliance (Brigham & Brown, 1980; Mazmanian & Sabatier, 1981) attend to shaping individual behavior.

While human relations theorists have traditionally viewed interpersonal conflict as an unhealthful state of human affairs that warrants diagnosis and treatment, the *political lens* accepts conflict as a natural ingredient of human relations. This lens focuses primarily on groups, including interpersonal behaviors as they affect the group and relations between and among groups. Its dominant metaphor could be seen as a war or battle. Power, influence, interests, coalition building, negotiation, and bargaining are key analytic terms that the political lens uses to analyze relations within groups, as well as between them. The games Bardach's (1977) implementors play are manifestations of the power and influence they possess or want opponents to believe they possess. Ripley and Franklin (1982) target the omnipresent bargaining norm and the intentional inclusion of interest groups as factors in implementation delay and failure. Murphy (1971) and Hasenfeld (1980) attribute implementation failure to the absence of developed sources of power and influence to support the proposed changes. Lazin (1980) and T. B. Smith (1973) describe the pressures and counterpressures of various interest groups, opposition parties, and affected individuals and groups as impediments to implementation.

The *structural lens* focuses on the design of the organization itself as the crucial factor regulating relations among organizational actors, rather than psychological, social psychological, or political factors. It examines task allocation, lines of authority, and spans of control. This lens derives from the image of the organization as a well-regulated machine. Lipsky (1979), Prottas (1979), and Weatherly (1979) each found that the design of street-level bureaucrats' agencies built discretion into their jobs, with the result that they formulated policies in their daily interactions with clients at the same time as they implemented them. Edwards (1980) found bureaucratic structural elements to be problematic for implementation success.

The *systems lens* examines interdependencies among organizations and between organizational subunits. The systems lens derives its analytic concepts largely from two sources: (1) the ecological system with subsystems or cells with semipermeable membranes, in interaction with their respective environments; and (2) the cybernetic system of the goal-oriented, self-correcting machine or biological mechanism. Applied together to the organization, these analogies yield a picture of the organization as a black box whose innermost processes are not subject to investigation. It must draw feedback from its environment—specifically, error-detecting communications—while keeping an eye on its goal and correcting its aim toward that target. The lens focuses on goal definition, coordination, communication, and feedback. Bunker (1972) and Edwards (1980) are among those who cited blocked information flows and inadequate communications as implementation problems. Derthick (1972) and Ripley and Franklin (1982) noted such problems as lack of goal consensus or coordination in intergovernmental relations and the multiple interrelated entities of the federal system. For Larson (1980) vague or unrealistic goals, complexities of intergovernmental relations, and environmental pressures from economic forces are possible reasons for failure. Nakamura and Smallwood's (1980) systems framework for implementation analysis highlights communications and compliance linkages within each of three important environments and the potential for garbled messages, misinterpretations, and transmission breakdowns. Pressman and Wildavsky (1973) found a plethora of decision points, each a possible source of delay.[2] The four lenses can be summarized as in Table 14.1.

Each lens embodies an idea of what is of key importance in studying implementation. Each lens uses a particular set of concepts and a distinct terminology to discuss these concepts. The lens largely determines what questions the researcher asks and what data he or she attends to. For example, an implementation analyst who identifies the problem under study as poor coordination among related agencies is more likely to discuss it as a systems problem than as one of human relations. Political theorists put contesting interests, power, and negotiation at the center of their analytic focus, from a point of view that accommodates neither the human relationists' emphasis on the dysfunctionality of conflict nor the structuralists' theories about authority and control. "Norms" do not explain inputs, outputs, and feedback loops; "bargaining" does not describe very well technology or task.

Furthermore, each lens includes a prescription for rectifying the problems which it has defined. The prescriptions for change which the theorist poses in the case of poor interagency coordination will most likely derive from the interorganizational field, using the terminology of the systems lens (for example, improving collection of or attention to feedback). Neither the problem diagnosis nor the proposed remedy is likely to discuss the needs of the individual actors in the case or the bargaining activities of groups within the different agencies, because neither the research focus nor the language of the systems lens makes such a discussion possible. Observation, analysis, and prescription are typically connected in this fashion in each theoretical frame.[3]

It is important to note that these four lenses are fully distinct chiefly in an analytic sense. In implementation analysis as well as in organizational diagnosis, the lenses are often used in various combinations. Implementation analyses that have focused on intergovernmental relations describe problems that amalgamate elements from the systems, structural, and political lenses: multiple decision points, unclear communications, incomplete information, conflicting lines of authority and sources of power, and so forth. Human relations theorists have adopted systems language (feedback, communications) in applications to individual behavior; the political lens's attention to leaders has enhanced the human relationists' study of the leadership role, although the two lenses typically attend to different aspects of the phenomenon.

Table 14.1
Four Lenses of Implementation Analysis

ORGANIZATIONAL LEVEL OF ANALYSIS

	Individual	Interpersonal	Group	Inter-group	Organization	Inter-organization
Human Relations	Dispositions Desired behavioral change Implementors' needs	Leadership Motivation Incentives Expectation Roles				
Political			Massing assent Power, influence Negotiation Games	Bargaining norm Strategies, Tactics Interest groups Coalitions		
Structural					Bureaucratic structure, design Control model Authority Worker discreation Task allocation	
Systems						Ferderalism Inter-governmental relations Coordination Decisions, goals communcation Environments Linkages, feedback Information

SET OF ANALYTIC CONCEPTS

Each lens combines an organizational level of analysis with its related set of analytic concepts, yielding terminology for implementation analysis.

Nevertheless, for analytic purposes in lending some clarity to implementation studies, these distinctions are useful. They illustrate the extent to which there is an underlying order to the seeming disarray of analytic concepts used in the study of implementation, while highlighting some differences among them. In addition, seeing implementation studies in this way allows us to examine some underlying assumptions that they share.

THEORETICAL ASSUMPTIONS AND COUNTERASSUMPTIONS

The analytic use of these four lenses grows out of several shared assumptions about the nature of "the implementation problem." First, since implementation activities have been seen as beginning with the conclusion of the policymaking phase, the cause of implementation problems has been assumed to lie somewhere in that same post-policymaking realm. Problem-searching attention has begun with the dissemination of the new legislation, or when administrative agencies take over. Action prior to policy legislation has been taken to be irrelevant as a source of implementation problems. This assumption has led to a focus on agency behaviors as the primary source of implementation problems, to the exclusion of policymaking activities themselves. Such a focus is a carryover from earlier theories that considered implementation to be the simple execution of policy-makers' intentions. From that point of view, if policy is not being implemented, the problem must lie with its administrators (see Sharkansky, 1970, in Pressman & Wildavsky, 1973, p. 172; T. B. Smith, 1973, pp. 197–198).

A second assumption is that implementing agencies' and individuals' point of departure is the written language of their policy mandate—that is, its literal meaning. That the policy language was not clear and explicit enough for implementors to work with is a common research finding (see Edwards, 1980; Mazmanian & Sabatier, 1983; Nakamura & Smallwood, 1980). This, too, echoes an earlier view of implementation: ambiguous language does not carry sufficiently clear instructions for implementors' technical, administrative execution. It is not the implementor's task to interpret policy language, according to this assumption; if he does, he has done so erroneously, because he is expected to confine himself to the literal meanings of the policy language, which are the expressions of legislators' intentions.

This is linked with a third assumption common to the four lenses: that implementors begin with an intent to implement the policy as it is written; implementation problems are a result of something interfering with that intent. This also follows from the earlier conception of implementation as the technical administration of a policymaking phase. Legislators are expected to work out and resolve the complexities of a policy issue before its legislation; their intentions are then embedded in the policy language, in which prior disagreements no longer appear. Implementors are charged with carrying out these legislative intentions. If they are unable to do so, it is because something has interfered with their own administrative intent (e.g., an inadequate bureaucratic structure, a weak incentive system), not because implementors were affected by something outside of the literal policy language or their agency world.

These assumptions, however, do not accurately reflect other aspects of what is known about implementation and organizational behaviors. Specifically, we do not have evidence to support an assumption that implementors are isolated from the general historical and value context of the policy they are implementing, nor that they are blind to the multiple meanings of policy language that carry those contextual values. Two counterassumptions address these concerns.

First, the explanation of implementation success and failure cannot be confined to postlegislation factors alone. An implementing agency acts in the context of a specific policy issue's "culture," which includes the accumulated and often competing values and beliefs concerning that issue, collected over successive debates. While legislation may include a new formulation of a specific piece of policy, most policy issues are not new. The accretion of preexisting values influences policy debate over the new formulation. The issue culture of American immigration policy, for example, consists of a set of ideas and experiences that have accrued from prior debates about immigration policy: that this country was built by immigrants, that the United States has always offered sanctuary from religious and political persecution, as well as attitudes toward particular ethnic and racial groups. The beliefs and values embedded in this issue culture influence current policy debates about immigration.

Preexisting values and beliefs are embedded in contemporaneous debate about a specific policy, and that debate influences implementors. The battle to implement Prohibition was played out against a backdrop of beliefs inherited from earlier times about the link between religious affiliation and social status and their relationship to drink (Gusfield, 1963). As Love and Sederberg (1987) put it, "policies and organizations are thrust into an already structured social and physical ecology that may either resist or facilitate" the implementation of those policies.

In other words, implementation is affected not only by what happens after the legislative phase, but by what transpired before and during policy drafting as well. Baier et al. (1986) have noted that to assume that implementors are "innocent" of what transpired prior to implementation "suggests more clarity in the distinction between policy making and administration than can usually be sustained." Yet, not only the political forces of policy formulation (MacLennan, 1981) or the immediate policy formation environment (Nakamura & Smallwood, 1980) influence implementors, but so do the values and beliefs inherited from earlier debates, which are attached to the current concern. The issues over which legislators debated and compromised in drafting a policy do not die when the policy appears in the *Federal Register*. They survive the policymaking phase and are carried in the policy culture into the implementation phase, with the strong likelihood that they affect implementors' work.

Second, we cannot expect that implementors attend to the literal meanings of policy language alone. Language, which is symbolic and metaphoric, carries multiple meanings. Policy cultures are transmitted through the symbols and metaphors of policy language, as well as through other artifacts of the policy culture such as editorial cartoons (see Gamson & Lasch, 1980), oral and written media reports and editorials, public debates, stories, and so forth. Rather than dealing only with the literal meanings of policy language, implementors work with multiple meanings.[4] Implementors who are faced with the necessity of having to interpret policy language are not behaving improperly; neither are policymakers at fault for using ambiguous language. Purposeful ambiguity is at times a necessary recourse to accommodate conflicting interests in order to devise draftable legislation. An architect of various policies in different arenas of government and public administration offered his insight on this process. Faced with the need to compromise with the opposition and to accommodate them through intentional ambiguity, "you hope," he said, "that your people will be in there when the time comes" to make the interpretations that you would have made. (Ylvisaker, 1982)

ONTOLOGICAL AND INTERPRETIVE LOGICS

Central to the first set of assumptions is an unexamined, common logic of inquiry. That logic holds that implementation is an activity with factual characteristics in the real world; since they exist as objective facts, they can be discovered. This logic is "ontological" in nature, in that it is concerned with discovering the way implementation is in the world. In its terms, the key questions of implementation analysis are: What is the objective nature of implementation? Where are its problems to be found? The ontological response is that there is one and only one real, factual, correct answer to those questions. This may be seen in the way that each lens has generally restricted inquiry to its own domain: "implementation *is* a set of games," or "implementation *is* a bureaucratic problem," and so forth. That is, the four lenses are, essentially, competing frames of analysis, each claiming to present the single empirically verifiable and factual solution to a factual problem.

The ontological logic of organizationally grounded implementation analysis has also influenced the formulation of the debate between "top-down" and "bottom-up" theories. The "top-down" argument is informed by the analytic language of the structural lens, which expects implementation to be governed by the behavioral rules built into the structural design of the implementing organization. Under these rules, the bottom of the hierarchy executes the directives of the top. The "bottom-up" argument is informed largely by the analytic language of the human relations lens, which suggests that individual workers do not necessarily comply automatically with a policy directive. The top-down approach has been perhaps the more prevalent of the two because the structural lens is more widely represented in implementation research than the human relations lens.

The counterassumptions suggest a logic of inquiry that treats implementation as a set of activities in which multiple meanings are expected. This logic is essentially "interpretive," not ontological. Rather than asking, "What is the factual reality of implementation? Where can its shortcomings be seen empirically?" it asks, "How do we understand implementation? What meanings are made of this enabling policy by its implementing agency and other relevant publics?" The answers to these questions take the form of, "What meaning(s) did agency chiefs, legislators, front-line workers, and clients make of this policy? How did these meanings shape the policy's implementation?"[5] The ultimate success or failure of policy implementation, from this point of view, rests on the interpretations of its policy mandate.

Using interpretive logic, implementation analysis is no longer the search for a factual essence of the implementation problem. The lenses cease to be competing frames of reference. They are, instead, different aspects of a larger picture, which can supplement and balance each other rather than contradict and refute. Multiple meanings, multiple interpretations coexist, like the many facets of a cubist portrait. The role of the analyst is to investigate implementors' and other relevant publics' interpretations of the policy culture and to analyze the effects of these interpretations and meanings on implementation efforts. Indeed, the assumption shared by the four lenses regarding implementors' intent to implement as written requires analysts to discover what policymakers' intentions were, whether they were understood as such by implementors, and whether implementors' intentions were identical with legislators'. Such discovery of "original intent," whether of policy legislators or of agency actors, requires the researcher to make interpretations of actors' words and actions.[6] Since interpretations are not facts, they cannot be handled by a fact-oriented research methodology and require an interpretive logic, rather than an ontological one.

An interpretive approach to implementation analysis raises some differences with ontological logic which are of particular theoretical importance. Interpretive logic highlights several features of implementation which are not part of the ontological point of view: the fact of individual interpretations and shared, compatible, and conflicting meanings; interaction in meaning making, and the role of persuasion in the creation and destruction of shared meanings; and the ongoing reinterpretation of implementation activities.

First, implementors interpret policies. The agency executive, the manager, and the street-level bureaucrat as implementors make meanings of policies by interpreting policy language and one another's acts. From an interpretive perspective, implementation may be seen to be hampered when different implementors do not share the same meanings of symbols, metaphors, and other cultural artifacts of a policy issue. Two implementors may each be implementing something different, based on different interpretations of the policy or its artifacts. The more people involved, the greater the potential for varying interpretations. For example, the problem of different departments within an agency implementing a policy each in its own way may be explained as different meanings made by each department of the policy. Similarly, implementation difficulties arising between agency management and units of professionals within the agency may be due to different interpretations of the policy culture (Yanow, 1981). Pressman and Wildavsky's (1973) multiple decision points may be complicated by the larger number of interpretation points, yielding a thicker analysis of why implementation "gang aft agley" (often go wrong).

Second, implementing on the basis of multiple meanings may involve persuasion of one person to another's interpretation. For example, implementation of a policy designed to produce changes in the behavior of a target population depends on the "target" agreeing to the terms of the transition. Such agreement can be hampered if the two parties to the interpretation do not share the same or compatible meanings. Implementation of a voucher-based housing policy, for instance, may fail if tenants use vouchers improperly or if landlords refuse to accept them, based on the different meanings vouchers—as an artifact of the issue culture of housing policies—have for each group.

In this and in other cases, implementation activities include a critical element of persuasion, where an actor tries, consciously or not, to convince another to share his interpretation of events.[7] From this point of view, implementation succeeds when voting publics or legislative appropriations committees, to take two examples, are convinced of that success. Pressman and Wildavsky (1973), for instance, found that spending allocated budgets was interpreted as a sign of the agency's success in implementing its mandate. Sapolsky (1972) noted that Polaris supporters intentionally sought to create the impression that the missile was successful in order to persuade members of Congress to vote the funds necessary to continue work on it. Congressional support itself became an indicator of successful implementation. In both cases, policy-relevant publics could have declined to be persuaded of the implementing agency's success.

Seeing implementation as an interactive process means that we yield some control over the definition of success of implementation activities to actors other than those conceived of traditionally as implementors. The enlarged scope includes actors external to the implementing agency, including policy target groups, agency clients and potential clients, and other policy-relevant publics whose interpretations of the policy and of agency acts contribute to the definition of implementation success and failure.

Third, from an interpretive point of view, implementation is also adaptive and iterative. Once an implementor (broadly defined) interprets a policy and acts on that interpretation, a second implementor is no longer dealing with the original policy. Each interpretation can yield a new view of the policy; it can be modified in some consequential way. Subsequent implementors engage a different policy from the one initially acted on. Palumbo and Harder (1981) noted that "successful implementation occurs in an evolutionary way" through successive reinterpretations. Interpretive logic suggests that these interpretations do not occur at random; they evolve within the culture of the policy issue.

Finally, interpretive logic treats implementation, and indeed the policy process as a whole, as other than solely a goal-directed activity. From this point of view, policies are statements of negotiated public consensus at a particular point in time and express public values and beliefs. The first four lenses share, to some extent, a view of implementation behavior as essentially rational behavior, in the sense that it is goal-oriented, involving the conscious and deliberate adjustment of agency means to the realization of explicitly stated policy ends.[8] Interpretive logic suggests that agency behaviors are not always exclusively goal-oriented; sometimes they are expressive acts. If such acts can be expressive as well as rational, a rational analysis will not help us understand their expressive, nonrational aspects. For this, we need an appropriate interpretive "science," and this is what an interpretive methodology affords us.

IMPLICATIONS FOR A RESEARCH AGENDA

The expressive side of human behavior takes place within organizations and around and about them, and as it figures in implementation, we are in need of an appropriate analytic view of it. For example, attendance figures and other numbers may be simple, rational devices for reporting weekly activities and useful as a measure of implementation success. Evaluators have generally assumed that reported numbers are accurate, but numbers have also been reported in such a way as to support desired organizational images or to create and manage impressions (Stone, 1988; Yanow, 1982). Rational planning systems adopted by an agency to manage implementation may at times produce invalid information, rather than more accurate information, adversely affecting implementation of the program innovation (McGowan, 1976). An interpretive analysis would be sensitive to the reasons for such use. In other words, organizations may seem often to be purposive and goal-oriented, but not all human behavior is.

An interpretive approach to implementation analysis requires a longer time perspective than that taken by most studies. Research needs to trace the multiple policy interpretations made by the several stakeholders in the policy, to explore how the meanings evolve during implementation, to trace the historical development of the issue culture, as well as to explore implementation across levels of the implementing bureaucracy and across intergovernmental lines.[9]

The analysis of the four lenses posits that it is not merely that different analytic approaches to the study of implementation exist. More than that, to the extent that implementation analysis concerns itself with the actions of implementing agencies and of implementors acting as agents for organizations, the four analytic approaches are linked inextricably with the level of the organization which is under analysis.

Not only has the nature of organizational theories lent an analytic design to implementation studies; it has also brought two other concepts into the field. First, the arrangement of analysis according to organizational level has emphasized the predilection to study implementation "top down" and to react to that from the "bottom up," a predilection already inherent in implementation analysis based on earlier views that implementation was the simple administrative enactment of legislative intent.

The second area of influence is seen in the debate between "fidelity" to an original intent and implementive "adaptation." This juxtaposition is parallel to the debate in social science between ontological "realism" and "naturalism," called here interpretation (J. K. Smith, 1984). The distinction reflects fundamental differences of epistemology between what I have called ontological logic and interpretive logic. In summary, the major point of the debate is that ontological positivism believes that social science is capable of capturing reality in a way that is completely faithful to it, whereas interpretive social science believes that all reality, and all science, is interpretive. With respect to implementation this means that the two points of view cannot be reconciled. From the first, implementing activities will always be expected to replicate their policy mandate, and they will be judged against their ability to reach those goals. From the interpretive point of view, all implementing activities are interpretations of a policy statement, which itself is an interpretation of prior political statements and debates.

Another way to put it is to examine the nature of goals and goal-seeking actions. To a great extent, research has defined implementation as a mechanism for attaining goals and defined those goals as the literal meanings of explicit policy statements. Implementation is judged a success to the extent that it reaches those goals. An ontological approach assumes the literal and objective nature of such goals. An interpretive approach assumes that goals are cultural creations subject to multiple interpretations, an extreme view of which is that goals "are not meant to be realized" (Etzioni, 1960).

Methodological choices are a function of epistemology. If one believes that reality is objective and based on facts which may be perceived directly by the senses, one will choose among a set of ontologically oriented methods. If one believes that reality is socially constructed, subject to interpretation, one will choose a different sort of method. We may be able to reach some consensus on what type of problem implementation is and to narrow the choice among methods. But there will remain a fundamental difference in what appears on the choice menu depending on one's orientation to ontological positivism or interpretation.

Similarly, the debate between the discoverability of general laws of implementation versus contextual specificity is marked by the same distinction between ontological and interpretive logics. Ontological realism makes possible the generalization of observations across sites and experiences, because the experience proves the validity of a fact. Interpretation, on the other hand, restricts generalizability, although to the extent that verifiability depends on consensus (the hermeneutical circle), findings may be generalized as long as the consensus holds up.

There is a degree of determinism that describes the relationship between how one perceives the nature of reality (one's ontological view) and how one believes that reality can be known (epistemology) and the standardized pattern of research one takes to acquire that knowledge (methodology). They reinforce one another in a circular fashion, as in the phrase, "seeing is believing, and believing is seeing."

So, one who perceives the world as socially constructed will most likely choose to research different interpretations of policy implementation, using various available interpretive methodologies (ethnography, ethnomethodology, case study methods, critical theory, hermeneutics). Whereas an ontological positivist who sees implementation success or failure as a matter of objective fact rather than individual interpretation will define the problems and determine a research agenda using methodologies more traditionally found in policy analysis.

Currently, policy analysts sound as though we were in search of a paradigm (see Palumbo, 1987). Signs point to pluralism as the new paradigm (a seeming irony). If this is true, it suggests that trying to determine the one best research agenda is a misguided effort. Rather, we should continue to develop many research strands at one and the same time.

CONCLUSION

Implementation studies set out to find the source of the implementation "problem," where the working definition of problem is that outcomes do not match intent. Analysis began in the 1970s with an ideological *crie de coeur* about the need to fix something that was working improperly: desired policy objectives, after being hammered through legislation, were not being achieved. The metaphor of the "gap" between intent and outcome has its roots in theories that view implementation as the rational bureaucratic execution of policies, reinforced by the ontological view that an objectively discoverable implementation problem has an objective, factual solution. The imagery foreordains the solution: close the gap. Accordingly, the four lenses of ontologically oriented theories propose variations on how to close it. Even the "second generation" of implementation studies, which abandoned the assumptions of technical bureaucratic execution and implementation of legislators' intent in favor of implementation as "evolution" (Majone & Wildavsky, 1984) or "adaptation" (Berman, 1980), still retain, by and large, the feeling that such interpretation is somehow unfortunate, if not wrong, and should be controlled.

Interpretive logic suggests that if we continue to base our implementation analyses only on narrowing the gap between policy intentions and agency outcomes, we will come no closer to understanding implementation failures and successes. From the interpretive point of view, the gap is expected, because the "problem" of implementation is the ongoing working out of societal values about the policy issue which is being implemented, values that change over time and exist in multiple versions simultaneously.

It has been said that attention to implementation began when we saw that we could martial resources to put a man on the moon but were incapable of winning the war on poverty at home. We could put a man on the moon because there was little clash of values to impede that mission. We have not been able to win the war on poverty because of the clash of values and the varying beliefs concerning what is poverty, who are the poor, whether government should help them—to name only a few points of contention. Competing values coexist, even after policy is legislated, and influence implementors and implementation. This cannot be understood ontologically: values are not objective facts. They can only be interpreted.

The influence that ontological logic has had on implementation studies has left them largely powerless to deal with meaning making and interpretation in social behavior. Rather than being a manifestation of error, the gap may be the expression of the lack of consensus in support of policy values. If we continue to ignore the interpretive aspects of policies, slippage between intent and outcome is likely to seem to be a perennial substantive problem. With interpretive logic, the "gap" is expected, since we are encouraged to anticipate differences in meaning and interpretation. In fact, we might often be surprised if we did not find a gap. With interpretive analysis, the study of implementation is no longer limited to a fight against unanticipated consequences or to an attempt to explain the gap away, rather than to explain it.

Implementation analysis has been traveling two roads simultaneously. As the public sector branch of organizational analysis, its unique contribution is the examination of a set of organizations linked across geographic and governmental lines by a policy thread. As part of the analysis of the policymaking process, it continues to revise earlier linear concepts of policy execution in favor of a more complex, iterative model. An interpretive approach suggests a way of linking the two paths, where organizational events are seen to be influenced by beliefs and values prevalent during the policymaking phase, including those inherited from prior debates. It offers a new set of research questions, which expand the analysis of implementation.

NOTES

1. Others have proposed various divisions of the organizational literature (Van Maanen, 1975; Cook, 1977; Elmore, 1978; Bolman & Deal, 1984). Scheirer's (1981) discussion of implementation distinguishes among individual, intermediate, and macro-organizational levels. Lynn (1987) argues that public executives' decision making is affected by individual, group, structural, political, and societal factors, including interpretations of policies by various actors in the policymaking process. Some of the ideas expressed in this section grew out of collaboration with Scott Cook, and I gratefully acknowledge that intellectual debt.

2. Lipsky (1978) has noted that many implementation studies share assumptions that derive from a systems perspective, such as the assumption that agency components of a policy system share mutual and congruent interests and therefore will contribute to unobstructed information flows.

3. Others have used concepts similar to "lens" to discuss related issues. Bolman and

Deal (1984) used the perspective of "frames" in discussing organizational theory. Goffman (1974) used the term "frame" to connote the individual's observational and interpretive focus on everyday experience. Rein's (1983) "frames" are closer in meaning to a general *weltanschauung*. Allison (1971) offers three "models," "frames of reference," or "conceptual lenses" on governmental foreign policy behavior. Kuhn's (1970) "paradigm" presupposes a well-developed, dominant disciplinary point of view, which neither organizational studies nor implementation possesses, given the interdisciplinary nature of each.

One could, of course, argue that the several contending lenses represent the battle within each field for a paradigm. It seems to me that what is "paradigmatic" for each is an ontological predisposition, which I discuss in the next section. In any event, I see these as different terms expressing a similar notion: that research questions and solutions are determined by one's face on the world, even when this research is as informal as making meaning of everyday life.

4. There is, in fact, extensive debate within circles of literary criticism and philosophy as to whether it is even meaningful to talk about the "literal" meaning of language of any sort. One opinion is that each reader of a text creates a new interpretation. This would be as true for an implementor reading a piece of legislation as it would be for someone reading Charles Dickens or William Shakespeare. By extension, in treating legislators' or implementors' actions or behavior as text, we again consider that each "reader"—in this case, an implementor or a policy analyst—creates a new interpretation. I have dealt with this below and in Yanow (1982); see also Rabinow and Sullivan (1987) for a discussion of some of these issues.

5. Sharp's (1981) case analysis section provides a good illustration of the different kinds of questions that might be raised in conducting research using these two different logics. Neither Sharp nor Berman (1980), however, suggest that "programmed" and "adaptive" implementation approaches are undergirded by different ontological logics.

6. This is remarkably similar to the line of argument in constitutional interpretation that seeks to establish what the framers' intent was when they drafted that document. Ironically, from the point of view of this chapter, legal "interpretivism" refers to reading the letter of the law, while "noninterpretivism" goes beyond the literal language (Baer, 1988).

7. The foregoing discussion suggests a meaning of "implementation" similar to its usage in operations research, where "to implement" is to convince a client to use the system that has been designed (e.g., Siebert, 1973).

8. For a discussion of traditional views of rationality in organizations, and some alternative perspectives, see Brown (1978), pages 368–370.

9. Lester et al. (1987), for example, suggest expanding the longitudinal time frame across a decade or more.

Bibliography

Ackoff, R. (1974). *Redesigning the future*. New York: John Wiley.

Ackoff, R. (1978). *The art of problem solving*. New York: John Wiley.

Agranoff, R. (1985). Services integration is still alive: Local intergovernmental bodies. *New England Journal of Human Services, 5*, 16–25.

Alexander, C. (1964). *Notes on the synthesis of form*. Cambridge, MA: Harvard University Press.

Alexander, C. (1965). A city is not a tree. *Architectural Forum, 122*.

Alexander, E. R. (1982). Design in the decision-making process. *Policy Sciences, 14*, 279–292.

Alexander, E. R. (1985). From idea to action: Notes for a contingency theory of the policy implementation process. *Administration & Society, 16*(4), 403–426.

Allison, G. (1971). *Essence of decisionmaking: Explaining the Cuban missile crisis*. Boston: Little, Brown.

American Dental Association, Council on Dental Therapeutics. (1975). Council classifies fluoride mouthrinse. *Journal of the American Dental Association, 91*, 1, 250.

Arrow, K., Hurwicz, L., & Uzawa, H. (1958). *Studies in linear and non-linear programming*. Stanford, CA: Stanford University Press.

Ashford, D. (1977). Political science and policy studies: Toward a structural solution. *Policy Studies Journal, 5*, 570–582.

Atkinson, M. M., & Chandler, M. A. (1983). *The politics of Canadian public policy*. Toronto: University of Toronto Press.

Aubert, V. (1982). *Retssociologi*. Oslo: Universitetsforlaget.

Auerbach, J. (1985, Spring). Commentary on Gilligan's *In a different voice*. *Feminist Studies, 11*.

Austin, D. M. (1978). Consolidation and integration. *Public Welfare, 36*(3), 20–28.

Austin, D. M. (1983). Program design issues in the improved administration of human services program. *Administration in Social Work, 7*, 1–11.

Ayer, A. J. (Ed.). (1959). *Logical positivism*. New York: The Free Press.

Ayers, R. (1986, July). The "social pact" as anti-inflation policy. *World Politics*, *28*(4).

Bachrach, P. (1967). *The theory of democratic elitism*. Boston: Little, Brown.

Bachrach, P., & Baratz, M. (1970). *Power and poverty*. New York: Oxford University Press.

Baer, J. (1988). *Reading the 14th Amendment: The inevitability of noninterpretivism*. Paper delivered at the annual meeting of the Western Political Science Association, San Francisco, CA.

Baier, V. E., March, J. G., & Setren, H. (1986). Implementation and ambiguity. *Scandinavian Journal of Management Studies*, *2*.

Bailey, S. K., & Mosher, E. K. (1968). *ESEA: The Office of Education administers a law*. Syracuse, NY: Syracuse University Press.

Balestra, P., & Nerlove, M. (1966). Pooling cross-section and time series data in the estimation of a dynamic model: The demand for natural gas. *Econometrica*, *34*, 585–612.

Barber, B. (1978). Control and responsibility in the powerful professions. *Political Science Quarterly*, *93*, 597–612.

Barber, G. (1986). Correlates of job satisfaction among human service workers. *Administration in Social Work*, *10*, 25–38.

Bardach, E. (1979). *The implementation game*. Cambridge, MA: MIT Press.

Bardach, E. (1980). On designing implementable programs. In G. Majone & E. S. Quade, *Pitfalls of analysis*. New York: John Wiley.

Barrett, S., & Fudge, C. (1981). *Policy and action*. London: Methuen.

Barthes, R. (1972). *Mythologies*. New York: Hill and Wang.

Baum, L. (1976). Implementation of judicial decisions: An organizational analysis. *American Politics Quarterly*, *4*, 86–114.

Bauer, R. (1966). *Social indicators*. Cambridge, MA: MIT Press.

Bauer, R., de Sola Pool, I., & Dexter, L. A. (1967). *American business and public policy*. New York: Atherton.

Behn, R. (1986). Ira Jackson and the Massachusetts Department of Revenue. *Case Material of Duke University*.

Bendor, J., & Moe, T. (1985). An adaptive model of bureaucratic politics. *American Political Science Review*, *79*, 755–774.

Berman, P. (1978). The study of macro and micro implementation. *Public Policy*, *27*, 157–184.

Berman, P. (1980). Thinking about programmed and adaptive implementation: Matching strategies to situations. In H. Ingram & D. Mann (Eds.), *Why policies succeed or fail*. Beverly Hills, CA: Sage.

Berman, P., & McLaughlin, M. (1976). Implementation of educational innovation. *The Education Forum*, *40*, 345–370.

Berry, J. (1984). *Feeding hungry people: Rulemaking in the food stamp program*. New Brunswick, NJ: Rutgers University Press.

Berry, W. D., & Feldman, S. (1985). *Multiple regression in practice*. Beverly Hills, CA: Sage.

Bickman, L. (1987). The functions of program theory. In L. Bickman (Ed.), *Using program theory in evaluation* (pp. 5–19). San Francisco: Jossey-Bass.

Blakely, C., Mayer, J., Gottschalk, R., Roitman, D., Schmitt, N., & Davidson, W. (1984). *Salient processes in the dissemination of social technologies* (Final report submitted to the National Science Foundation from Grant No. ISI–7920576–01). Lansing: Michigan State University.

Blankenburg, E. (1985). Research concept for the study of implementation. *Tidskrift för Rättssociologi, 2*(3/4), 205–226.

Bledstein, J. (1976). *The culture of professionalism.* New York: Norton.

Bobrow, D., & Dryzek, J. (1987). *Policy analysis by design.* Pittsburgh: University of Pittsburgh Press.

Bolman, L., & Deal, T. (1984). *Modern approaches to understanding and managing organizations.* San Francisco: Jossey-Bass.

Bowers, J., & Mills, G. (1981). William Ruckelshaus and the EPA. *Case Material of J.F. Kennedy School of Government.*

Bowman, A. O'M., Goggin, M. L., Lester, J. P., & O'Toole, L. J., Jr. (1987). *Third-generation implementation studies: Conceptual and methodological issues.* Paper presented at the 1987 annual meeting of the Midwest Political Science Association, Chicago, IL.

Bowman, A. O'M., & Lester, J. P. (1987). *Implementing intergovernmental policy: The Resource Conservation and Recovery Act of 1976.* Presented at the 1987 annual meeting of the Southern Political Science Association, Charlotte, NC.

Box, G.E.P., & Tiao, G. C. (1975). Intervention analysis with applications to economic and environmental problems. *Journal of the American Statistical Association, 70,* 70–79.

Braybrooke, D., & Lindblom, C. (1963). *A strategy of decision: The cognitive maps of political elites.* New York: The Free Press.

Brigham, J., & Brown, D. W. (1980). *Policy implementation: Penalties or incentives?* Beverly Hills, CA: Sage.

Brodkin, E. Z. (1986). *The false promise of administrative reform: Implementing quality control in welfare.* Philadelphia: Temple University Press.

Brown, B. (1983, June). Review of Carol Gilligan's *In a different voice. Sex Roles,* 9.

Brown, R. H. (1978). Bureaucracy as praxis: Toward a political phenomenology of organizations. *Administrative Science Quarterly, 23.*

Browne, A., & Wildavsky, A. (1984). Implementation as mutual adaptation. In J. L. Pressman & A. Wildavsky (Ed.), *Implementation* (3d ed.). Berkeley: University of California Press.

Buchanan, J., & Tullock, G. (1962). *The calculus of consent.* Ann Arbor: University of Michigan Press.

Bullock, C. S., & Lamb, C. M. (1984). A search for variables important in policy implementation. In C. S. Bullock & C. M. Lamb (Eds.), *Implementation and civil rights policy* (pp. 1–19). Monterey, CA: Brooks/Cole.

Bullock, C. S., III, & Lamb, C. M. (1984). *Implementation of civil rights policy.* Belmont, CA: Wadsworth.

Bunker, D. R. (1972). Policy sciences perspectives on implementation processes. *Policy Sciences, 3.*

Burke, J. P. (1986). *Bureaucratic responsibility.* Baltimore, MD: Johns Hopkins University Press.

Burke, J. P. (1987). A prescriptive view of the implementation process: When should bureaucrats exercise discretion? *Policy Studies Review, 7,* 217–231.

Burnham, W. D. (1980). American politics in the 1980s. *Dissent, 27,* 149–160.

Califano, J. A., Jr. (1981). *Governing America.* New York: Simon and Schuster.

Calista, D. J. (1986a, August). Linking policy intention and policy implementation: The role of the organization in the integration of human services. *Administration and Society*, *18*(2), 263–286.

Calista, D. J. (1986b). On the orthodoxy and tentativeness of reform. In D. J. Calista (Ed.), *Bureaucratic and governmental reform* (pp. 3–19). Greenwich, CT: JAI Press.

Calista, D. J. (1986c). Reorganization as reform: The implementation of integrated human services agencies. In D. J. Calista (Ed.), *Bureaucratic and governmental reform*. Greenwich, CT: JAI Press.

Calista, D. J. (1987). Resolving public sector implementation paradoxes through transaction costs analysis: Theory and application. *Policy Studies Review*, *7*, 232–245.

Campbell, D. T., & Stanley, J. C. (1966). *Experimental and quasi-experimental designs for research*. Chicago: Rand McNally.

Chen, H., & Rossi, P. H. (1980). The multi-goal, theory-driven approach to evolution: A model sinking basic and applied social science. *Social Forces*, *59*, 106–122.

Chi, K. S. (1987). What has happened to the comprehensive human services agency? *New England Journal of Human Services*, *7*, 24–30.

Chodorow, N. (1978). *The reproduction of mothering*. Berkeley: University of California Press.

Christensen, P. B. (1987). Organisationskultur og omstilling. *Politica*, *19*(4), 420–434.

Christensen, S., & Kreiner, K. (1984, June). *On the origin of organizational culture*. Paper prepared for the First International Conference on Organizational Symbolism and Corporate Culture, Lund, Sweden, Copenhagen School of Economics and Business Administration.

Chubb, J. E. (1985). The political economy of federalism. *American Political Science Review*, *79*, 994–1015.

Cingranelli, D., Hofferbert, R., & Ziegenhagen, E. (1981). Goal evolution through implementation: The problem for policy evaluation. In D. Palumbo, S. Fawcett, & P. Wright (Eds.), *Evaluating and optimizing public policy*. Lexington, MA: D.C. Heath.

Cobb, R., and Elder, C. (1984). *Participation in American politics: The dynamics of agenda building* (2d ed). Baltimore, MD: Johns Hopkins Press.

Cohen, A., et al. (1970). The human dimensions of administrative reform: Towards more differentiated strategies for change. *Development and change*, *2*, 2.

Cook, S. (1977). *A toxonomy of organizations: A conceptual review of the literature*. Manuscript.

Cook, T. D. (1985). Postpositivist critical multiplism. In R.L. Shotland & M.M. Mark (Eds.), *Social science and social policy* (pp. 21–62). Beverly Hills, CA: Sage.

Cook, T. D., & Shadish, W. (1986). Program evaluation: The worldly science. *Annual Review of Psychology*, *37*, 193–232.

Cronback, L. J., et al. (1980). *Toward reform of program evaluation*. San Francisco: Jossey-Bass.

Crotty, P. M. (1988, March/April). Assessing the role of federal administrative regions: An exploratory analysis. *Public Administration Review*, *48*, 642–648.

Cyert, R., & March, J. G. (1963). *A behavioral theory of the firm*. Englewood Cliffs, NJ: Prentice-Hall.

Dahl, R. A. (1971). *Polyarchy*. New Haven, CT: Yale University Press.

Dahl, R. A., & Lindblom, C. E. (1953). *Politics, economics, and welfare*. New York: Harper & Row.

Dalbert-Larsen, J. (1973). *Retssociologi*. Copenhagen: Akademisk Forlag.

Damgaard, E. (1981). Politiske sektorer: Jerntrekanter eller løse netværk? *Nordisk Administrativt Tidsskrift, 396*–411.

Danziger, J., Dutton, W., Kling, R., & Kraemer, K. (1982). *Computers and politics: High technology in American local governments.* New York: Columbia University Press.

Davis, C. E., & Lester, J. P. (1987). Decentralizing federal environmental policy. *Western Political Quarterly, 40,* 555–565.

de Haven-Smith, L., & Van Horn, C. E. (1984). Subgovernment conflict in public policy. *Policy Studies Journal, 12,* 627–642.

Denhardt, R. (1984). *Theories of public organization.* Monterey, CA: Brooks/Cole.

Derthick, M. (1972). *New towns in town.* Washington, DC: The Urban Institute.

Destler, I. M., & Sato, H. (Eds.). (1982). *Coping with U.S. Japanese economic conflicts.* Lexington, MA: Lexington Books.

Diesing, P. (1982). *Science and ideology in the policy sciences.* New York: De Gruyter/Aldine.

Dodd, L. C., & Schott, R. L. (1979). *Congress and the administrative state.* New York: John Wiley.

Domhoff, G. W. (1979). *The powers that be: Processes of ruling class domination in America.* New York: Vintage.

Donnel, A., & Hill, J. (1980, Spring). Women vs. managers: A significant case of no significant difference. *Organizational Dynamics.*

Downs, A. (1967). *Inside bureaucracy.* Boston: Little, Brown.

Downs, G. (1976). *Bureaucracy, innovation and public policy.* Lexington, MA: Lexington Books.

Dror, Y. (1984). *Policymaking under adversity.* New Brunswick, NJ: Transaction Books.

Dryzek, J. (1983). Don't toss coins into garbage cans: A prologue to policy design. *Journal of Public Policy, 3,* 345–367.

Dye, T. R. (1988). *Politics in states and communities.* Glenview, IL: Scott, Foresman/Little, Brown.

Dye, T. R., & Zeigler, H. (1987). *The irony of democracy* (7th ed.). Monterey, CA: Brooks/Cole.

Edelman, M. (1964). *The symbolic uses of politics.* Champaign: University of Illinois Press.

Edelman, M. (1988). *Constructing the political spectacle.* Chicago: University of Chicago Press.

Edwards, G. C., III. (1980). *Implementing public policy.* Washington, DC: Congressional Quarterly Press.

Elder, C., & Cobb, R. (1983). *The political uses of symbols.* New York: Longman.

Elmore, R., Gustafsson, G., & Hargrove, E. (1986). Comparing implementation processes in Sweden and the United States. *Scandinavian Political Studies, 9*(3), 209–233.

Elmore, R. F. (1978). Organizational models of social program implementation. *Public Policy, 26*(2), 185–228.

Elmore, R. F. (1982). Backward mapping: Implementation research and policy decisions. In W. Williams (Ed.), *Studying implementation: Methodological and administrative issues* (pp. 18–35). Chatham, NJ: Chatham House Publishers, Inc.

Elmore, R. F. (1985). Forward and backward mapping: Reversible logic in the analysis of public policy. In K. Hanf & T.A.J. Toonen (Eds.), *Policy implementation in federal and unitary systems* (pp. 33–70). Dordrecht: Martinus Nijhoff.

Elmore, R. F. (1986). Youth employment: National policy and local delivery in three US settings. In R.C. Rist (Ed.), *Finding work: Cross national perspectives on employment and training* (pp. 87–108). London: The Falmer Press.

Elmore, R. F. (1987a). Instruments and strategy in public policy. *Policy Studies Review*, 7(1), 174–186.

Elmore, R. F. (1987b). Implementation. *Journal of Policy Analysis and Management*, 6, 278–279.

Etzioni, A. (1960). Two approaches to organizational analysis. *Administrative Science Quarterly*, 5.

Eveland, J., Klepper, C., & Rogers, J. (1977). *The innovation process in public organizations*. Ann Arbor: University of Michigan.

Feller, I., Mezel, D., & Engel, A. (1974). *Diffusion of technology in state mission-oriented agencies*. University Park: Pennsylvania State University, Center for the Study of Science Policy.

Fenno, R. (1978). *Homestyle*. New York: Little, Brown.

Ferman, B., & Levin, M. A. (1987). Dilemmas of innovation and accountability: Entrepreneurs and chief executives. *Policy Studies Review*, 7, 187–199.

Finer, H. (1941). Administrative responsibility in democratic government. *Public Administration Review*, 1, 335–350.

Fiorena, M. P. (1977). *Congress: The electoral connection*. New Haven, CT: Yale University Press.

Flora, P., & Heidenheimer, A. J. (1981). *The development of welfare states in Europe and America*. New York: Transaction Books.

Florig, D. (1986, Spring). The concept of equal opportunity. *Polity*, 18(3).

Fox, C. J. (1980). The existential-phenomenological alternative to dichotomous thought. *Western Political Quarterly*, 33, 357–379.

Fox, C. J. (1987). Biases in public policy implementation evaluation. *Policy Studies Review*, 7(1), 128–141.

Fox, C. J. (1989). Free to choose, free to win, free to lose: The phenomenology of ethical space. *International Journal of Public Administration*.

Friedrich, C. J. (1940). Public policy and the nature of administrative responsibility. In E.S. Mason & C.J. Friedrich (Eds.), *Public policy, 1940* (pp. 3–24). Cambridge, MA: Harvard University Press.

Friedson, E. (1970). *Professional dominance*. New York: Atherton.

Fukui, H. (1977). Studies in policymaking: A review of the literature. In T.J. Pempel (Ed.), *Policymaking in contemporary Japan*. Ithaca, NY: Cornell University Press.

Gamson, W. A., & Lasch, K. E. (1980). *The political culture of social welfare policy* (Working paper no. 221, University of Michigan, Center for Research on Social Organization). Paper delivered at the Pinhas Sapir International Conference on Development, Tel Aviv University, Israel.

Gans, S. P., & Horton, G. T. (1975). *Integration of human services: The state and municipal levels*. New York: Praeger.

Gilligan, C. (1982). *In a different voice*. Cambridge, MA: Harvard University Press.

Glisson, C., & Durick, M. (1988). Predictors of job satisfaction and organizational commitment in human service organizations. *Administrative Science Quarterly*, 33, 61–81.

Glynn, T. (1977). *The implementation of public policy: The role of executive leadership*. Unpublished Ph.D. dissertation, Brandeis University.

Goffman, E. (1959). *The presentation of self in everyday life*. New York: Doubleday.

Goffman, E. (1967). *Interaction ritual: Essays in face to face behavior*. New York: Doubleday.

Goffman, E. (1974). *Frame analysis*. New York: Harper & Row.

Goggin, M. L. (1986). The "too few cases/too many variables" problem in implementation research. *Western Political Quarterly, 39*(2), 328–347.

Goggin, M. L. (1987). *Policy design and the politics of implementation: The case of child health policy in the American states*. Knoxville: University of Tennessee Press.

Goggin, M. L. (1988). *Policy redesign: A concept and its empirical referents*. Paper presented at the 1988 annual meeting of the Western Political Science Association, San Francisco, CA.

Goggin, M. L., Bowman, A. O'M., Lester, J. P., & O'Toole, L. J., Jr. (1990). *Implementation theory and practice: Toward a third generation*. Glenview, IL: Scott, Foresman/Little, Brown.

Goldberg, V. (1976). Regulation and administered contracts. *The Bell Journal of Economics, 7*, 426–448.

Golembiewski, R. T. (1965). *Men, management, and morality: Toward a new organizational ethic*. New York: McGraw-Hill.

Golembiewski, R. T. (1970). Organizational patterns of the future: What they mean to personnel administration. In R.T. Golembiewski & M. Cohen (Eds.), *People in public service* (pp. 198–216). Itasca, IL: F.E. Peacock.

Gormley, W., & Peters, B. G. (1986). *Policy problems and their remedies*. Paper presented at Annual Meeting of Midwest Political Science Association, Chicago, IL.

Gormley, W. T. (1986). Regulatory issue networks in a federal system. *Polity*.

Greenstein, F. (1981). *The hidden hand presidency*. New York: Basic Books.

Greer, A. L. (1977). Advances in the study of diffusion of innovation in health care organizations. *Milbank Memorial Fund Quarterly, Health and Society, 55*, 505–532.

Grodzins, M. (1963). Centralization and decentralization in the American federal system. In R. Goldwin (Ed.), *A nation of states*. Chicago: Rand McNally.

Gulick, L. (1933). Politics, administration, and the New Deal. *Annals, 169*, 55–66.

Gunnell, J. G. (1975). *Philosophy, science, and political inquiry*. Morristown, NJ: General Learning Press.

Gusfield, J. R. (1963). *Symbolic crusade*. Chicago: University of Illinois Press.

Halberstam, D. (1986). *The reckoning*. New York: Norton.

Hall, G. E., & Loucks, S. F. (1978). *Innovation configuration: Analyzing the adaptations of innovations*. Austin: University of Texas at Austin, Research and Development Center for Teacher Education.

Hall, J., & MacManus, S. (1982). Tracking decisions and consequences: The field network evaluation approach. In W. Williams (Ed.), *Studying implementation*. Chatham, NJ: Chatham House.

Hargrove, E. (1975). *The missing link*. Washington, DC: The Urban Institute.

Harrington, J. L. (1988). *Politics and policy in states and communities*. Glenview, IL: Scott, Foresman/Little, Brown.

Hartz, L. (1955). *The liberal tradition in America*. New York: Harcourt, Brace & World.

Hasenfeld, Y. (1980). Implementation of change in human service organizations. *Social Service Review, 54.*

Hayek, F. (1945). The use of knowledge in society. *American Economics Review, 45,* 519–530.

Heclo, H. (1974). *Modern social politics in Britain and Sweden.* New Haven, CT: Yale University Press.

Heclo, H. (1978). Issue networks and the executive establishment. In A. King (Ed.), *The new American political system.* Washington, DC: American Enterprise Institute.

Heclo, H. (1984). Comments: An executive's success can have costs. In L. Salamon & M. Lund (Eds.), *The Reagan presidency and the governing of America* (pp. 371–374). Washington, DC: The Urban Institute.

Hicks, J. (1946). *Value and capital* (2d ed.). Oxford: Clarendon Press.

Hirschman, A. (1970). *Exit, voice and loyalty.* Cambridge, MA: Harvard University Press.

Hjern, B. (1978). *Implementation and network analysis.* Discussion paper. International Institute of Management, Wissenschaftzentrum, Berlin.

Hjern, B. (1982a). Review of Mazmanian & Sabatier (Eds.), *Effective policy implementation. Journal of Public Policy, 2,* 301–308.

Hjern, B. (1982b, August). Implementation research—The link gone missing. *Journal of Public Policy, 2*(3), 301–308.

Hjern, B. (1987). *Policy analysis: An implementation approach.* Paper presented at the 1987 annual meeting of the American Political Science Association, Chicago, IL.

Hjern, B., Hanf, K., & Porter, D. (1978). Local networks of manpower training in the FRG and Sweden. In K. Hanf & F.W. Scharpf (Eds.), *Interorganizational policy making* (pp. 304–341). London: Sage.

Hjern, B., & Hull, C. (1980). *Coordination and control in the mixed economy: Implementation structures as a way of getting at what's going on out there.* Discussion papers. International Institute of Management, West Berlin.

Hjern, B., & Hull, C. (1982, June). Implementation research as empirical constitutionalism. *European Journal of Political Research, 10,* 105–116.

Hjern, B., & Hull, C. (1983, September 1–4). *Going interorganizational: Weber meets Durkheim.* Paper presented at the 1983 annual meeting of the American Political Science Association.

Hjern, B., & Hull, C. (1985). Small firm employment creation: An assistance structure explanation. In K. Hanf & T.A.J. Toonen (Eds.), *Policy implementation in federal and unitary systems: Questions of analysis and design* (pp. 131–156). Dordrecht: Martinus Nijhoff.

Hjern, B., & Porter, D. (1981). Implementation structures: A new unit of administrative analysis. *Organization Studies, 2,* 211–227.

Hogwood, B. W., & Peters, B. G. (1985). *The pathology of public policy.* Oxford: Oxford University Press.

Hood, C. (1983). *The tools of government.* London: Macmillan.

Hood, C. (1986). *Administrative analysis.* Brighton, Sussex: Wheatsheaf.

Hoppe, R., van de Graaf, H., & van Dijk, A. (1987). Implementation research and policy design: Problem tractability, polity theory and feasibility testing. *International Review of Administrative Sciences, 53,* 581–604.

Horkheimer, M., & Adorno, T. A. (1972). *Dialectic of enlightenment*. New York: Herder and Herder.

Horowitz, H. S. (1973). A review of systemic and topical fluorides for the prevention of dental caries. *Community Dental Oral Epidemiology*, *1*, 104–114.

Howe, I. (1982). *Beyond the welfare state*. New York: Schocken Books.

Huitt, R. (1969). *Studies of Congress and congressional committees*. In R. Huitt & R. Peabody (Eds.), *Two decades of analysis of Congress*. New York: Harper & Row.

Hull, C., & Hjern, B. (1987). *Helping small firms grow, an implementation perspective*. London: Croom Helm.

Huntington, S. (1981). *American politics: The promise of disharmony*. Cambridge, MA: Harvard University Press.

Huntington, S. P. (1975). The United States. In M. Crozier, S. Huntington, & J. Watanuki (Eds.), *The crisis of democracy* (pp. 59–118). New York: New York University Press.

Hurwicz, L. (1960). Optimality and informational efficiency in resource allocation processes. In K. Arrow, S. Karlin, & P. Suppes (Eds.), *Mathematical methods in the social sciences*. Stanford, CA: Stanford University Press.

Husserl, E. (1954). *Die krisis der europanaische Wissenschaft und die transzendentale Phanomenologie*. The Hague: Martinus Nijhoff.

Ianello, K. (1987). *Making sense of decentralized participation*. Unpublished manuscript, Dartmouth College, Department of Government.

Imershein, A. W. (1985). The influence of Reagan's new federalism on human services in Florida. *New England Journal of Human Services*, *5*, 17–24.

Imershein, A. W., Chackerian, R., Martin, P., & Frumpkin, M. (1983). Measuring organizational change in human services. *New England Journal of Human Services*, *3*, 21–29.

Ingraham, P. (1987). Policy implementation and the public service. In R. B. Denhardt & E. T. Jennings, Jr. (Eds.), *The revitalization of the public service*. Columbia: University of Missouri.

Ingraham, P. W. (1987). Toward more systematic consideration of policy design. *Policy Studies Journal*, *15*, 611–628.

Ingram, H. (1977). Policy implementation through bargaining: The case of federal grants-in-aid. *Public Policy*, *25*, 499–526.

Ingram, H., & Mann, D. (1980). Policy failure: An issue deserving analysis. In H. Ingram & D. Mann (Eds.), *Why policies succeed or fail* (pp. 11–32). Beverly Hills, CA: Sage Publications.

Jayaratne, S., & Chess, W. A. (1983). Job satisfaction and turnover among social work administrators: A national survey. *Administration in Social Work*, *7*, 11–22.

Jenkins-Smith, H. C., St. Clair, G., & Martin, D. B. (1987, April 9–11). *Change and continuity in elite belief systems: The 1973–1979 OSC leasing debate*. Paper presented at the 1987 annual meeting of the Midwest Political Science Association, Chicago, IL.

Jennings, B. (1983). Interpretive social science and policy analysis. In D. Callahan & B. Jennings (Eds.), *Ethics, the social sciences and policy analysis*. New York: Plenum.

Jick, T. (1979). Mixing qualitative and quantitative methods: Triangulation in action. *Administrative Science Quarterly*, *24*(4), 602–611.

Johansen, L. N., & Kristensen, O. P. (1982). Corporatist traits in Denmark, 1946–1976.

In G. Lembruch & P. C. Schmitter (Eds.), *Patterns of corporatist policy-making.* London: Sage.

Johnson, C. (1982). *MITI and the Japanese Miracle.* Palo Alto, CA: Stanford University Press.

Johnson, C. (1986). The institutional foundations of Japanese industrial policy. In C. Barfied & W. Schambra (Eds.), *Politics of industrial policy.* Washington, DC: American Enterprise Institute.

Johnson, R. W., & O'Connor, R. E. (1979). Inter-agency limitations on policy implementation: You can't always get what you want, but sometimes you get what you need. *Administration and Society, 11,* 193–215.

Johnson, T. (1972). *Professions and power.* London: Macmillan.

Jones, C. O. (1974). Speculative augmentation in federal air pollution policy-making. *Journal of Politics, 36,* 438–464.

Judd, D. (1988). *The politics of American cities* (3rd ed.). Boston: Scott, Foresman.

Kaufman, F. X., Majone, G., & Ostrom, V. (Eds.). (1986). *Guidance, control and evaluation in the public sector.* Berlin: De Gruyter/Aldine.

Kaufman, H. (1964). Organization theory and political theory. *American Political Science Review, 58.*

Kaufman, H. (1977). *Red tape.* Washington, DC: The Brookings Institution.

Kilman, R., & Mitroff, I. (1977). *Systems design: Normative theory and the MAPS design technology.* New York: Elsevier.

King, A. (1975). Overload: Problems of governing in the 1970s. *Political Studies, 23,* 284–296.

Kingdon, J. W. (1984). *Agendas, alternatives, and public politics.* Boston: Little, Brown.

Kirk, J., & Miller, M. L. *Reliability and validity in quantitative research.* Beverly Hills, CA: Sage.

Kirschen, E. S. (1964). *Economic policy in our time.* Amsterdam: North-Holland.

Kirst, M., & Jung, R. (1982). The utility of a longitudinal approach in assessing implementation: A thirteen year view of Title 1, ESEA. In W. Williams (Ed.), *Studying implementation: Methodological and administrative issues* (pp. 119–148). Chatham, NJ: Chatham Publishers, Inc.

Knoepfel, P., & Weidner, H. (1982). A conceptual framework for studying implementation. In P. Downing & K. Hanf (Eds.), *The implementation of pollution control programs.* Tallahassee, FL: Policy Studies Program.

Koopmans, T. (1951). *Activity analysis of production and allocation.* New York: John Wiley.

Kowalewski, D. (1980). The protest uses of symbolic politics in the USSR. *Journal of Politics, 42.*

Kuhn, T. (1970). *The structure of scientific revolutions* (2nd ed.). Chicago: University of Chicago Press.

Lambright, H. (1979). *Technology transfer to cities: Process of choice at the local level.* Boulder, CO: Westview Press.

Lane, J. E. (1983). The concept of implementation. *Statsvetenskaplig Tidskrift, 86,* 17–40.

Langbein, L. I. (1980). *Discovering whether programs work: A guide to statistical methods for program evaluation.* Santa Monica, CA: Goodyear.

Larson, J. S. (1980). *Why government programs fail: Improving policy implementation.* New York: Praeger.

Lawrence, P., & Lorsch, J. (1969). *Organization and environment*. Homewood, IL: Irwin.

Lazin, F. (1980). The effects of administrative linkages on implementation: Welfare policy in Israel. *Policy Sciences, 12*.

Lerner, A. (1944). *The economics of control*. New York: Macmillan.

Lester, J. P. (1985a). Hazardous waste and policy implementation: The subnational role. *Hazardous waste and hazardous materials, 2*, 381–397.

Lester, J. P. (1985b). New federalism and environmental policy. *Publius, 16*, 149–165.

Lester, J. P., & Bowman, A. O'M. (1989). Implementing intergovernmental policy: A test of the Sabatier-Mazmanian model. *Polity*.

Lester, J. P., Bowman, A. O'M., Goggin, M. L., & O'Toole, L. J., Jr. (1987). Public policy implementation: Evolution of the field and agenda for future research. *Policy Studies Review, 7*(1), 200–216.

Levin, M., & Ferman, B. (1985). *The political hand: Policy implementation and youth employment programs*. Elmsford, NY: Pergamon Press.

Levin, M., & Hausman, B. (1985). *Gordon Chase: The best and the brightest doing good deeds in New York*. Association for Public Policy Analysis and Management Research Conference Presentation.

Levi-Strauss, C. (1963). *Structural anthropology*. New York: Basic Books.

Levy, F., Meltzner, A., & Wildavsky, A. (1974). *Urban outcomes*. Berkeley: University of California Press.

Lewis-Beck, M. S. (1980). *Applied regression: An introduction*. Beverly Hills, CA: Sage.

Leys, W.A.R. (1943). Ethics and administrative discretion. *Public Administration Review, 3*, 10–23.

Lincoln, Y. & Guba, E. (1986). *Naturalistic inquiry*. Beverly Hills, CA: Sage.

Lindblom, C. (1959). The science of muddling through. *Public Administrative Review*, 79–88.

Lindblom, C. (1977). *Politics and markets*. New York: Basic Books.

Lindblom, C. (1980). *The policymaking process* (2nd ed.). Englewood Cliffs, NJ: Prentice-Hall.

Linder, S. H., & Peters, B. G. (1984). From social theory to policy design. *Journal of Public Policy, 4*, 237–259.

Linder, S. H., & Peters, B. G. (1986). *Policy formulation and the challenge of conscious design*. Paper presented at Annual Research Meeting of the Association for Public Policy Analysis and Management, Austin, TX.

Linder, S. H., & Peters, B. G. (1987a). A design perspective on policy implementation: The fallacies of misplaced prescription. *Policy Studies Review, 6*(3), 459–475.

Linder, S. H., & Peters, B. G. (1987b). Relativism, contingency, and the definition of success in implementation research. *Policy Studies Review, 7*(1), 16–27.

Lipsky, M. (1978). Standing the study of implementation on its head. In W. D. Burnham & M. Weinberg (Eds.), *American politics and public policy*. Cambridge, MA: MIT Press.

Lipsky, M. (1980). *Street-level bureaucracy: Dilemmas of the individual in public services*. New York: Russell Sage Foundation.

Long, N. (1986). Power and administration. In P. Nivola & D. Rosenbloom (Eds.), *Classic readings in American politics* (pp. 448–458). New York: St. Martin's Press.

Love, J., & Sederberg, P. C. (1987, Autumn). Euphony and cacophony in policy implementation. *Policy Studies Review*, 7(1), 155–174.

Lowi, T. (1964). American business, public policy, case studies, and political theory. *World Politics*, *16*, 677–715.

Lowi, T. (1969). *The end of liberalism*. New York: W. W. Norton.

Lundquist L. (1980). *The hare and the tortoise: Clean air policies in the United States and Sweden*. Ann Arbor: University of Michigan Press.

Lynn, L. (1980). *Designing public policy*. Santa Monica, CA: Goodyear.

Lynn, L. (1987). *Managing public policy*. Boston: Little, Brown.

Lynn, L. E., Jr. (1984). The Reagan administration and the renitent bureaucracy. In L. Salamon & M. Lund (Eds.), *The Reagan presidency and the governing of America* (pp. 339–370). Washington, DC: The Urban Institute Press.

Lynn, L. E., Jr. (1986). *Public executives as policy makers: Observations on theory and practice*. Paper presented at the Deuxième Colloque International de la Revue Politiques and Management Public, Lyon, France.

McDonnell, L., & Elmore, R. (1987, November). *Alternative policy instruments*. Unpublished paper.

McGowan, E. F. (1976). Rational fantasies. *Policy Sciences*, *7*.

McKelvey, B. (1982). *Organizational systematics: Taxonomy, evolution, classification*. Berkeley: University of California Press.

McLaughlin, M. (1976). Implementation as mutual adaptation. *Teachers College Record*, *77*, 339–351.

MacLennan, B. W. (1981). Political power and policy formulation, implementation, and evaluation. In D. J. Palumbo & M. A. Harder (Eds.), *Implementing public policy*. Lexington, MA: Lexington Books.

McMahon, L., Barrett, S., & Hill, M. (1983). Power bargaining models in policy analysis. *Public Administration Bulletin*, *43*, 197–212.

McNeely, R. L., Feyerherm, W. H., & Johnson, R. E. (1986). Services integration and job satisfaction reactions in a comprehensive human resource agency. *Administration in Social Work*, *10*, 39–53.

Maddala, G. S. (1971). The use of variance components models in pooling cross section and time series data. *Econometrica*, *39*, 341–358.

Majone, G., & Wildavsky, A. (1978). Implementation as evolution. In H. E. Freeman (Ed.), *Policy Studies Annual Review* (Vol. 2). Beverly Hills, CA: Sage.

Majone, G., & Wildavsky, A. (1984). Implementation as evolution. In J. Pressman & A. Wildavsky (Eds.), *Implementation* (3d ed.). Berkeley: University of California Press.

March, J., & Olsen, J. P. (1985). The new institutionalism: Organizational factors in political life. *APSR*, *77*, 281–296.

March, J., & Simon, H. A. (1958). *Organizations*. New York: John Wiley.

Marcus, A. A. (1980). *Promise and performance: Choosing and implementing environmental policy*. Westport, CT: Greenwood Press.

Marcuse, H. (1964). *One dimensional man*. Boston: Beacon.

Marschak, J., & Radner, R. (1971). *The economic theory of teams*. New Haven, CT: Yale University Press.

Marschak, T. (1965). Economic theories of organization. In J. G. March (Ed.), *Handbook of organizations*. Chicago: Rand McNally.

Martin, P. Y., Chackerian, R., Imershein, A. W., & Frumpkin, M. L. (1983). The concept of "integrated" services reconsidered. *Social Sciences Quarterly, 64,* 747–763.

Matthews, D. (1960). *United States senators and their world.* New York: Vintage.

Matthews, D., & Stimson, J. (1975). *Yeas and nays: Normal decision-making in the U.S. House of Representatives.* New York: John Wiley.

May, J., & Wildavsky, A. (Eds.). (1978). *The policy cycle.* Beverly Hills, CA: Sage.

Mayhew, D. (1974). *Congress: The electoral connection.* New Haven, CT: Yale University Press.

Mazmanian, D. A., & Sabatier, P. A. (1981). *Effective policy implementation.* Lexington, MA: Lexington Books.

Mazmanian, D. A., & Sabatier, P. A. (1983). *Implementation and public policy.* Glenview, IL: Scott, Foresman.

Meltsner, A. J., & Bellavita, C. (1983). *The policy organization.* Beverly Hills, CA: Sage.

Merleau-Ponty, M. (1962). *The phenomenology of perception.* London: Routledge and Kegan Paul.

Merton, R., Fiske, M., & Kendall, P. K. (1956). *The focused interview.* Glencoe, IL: The Free Press.

Miller, T. C. (Ed.). (1984a). *Public sector performance: A conceptual turning point.* Baltimore, MD: Johns Hopkins University Press.

Miller, T. C. (1984b). Conclusion: A design science perspective. In T. C. Miller (Ed.), *Public sector performance: A conceptual turning point.* Baltimore, MD: Johns Hopkins University Press.

Milward, H. B. (1980). Policy entrepreneurship and bureaucratic demand creation. In H. Ingram & D. Mann (Eds.), *Why policies succeed or fail.* Beverly Hills, CA: Sage.

Mishan, E. (1971). *Cost benefit analysis.* New York: Praeger.

Mladenka, K. R. (1980). The urban bureaucracy and the Chicago political machine. *American Political Science Review.*

Moe, T. M. (1985). Control and feedback in economic regulation: The case of the NLRB. *The American Political Science Review, 79,* 1094–1116.

Mohr, L. B. (1967). The concept of organizational goal. *American Political Science Review, 67,* 470–481.

Mohr, L. B. (1978). Process theory and variance theory in innovation research. In M. Radnor et al. (Eds.), *The diffusion of innovations: An assessment* (Report prepared for the National Science Foundation, NTIS No. PB–287 687). Evanston, IL: Northwestern University.

Molineu, H. (1980, Summer). Carter and human rights: Administrative impact of a symbolic policy. *Policy Studies Journal, 9*(6).

Monahan, J., & Scheirer, M. A. (1988). The role of linking agents in the diffusion of health promotion programs. *Health Education Quarterly, 15,* 417–433.

Montjoy, R. S., & O'Toole, L. J., Jr. (1979). Toward a theory of policy implementation: An organizational perspective. *Public Administration Review, 39,* 46576.

Montjoy, R. S., & O'Toole, L. J., Jr. (1986). Policy recommendations for multi-actor implementation: An assessment of the field. *Journal of Public Policy, 6,* 181–210.

Moore, S. (1987). *Street-level tasks: A decision making approach.* Paper presented at American Political Science Association meeting.

Morris, C. (1980). *The cost of good intentions*. New York: Norton.

Morse, R., & Olson, E. (1983, Fall). Japan's bureaucratic edge. *Foreign Policy*, 171.

Mosher, F. (1968). *Democracy and the public service*. New York: Oxford University Press.

Mosher, F. (1980). The changing responsibilities and tactics of the federal government. *Public Administration Review*, *40*, 541–553.

Mouzelis, N. P. (1967). *Organization and bureaucracy*. Chicago: Aldine.

Moynihan, D. P. (1969). *Maximum feasible misunderstanding*. New York: Free Press.

Murphy, J. (1971). Title I of ESEA: The politics of implementing federal education reform. *Harvard Education Review*, *2*, 35–63.

Murphy, J. (1971). Title I of ESEA: The politics of implementing federal education reform. *Harvard Education Review*, *41*, 35–63.

Musgrave, R. (1959). *The theory of public finance: A study in political economy*. New York: McGraw-Hill.

Musheno, M. C. (1981). On the hazards of selecting intervention points: Time series analysis of mandated policies. In D. J. Palumbo & M. Harder (Eds.), *Implementing public policy* (pp. 77–91). Lexington, MA: D. C. Heath.

Musheno, M. C., Palumbo, D. J., Maynard-Moody, S., & Levine, J. P. (1989, May). Community corrections as an organizational innovation: What works and why. *Journal of Research in Crime and Delinquency*, *26*, 136–167.

Mutschler, E., & Cnaan, R. A. (1985). Success and failure of computerized information systems: Two case studies in human service agencies. *Administration in Social Work*, *9*, 67–79.

Myrtle, R. C. (1983). A managerial view of policy implementation. *American Review of Public Administration*, *17*, 17–32.

Nachmias, D. (1979). *Public policy evaluation: Approaches and methods*. New York: St. Martin's Press.

Nakamura, R. T. (1980, May). Beyond purism and professionalism. *American Journal of Political Science*.

Nakamura, R. T. (1985). *JETRO and import promotion: A case of policy implementation in Japan*. Paper delivered at the International Political Science Association World Congress.

Nakamura, R. T. (1987). The textbook policy process and implementation research. *Policy Studies Review*, *7*(1), 142–154.

Nakamura, R. T., & Pinderhughes, D. (1981). Changing anacosta. In D. Palumbo & M. Harder (Eds.), *Implementing public policies*. Lexington, MA: D. C. Heath.

Nakamura, R. T., & Smallwood, F. (1980). *The politics of policy implementation*. New York: St. Martin's Press.

Nathan, R. P. (1983). *The administrative presidency*. New York: John Wiley.

Nathan, R. P. (1984). Comments: Political administration is legitimate. In L. Salamon & M. Lund (Eds.), *The Reagan presidency and the governing of America*. Washington, DC: The Urban Institute Press.

Nathan, R. P., et al. (1983). *The consequences of cuts: The effects of the Reagan domestic program on state and local governments*. Princeton, NJ: Princeton University Press.

National Journal. (1988, March 5).

Niskanen, W. (1971). *Bureaucracy and representative government*. Chicago: Aldine/Atherton.

Noll, R. (1971). *Reforming regulation*. Washington, DC: The Brookings Institution.

Nystrom, P. C., & Starbuck, W. H. (1981). *Handbook of organizational design*. New York: Oxford University Press.

Offe, C. (1984). *Contradictions of the welfare state*. Cambridge, MA: MIT Press.

Olsen, J. P. (1972). Public policy-making and theories of organizational choice. *Scandinavian Political Studies*, *7*, 45–62.

Orfield, G. (1972). *The reconstruction of southern education*. New York: John Wiley.

Orfield, G. (1975). How to make desegregation work. *Law and Contemporary Problems*, *39*, 314–340.

Ostrom, V. (1974). *The intellectual crisis in American public administration*. University: University of Alabama Press.

O'Toole, L., & Montjoy, R. (1984). Interorganizational policy implementation: A theoretical perspective. *Public Administration Review*, *49*(b), 491–503.

Palumbo, D. J. (1987). Implementation: What have we learned and still need to know? (Introduction to symposium). *Policy Studies Review*, *7*(1), 91–102.

Palumbo, D. J. (1988). *Public policy in America: Government in action*. San Diego: Harcourt Brace Jovanovich.

Palumbo, D. J., & Calista, D. (1987). Implementation: What have we learned and still need to know? (symposium). *Policy Studies Review*, *7* (1), 91–247.

Palumbo, D. J., & Harder, M. (Eds.). (1981). *Implementing public policy*. Lexington, MA: D. C. Heath.

Palumbo, D. J., Maynard-Moody, S., & Wright, P. (1984, February). Measuring degrees of successful implementation: Achieving policy versus statutory goals. *Evaluation Review*, *8*(1), 45–74.

Palumbo, D. J., Musheno, M., & Maynard-Moody, S. (1985). Public sector entrepreneurs: The doers and shakers of program innovation. In J. Wholey, M. Abrahamson, & C. Bellavita (Eds.), *Creating excellence: The role of evaluators and managers* (pp. 69–83). Lexington, MA: Lexington Books.

Palumbo, D. J., & Nachmias, D. (1983). The preconditions for successful evaluation: Is there an ideal paradigm? *Policy Sciences*, *16*, 67–79.

Palumbo, D. J., & Olivario, A. (1989, June). Implementing theory and the theory-drive approach to validity. *Evaluation and Program Planning*.

Patrick, H. (1982). The economic dimensions of the US Japan alliance: An overview. In D. Okimoto (Ed.), *Japan's economy*. Boulder, CO: Westview.

Patterson, J. (1981). *America's struggle against poverty 1900–1980*. Cambridge, MA: Harvard University Press.

Pechman, J. A., & Timpane, M. P. (1975). *Work incentives and income guarantees: The New Jersey negative income tax experiment*. Washington, DC: The Brookings Institution.

Pempel, T. J. (1982). *Policy and politics in Japan*. Philadelphia: Temple University Press.

Perry, J. L., & Rainey, H. G. (1988). The public-private distinction in organization theory: A critique and research strategy. *Academy of Management Review*, *13*, 182–200.

Peters, T. J., & Waterman, R., Jr. (1982). *In search of excellence: Lessons from America's best-run companies*. New York: Harper & Row.

Pinchot, G. (1985). *Intrapreneuring: Why you don't have to leave the corporation to become an entrepreneur*. Cambridge, MA: Harper & Row.

Plovsing, J. (1985). Socialreformens idealer og praksis. *Politica, 17*(4), 502–519.

Polsby, N. W. (1984). *Political innovation in America.* New Haven, CT: Yale University Press.

Popper, K. R. (1968). *Conjectures and refutations: The growth of scientific knowledge.* New York: Harper.

Posner, R. (1972). *Economic analysis of law.* Boston: Little, Brown.

Premfors, R. (1981). *Genomförande och utvardering av offentlig politik.* Stockholm: University of Stockholm, Department of Political Science.

Pressman, J. (1975). *Federal programs and city politics.* Berkeley: University of California Press.

Pressman, J. L., & Wildavsky, A. (1986). *Implementation.* Berkeley: University of California Press.

Price, D. K. (1965). *The scientific estate.* Cambridge, MA: Harvard University Press.

Prottas, J. M. (1979). *People-processing.* Lexington, MA: Lexington Books.

Rabinow, P., & Sullivan, W. M. (1987). The interpretive turn. In P. Rabinow & W. M. Sullivan (Eds.), *Interpretive social science: A second look.* Berkeley: University of California Press.

Rainey, G. W., Jr., & Rainey, H. G. (1984, April 8–11). *Organizational redesign in the public sector: Modularization of the social security claims process vs. the presumed inviolability of classical hierarchy.* Paper presented at the national conference of the American Society for Public Administration, Denver, CO.

Rainey, G. W., Jr., & Rainey, H. G. (1986a). Breaching the hierarchical imperative: The modularization of the social security claims process. In D. J. Calista (Ed.), *Bureaucratic and governmental reform* (pp. 171–195). Greenwich, CT: JAI Press.

Rainey, G. W., Jr., & Rainey, H. G. (1986b). Structural overhaul in a government agency: Implications of social security claims modularization for central OD principles and techniques. *Public Administration Quarterly, 10,* 206–228.

Rasmussen, C. (1986). *Barrierr for iværksætteise.* Unpublished master's thesis. Aarhus: University of Aarhus, Institute of Political Science.

Reid, H. (1980–1981). Appalachian policy, the corporate state, and American values: A critical perspective. *Policy Studies Journal, 9,* 622–637.

Rein, M. (1983). Action frames and problem setting. In *From policy to practice.* London: Macmillan.

Rein, M., & Rabinovitz, F. (1978). Implementation: A theoretical perspective. In W. D. Burnham & M. W. Weinberg (Eds.), *American politics and public policy* (pp. 307–335). Cambridge, MA: MIT Press.

Ricci, D. M. (1984). *The tragedy of political science.* New Haven, CT: Yale University Press.

Richardson, J. J. (1982). *Policy styles in Western Europe.* London: Allen and Unwin.

Rimlinger, G. V. (1971). *Welfare policy and industrialization in Europe, America, and Russia.* New York: John Wiley.

Ripley, R. P. (1985). *Policy analysis in political science.* Chicago: Nelson Hall.

Ripley, R. B., & Franklin, G. A. (1982). *Bureaucracy and policy implementation.* Homewood, IL: Dorsey Press.

Ripley, R. B., & Franklin, G. A. (1986). *Policy implementation and bureaucracy.* Chicago: Dorsey.

Roberts-Gray, C., & Scheirer, M. A. (1988, Winter). Checking the congruence between a program and its organizational environment. In K. J. Conrad & C. Roberts-Gray (Eds.), *Evaluating program environments* (New Directions in Program Evaluation, No. 40). San Francisco: Jossey-Bass.

Robertson, D. B. (1984, May). Program implementation versus program design: Which accounts for policy 'failure'? *Policy Studies Review, 3*(3–4), 391–406.

Robertson, D. B. (1984, Winter). Planned incapacity to succeed? Policymaking structure and policy failure. *Policy Studies Review, 8*(4).

Robinson, J. (Ed.). (1973). *State legislative innovation: Case studies of Washington, Ohio, Florida, Illinois, Wisconsin, and California.* New York: Praeger.

Robinson, M. (1967). *Health centers and community needs* (Inter-University Case Program #105). Indianapolis: Bobbs-Merrill.

Rodgers, H. R., & Bullock, C. S. (1972). *Law and social change: Civil rights laws and their consequences.* New York: McGraw-Hill.

Rogers, E. M. (1983). *The diffusion of innovations* (3d ed.). New York: The Free Press.

Rohr, J. (1988, July). Bureaucratic morality in the United States. *International Political Science Review, 9* (3), 167–179.

Romer, T., & Rosenthal, H. (1978). Political resource allocation, controlled agendas, and the status quo. *Public Choice, 33,* 27–44.

Romzek, B. S., & Dubnick, M. J. (1987). Accountability in the public sector: Lessons from the Challenger tragedy. *Public Administration Review, 47,* 227–238.

Rourke, F. (1984). *Bureaucracy, politics and public policy* (3d ed.). Boston: Little, Brown.

Russell, P. A., Lankford, M. W., & Grinnel, R. M., Jr. (1984). Administrative styles of social work supervisors in a human service agency. *Administration in Social Work, 8,* 1–16.

Sabatier, P. A. (1986). Top-down and bottom-up approaches to implementation research: A critical analysis and suggested synthesis. *Journal of Public Policy, 6*(1), 21–48.

Sabatier, P. A., Brasher, A., & Jenkins-Smith, H. (1987). *Measuring change over time in elite beliefs and public policy: Content analysis of public documents.* Paper presented at the annual meeting of the Midwest Political Science Association, Chicago, IL.

Sabatier, P. A., & Mazmanian, D. A. (1979). The conditions of effective implementation: A guide to accomplishing policy objectives. *Policy Analysis, 5,* 481–504.

Sabatier, P. A., & Mazmanian, D. A. (1980). The implementation of public policy. *Policy Studies Journal, 8,* 531–653.

Sabatier, P. A., & Mazmanian, D. A. (1983). Policy implementation. In S. Nagel (Ed.), *The encyclopedia of policy studies* (pp. 143–169). New York: Marcel Dekker.

Sætren, H. (1983). *Iverksettning av offentlig politik.* Oslo: Universitetsforlaget.

Salamon, L. (1981). Rethinking public management: Third party government and the changing forms of government action. *Public Policy, 29,* 255–275.

Salisbury, R. (1968). The analysis of public policy: A search for theories and roles. In A. Ranney (Ed.), *Political science and public policy.* Chicago: Markham.

Sapolsky, H. M. (1972). *The Polaris system development.* Cambridge, MA: Harvard University Press.

Schattsneider, E. (1960). *The semi-sovereign people.* New York: Holt, Rinehart and Winston.

Schein, E. H. (1985). *Organizational culture and leadership*. San Francisco: Jossey-Bass.

Scheirer, M. A. (1981). *Program implementation: The organizational context*. Beverly Hills, CA: Sage.

Scheirer, M. A. (1987). Program theory and implementation theory: Implications for evaluators. In L. Bickman (Ed.), *Using program theory in evaluation*. San Francisco: Jossey-Bass.

Scheirer, M. A. (1988). The life cycle of an innovation: Adoption versus discontinuation of the fluoride mouthrise program in schools. In M. A. Scheirer et al. (Eds.), *Surveys of dissemination processes for the fluoride mouthrinse program* (Final report submitted to the National Institute of Dental Research from Grant DE-06895).

Schlesinger, J. (1966). Systems analysis and the political process. *Journal of Law and Economics*.

Scholz, J. T., & Wei, F. H. (1986). Regulatory enforcement in a federalist system. *American Political Science Review, 80*, 1249–1270.

Schwartz, J. (1983). *America's hidden success: A reassessment of twenty years of public policy*. New York: Norton.

Seidelman, R. (1985). *Disenchanted realists*. Albany: State University of New York Press.

Seidman, H., & Gilmour, R. (1986). *Politics, power and position* (4th ed.). New York: Oxford University Press.

Shaffer, W., & Weber, R. (1974). *Policy responsiveness in the American states*. Beverly Hills, CA: Sage.

Sharkansky, I. (1970). *Public administration*. Chicago: Markham.

Sharp, E. B. (1981). Models of implementation and policy evaluation. In D. J. Palumbo & M. A. Harder (Eds.), *Implementing public policy* (pp. 99–117). Lexington, MA: Lexington Books.

Shavell, S. (1980). Strict liability versus negligence. *Journal of Legal Studies, 9*, 1–14.

Sieber, S. D. (1973). The integration of fieldwork and survey methods. *American Journal of Sociology, 78*, 1335–1359.

Sieber, S. D. (1981). *Fatal remedies*. New York: Plenum.

Siebert, G. (1973). *Implementation of evaluation and the systems approach in government* (Working Paper No. 20). Berkeley: University of California, Institute of Urban and Regional Development.

Silversin, J. B., Coombs, J. A., & Drolette, M. E. (1980a). Achievements of the seventies: Self-applied fluorides. *Journal of Public Health Dentistry, 40*, 248–257.

Silversin, J. B., Coombs, J. A., & Drolette, M. E. (1980b). Adoption of dental preventive measures in United States schools. *Journal of Dental Research, 59*, 2233–2242.

Simon, H. A. (1947). *Administrative behavior*. New York: Macmillan.

Simon, H. A. (1957). *Administrative behavior: A study of decision-making processes in administrative organization* (2d ed.). New York: The Free Press.

Simon, H. A. (1972). *The architecture of complexity*. Cambridge, MA: MIT Press.

Skocpol, T. (1985). Bringing the state back in: Strategies of analysis in current research. In P. B. Evans, D. Rucschemeyer, & T. Skocpol (Eds.), *Bringing the state back in* (pp. 3–37). Cambridge: Cambridge University Press.

Skocpol, T., & Finegold, K. (1982). State capacity and economic intervention in the early New Deal. *Political Science Quarterly, 97*, 225–278.

Skocpol, T., & Ikenberry, J. (1983). The political formation of the American welfare state in historical and comparative perspective. *Comparative Social Research, 6,* 87–148.

Smith, J. K. (1984). The problem of criteria for judging interpretive inquiry. *Educational Evaluation and Policy Analysis, 6.*

Smith, T. B. (1973). The policy implementation process. *Policy Sciences, 4.*

Sosin, M. (1988). *The changing structure of the social services: An alternative perspective.* Draft working paper. Madison: University of Wisconsin, Institute for Research on Poverty.

Starr, P., & Esping-Anderson, G. (1979). Passive intervention. *Working Papers for a New Society, 7,* 14–25.

Stigler, G. (1971). The theory of economic regulation. *The Bell Journal of Economics and Management Science, 2,* 3–21.

Stone, C. (1980). The implementation of social programs: Two perspectives. *Journal of Social Issues, 36*(4), 13–34.

Stone, D. A. (1984). *The disabled state.* Philadelphia: Temple University Press.

Stone, D. A. (1988). *Policy paradox and political reason.* Glenview, IL: Scott, Foresman.

Suchman, E. (1967). *Evaluation research.* New York: Russell Sage Foundation.

Sutherland, J. (1977) . *Systems: Analysis, administration and architecture.* New York: Van Nostrand.

Thompson, F. (1982). Bureaucratic discretion and the National Health Service Corps. *Political Science Quarterly, 97,* 427–445.

Thompson, F., & Scicchitano, M. J. (1985). State implementation effort and federal regulatory policy: The case of occupational safety and health. *Journal of Politics, 47,* 686–703.

Thompson, F., & Scicchitano, M. J. (1987, May). State implementation and federal enforcement priorities. *Administration and Society, 19,* 95–124.

Tornatzky, L., Eveland, J., Boylan, M., Hetzner, W., Johnson, E., Roitman, D., & Schneider, J. (1983). *The process of technological innovation: Reviewing the literature.* Washington, DC: National Science Foundation.

Van Horn, C. E. (1979). *Policy implementation in the federal system: National goals and local implementors.* Lexington, MA: Lexington Books.

Van Horn, C. E., & Baumer, D. C. (1985). *The politics of unemployment.* Washington, DC: Congressional Quarterly Press.

Van Horn, C. E., & Van Meter, D. S. (1976). The implementation of intergovernmental policy. In *Public policy in the federal system.*

Van Maanen, J. (1975). *Behavior in organizations: Notes on the evolution of a systems framework.* Manuscript.

Van Meter, D. S., & Van Horn, C.E. (1975). The policy implementation process: A conceptual framework. *Administration & Society, 6,* 445–488.

Vander Schie, A. R. (1987). Reorganizing human services at the local level: The Kalamazoo County experience. *New England Journal of Human Services, 7,* 29–33.

Vidich, A. J. (1955). A comparison of participant observation and survey data. *American Sociological Review.*

Vig, N. J. (1984). The president and the environment: Revolution or retreat? In N. J. Vig & M. E. Kraft (Eds.), *Environmental policy in the 1980s* (pp. 77–95). Washington, DC: Congressional Quarterly Press.

Wade, L. L. (1972). *The elements of public policy*. Columbus, OH: Charles E. Merrill.

Walker, J. (1969). The diffusion of innovations among the American states. *American Political Science Review*, *63*, 880–889.

Walzer, M. (1981). Philosophy and democracy. *Political Theory*, *9*, 379–400.

Weatherly, R. A. (1979). *Reforming special education: Policy implementation from state level to street level*. Cambridge, MA: MIT Press.

Weatherly, R. A. & Lipsky, M. (1977). Street-level bureaucrats and institutional innovation: Implementing special education reform. *Harvard Educational Review*, *47*(2), 171–197.

Weber, M. (1949). Bureaucracy. In H. Gerth & C. W. Mills (Eds.), *From Max Weber: Essays in sociology*. New York: Oxford University Press.

Weber, R., & Uslander, E. (1977). *Patterns of decision-making in state legislatures*. New York: Praeger.

Weick, K. (1976). Educational organizations as loosely-coupled systems. *Administration Science Quarterly*, *21*, 1–9.

Weiss, C., & Bucuvalas, M. (1980). *Social science research and decision making*. New York: Columbia University Press.

Weiss, J. (1981, Winter). Substance vs. symbol in administrative reform: The case of human services coordination. *Policy Analysis*, *7*(1).

Weitzman, M. (1974). Prices vs. quantities. *Review of Economic Studies*, *41*, 477–491.

Whiteman, D. (1985). The fate of policy analysis in congressional decision making: Three types of use in committees. *Western Political Quarterly*, *38*, 294–311.

Wildavsky, A. (1964). *The politics of the budgetary process*. Boston: Little, Brown.

Wildavsky, A. (1966). The political economy of efficiency: Cost-benefit analysis, systems analysis, and program budgeting. *Public Administration Review*, *26*, 292–310.

Wilensky, H. (1975). *The welfare state and equality: Structural and ideological roots of public expenditures*. Berkeley: University of California Press.

Williams, W. (1980). *The implementation perspective: A guide for managing social service delivery systems*. Berkeley: University of California Press.

Williams, W. (Ed.). (1982). *Studying implementation: Methodological and administrative issues*. Chatham, NJ: Chatham House Publishers.

Williams, W., & Elmore, R. F. (Eds.). (1976). *Social program implementation*. New York: Academic Press.

Williamson, O. (1975). *Markets and hierarchies: Analysis and antitrust implications*. New York: The Free Press.

Wilson, J. Q. (1968). *Varieties of police behavior*. Cambridge, MA: Harvard University Press.

Wilson, W. J. (1988). *The truly disadvantaged: The inner city, the underclass, and public policy*. Chicago: University of Chicago Press.

Winham, G., & Kabashima, I. (1982). The politics of US Japanese auto trade. In I. M. Destler & H. Sato (Eds.), *Coping with US Japanese economic conflicts*. Lexington, MA: Lexington Books.

Winter, S. (1978). *The consequences for efficiency and effectiveness of a consolidation and despecialization of the Danish social welfare system*. Paper prepared for the ECPR workshop on "Interorganizational Networks in Public Policy Implementation," University of Aarhus, Institute of Political Science, Grenoble, France.

Winter, S. (1981). *Den sociale markarbejder og de politiske mal. Faktorer der hæmmer malrealiseringen*. Paper. University of Aarhus, Institute of Political Science.

Winter, S. (1984) . Flere ressourcer ingen garanti for bedre offentlig service. In J. Gunst (Ed.), *Debat om offentlig service* (pp. 121–133). Copenhagen: Kommunetryk.

Winter, S. (1985). Iværksættelsesbarrierer. *Politica, 17*(4), 367–387.

Winter, S. (1986a). Studying implementation of top-down policy from the bottom up: Implementation of Danish youth employment policy. In R. C. Rist (Ed.), *Finding work: Cross-national perspectives on employment and training* (pp. 109–138). London: The Falmer Press.

Winter, S. (1986b). How policy-making affects implementation: The decentralization of the Danish disablement pension administration. *Scandinavian Political Studies, 9*(4), 361–385.

Winter, S. (1987). Implementation of the Danish youth employment policy. In P. J. Pedersen & R. Lund (Eds.), *Unemployment: Theory, policy and structure* (pp. 259–284). Berlin: Walter de Gruyter & Co.

Wirt, F. M. (1970). *Politics of southern equality*. Chicago: Aldine.

Wittrock, B., & DeLeon, P. (1986). Policy as a moving target: A call for conceptual realism. *Policy Studies Review, 6*, 44–60.

Wood, B. D. (1988). Principals, bureaucrats, and responsiveness in clean air enforcement. *American Political Science Review, 82*, 213–234.

Yamashita, H. D. (1983, November). Japan: Obstacles and opportunities. *Speaking of Japan*.

Yanow, D. J. (1981). *Community organization in the Israel community center corporation* (Technical Report). Jerusalem: JDC-Israel.

Yanow, D. J. (1982). *Toward a symbolic theory of policy implementation: An analysis of symbols, metaphors, and myths in organizations*. Ph.D. dissertation, MIT.

Yanow, D. J. (1987). Toward a policy culture approach to implementation. *Policy Studies Review, 7*(1), 103–115.

Yates, D. (1985). *The politics of management*. San Francisco: Jossey-Bass.

Yates, D. T., Jr. (1981). Hard choices: Justifying bureaucratic discretion. In J. Fleishman et al. (Eds.), *Moral duties: The obligations of government officials* (pp. 32–51). Cambridge, MA: Harvard University Press.

Yin, R., Heald, K., & Vogel, M. (1977). *Tinkering with the system: Technological innovations in state and local services*. Lexington, MA: Lexington Books.

Yin, R. K. (1982). Studying the implementation of public programs. In W. Williams (Ed.), *Studying implementation: Methodological and administrative issues* (pp. 36–72). Chatham, NJ: Chatham House Publishers.

Ylvisaker, P. N. (1982). Personal communication.

York, R. O., & Henley, H. C. (1986). Perceptions of bureaucracy. *Administration in Social Work, 10*, 3–13.

Young, D., & Nelson, R. R. (1973). *Public policy for day care for small children*. Lexington, MA: Lexington Books.

Index

About the Editors and Contributors

ANN O'M. BOWMAN's research focuses on the implementation of environmental and economic development policy by state and local governments. Currently she is collecting data from city governments regarding their use of public capital to stimulate development.

EVELYN Z. BRODKIN is assistant professor at the University of Chicago, School of Social Service Administration and the Graduate School of Public Policy. She is author of *The False Promise of Administrative Reform: Implementing Quality Control in Welfare* (1986) and currently conducting research on the politics of dependency.

JOHN P. BURKE is associate professor of political science at the University of Vermont. He is the author of *Bureaucratic Responsibility* and coauthor (with Fred I. Greenstein) of *The Quality of Presidential Decision Making*.

DONALD J. CALISTA is director of both the master's of public administration program and the Graduate Center for Public Policy and Administration at Marist College. His current interests are developing the transaction costs economics model to explain public sector organizational formation. In 1989 he was a Fulbright Scholar in Japan. His most recent articles appear in *Policy Studies Journal* and *Policy Studies Review*. He is editor of the *Journal of Management Science & Policy Analysis*.

CARL P. CARLUCCI is secretary to the New York Assembly Ways and Means Committee. He was assistant professor of public administration at Baruch College and vice president for administration at Brooklyn College. He received his Ph.D.

in public administration from New York University. His most recent publication appears in the *Western Political Quarterly* on the voting rights act.

BARBARA FERMAN is assistant professor of political science and public administration at the Illinois Institute of Technology. She is currently working on a book on public-private partnerships in urban economic development. She is also doing research on affordable housing in Chicago and other U.S. cities. She is coauthor of *The Political Hand* (1985).

CHARLES J. FOX is assistant professor of political science and director of the master's of public administration program at Texas Tech University. He has published articles on the philosophy of social science, ethics, and implementation research. He is currently working on theories of administrative discretion, professionalism, and a labor-management relations study.

MALCOLM GOGGIN spent most of 1988 as a guest scholar at the Brookings Institution. Since his return to the University of Houston, he has undertaken two research projects: a comparative study of policy redesign by legislative amendment and an investigation of policy redesign by rule change using the "gag rule" as a case in point.

JAMES GRIFFITH received his Ph.D. in applied social and organizational psychology from the Claremont Graduate School in 1983. He has written several articles on social support and its moderating effects on the negative effects of stress on individual functioning. His current research interest involves examining relationships among coworker and supervisor support, leader behaviors, organizational commitment, and worker adaptation to organizational stress in U.S. Army units.

JAMES P. LESTER is associate professor of political science at Colorado State University. During 1989–1990, he was a visiting scholar at the University of Linkoping, Sweden, where he conducted research on Swedish environmental politics and policy. He has published numerous articles on environmental policy in *Polity*, *Western Political Quarterly*, *Publius*, *Policy Studies Review*, and *Policy Studies Journal*, among others.

MARTIN A. LEVIN, who has taught at the University of California, Berkeley, is professor of political science at Brandeis University and director of the Gordon Public Policy center. He is the author of *The Political Hand* (with Barbara Ferman), *Urban Politics and the Criminal Courts*, and numerous articles on urban politics, social policy implementation, the presidency, youth employment, crime, and the courts. He is currently working on a book on bureaucratic entrepreneurship.

STEPHEN H. LINDER is associate professor in management and policy sciences at the University of Texas School of Public Health. He received the Ph.D. in political science from the University of Iowa and has held faculty positions at UCLA and Tulane. His principal interest lies in policy analysis, currently focusing on policy design and implementation issues. His most recent work has appeared in *Policy Studies Review*, *Milbank Quarterly*, and *Journal of Policy Analysis and Management*.

ROBERT T. NAKAMURA is associate professor and chair of the Department of Political Science, Rockefeller College of Public Affairs, State University of New York at Albany. He is the coauthor of four books including the *Politics of Policy Implementation*.

LAURENCE J. O'TOOLE, JR., is professor of political science at Auburn University. One of his major fields of scholarly interest is interorganizational policy implementation. He serves currently on the editorial boards of *The Journal of Politics*, the *Public Administration Review*, and the *State and Local Government Review*. In 1989 he was research fellow at the Erasmus University at the University of Leiden, The Netherlands.

DENNIS J. PALUMBO is Regents professor of justice studies and director of the Ph.D. program in the School of Justice Studies at Arizona State University. His most recent publications are *Public Policy in America: Government in Action* and *The Politics of Program Evaluation*. He is co-editor of the *Policy Studies Review*.

B. GUY PETERS is the Maurice Falk professor of American government at the University of Pittsburgh. He received the Ph.D. in political science from Michigan State University and has taught at the University of Delaware, Emory and Tulane universities. His most recent book (with Brain Hogwood) is entitled *The Pathology of Public Policy*. He is currently the coeditor of *Governance: An International Journal of Policy and Administration*, and his research interests include the design of public policy and comparative public administration.

GLENN W. RAINEY, JR., is professor of public administration and political science in the Department of Government at Eastern Kentucky University. He has published articles in *Administration and Society*, *Public Administration Review*, *Public Personnel Management*, and *Public Administration Quarterly*.

BRYNA SANGER is associate professor and chair of the Programs in Nonprofit Management at the Graduate School of Management and Urban Policy, New School for Social Research. Her research interests are social welfare policy and public management. She is currently at work on a book with Martin Levin entitled *Bureaucratic Entrepreneurs: Innovations in Public Organizations* and is completing a manuscript on "Designing the Social Protection System." Dr. Sanger has published widely in policy and management journals and sits on the board of the *Journal of Policy Analysis and Management* and the *Policy Studies Journal*. She will spend the 1989/90 academic year as a senior research fellow at the Gordon Public Policy Center at Brandeis University.

MARY ANN SCHEIRER is an applied social psychologist and program evaluator, currently with the National Institutes of Health in Bethesda, Maryland. She has examined program implementation in a number of projects, including a cross-disciplinary assessment of implementation measurement, and in a book that field-tested a multivariable framework for assessing implementation processes, *Program Implementation: The Organizational Context*. In other studies, she has evaluated a variety of educational, health-related, and human resource programs, using methods ranging from intensive interviews to econometric modeling.

SØREN WINTER is associate professor at the Institute of Political Science, University of Aarhus, Denmark. He is currently working on comparative projects on the implementation of youth employment policies in Denmark and the United States and local government reforms. His most recent article appears in *Journal of Management Science & Policy Analysis*.

DVORA YANOW's current research interests include interpretive policy analysis, the role of policy cultures in implementation, and organizational culture and learning. She is on the faculty of the Department of Public Administration at California State University, Hayward, and received the Ph.D. in planning, policy, and organizational studies from M.I.T.

**Policy Studies Organization publications issued with
Greenwood Press/Quorum Books**

Policy Controversies in Higher Education
Samuel K. Gove and Thomas M. Stauffer, editors

Citizen Participation in Public Decision Making
Jack DeSario and Stuart Langton, editors

Energy Resources Development: Politics and Policies
Richard L. Ender and John Choon Kim, editors

Federal Lands Policy
Phillip O. Foss, editor

Policy Evaluation for Local Government
Terry Busson and Philip Coulter, editors

Comparable Worth, Pay Equity, and Public Policy
Rita Mae Kelly and Jane Bayes, editors

Dimensions of Hazardous Waste Politics and Policy
Charles E. Davis and James P. Lester, editors

Small Business in a Regulated Economy: Issues and Policy Implications
Richard J. Judd, William T. Greenwood, and Fred W. Becker, editors

Rural Poverty: Special Causes and Policy Reforms
Harrell R. Rodgers, Jr., and Gregory Weiher, editors

Fundamentals of the Economic Role of Government
Warren J. Samuels, editor

Policy Through Impact Assessment: Institutionalized Analysis as a Policy Strategy
Robert V. Bartlett, editor

Biomedical Technology and Public Policy
Robert H. Blank and Miriam K. Mills, editors